Adobe™ Illustrator®
Paths and Curves

Kenneth Batelman

John Wiley & Sons, Inc.
New York • Chichester • Brisbane • Toronto • Singapore

Publisher: Katherine Schowalter
Editor: Philip Sutherland
Assistant Editor: Allison Roarty
Assistant Managing Editor: Angela Murphy
Text Design & Composition: Benchmark Productions

This is printed on acid-free paper.

Published by John Wiley & Sons, Inc.

Library of Congress Cataloging-in-Publication Data:

Batelman, Kenneth.
   Adobe Illustrator paths and curves / Kenneth Batelman.
      p.   cm.
   Includes index.
   ISBN 0-471-12027-8 (paper : alk. paper)
     1. Computer Graphics.   2. Adobe Illustrator (Computer file)
3. Curves.   I. Title
T385.B379   1995
006.6'869—dc20

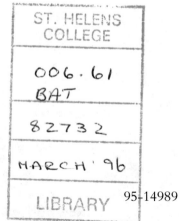

95-14989

Printed in the United States of America
10 9 8 7 6 5 4 3 2 1

To my wife Jill:
You inspire me. Thank you.

Acknowledgments

Special thanks to Paul Farrell, who came up with this idea and gave me the opportunity to write this book; and to Michelle-Mallin-Schayes, who literally touched every letter on these pages.

Contents

CHAPTER 3

Points   27

CHAPTER 4

Line Segments   45

CHAPTER 5

Paths 59

CHAPTER 6

Curves 107

CHAPTER 7

Single Ideal Curve   127

CHAPTER 8

More about Curves   135

CHAPTER 9

Drawing Consecutive Straight and Curved Line Segments   151

Introduction

The computer graphics field is growing at an extraordinary pace, with more powerful and user-friendly software being developed to cater to the needs of graphic artists. The tool icons and menus are presented so that one needn't be a computer expert to understand their use. Almost anyone with a minimal knowledge of computers can sit down and start using these software packages; in some cases, you don't even need to read the manual. Often, instinct and a working understanding of computers are enough to just sit down and be able to create graphics. If you want to draw a brush stroke, click on the icon that looks like a brush and drag it across the screen. If you want to create a circle, click on the circle icon and it will be created.

It is almost like using magic markers for the first time after you've used only a Number 2 pencil. They look and feel different, but instinctively you know to take off the cap, place the pointy end on the paper, and move your hand. The amount of different colors may overwhelm you at first, but you soon realize the greater potential compared to the gray of the pencil.

The computer is just like that marker—a new tool. Although software developers have attempted to make their product so that you can take the program out of the box (remove the marker cap, if you will) and start using it immediately, mastering all the features could take months or even years of hard work. Even if you read the manual cover to cover, becoming an expert will still take a long time.

As with any other tool, the limit of what can be done is dictated not by the power of the program, but by the person who uses it. Many software developers, including Adobe, admit that the images created with their programs have gone far beyond their original expectations. The imagination of users has pushed the limits of these applications far past their initially intended boundaries.

To return to the marker analogy, drawing simple figures—or drawing at all—with the marker is easy, but to get the most out of it and utilize it to its full potential and beyond may take a long time. You would need to explore the different kinds of papers available, the amount of pressure to apply for varying effects, how to mix different colors, and so on. Experimentation, trial, and error are the keys to unlocking the limitless possibilities. If you could get a magic-marker expert to show you these things, all that time would be saved and you could spend it on developing your own techniques and discovering new methods.

I have been using Adobe Illustrator for eight years. It is the most powerful illustration program on the market, and the most difficult one to learn. Even if you could memorize the whole manual and do everything described within its pages, you would still have only begun to learn Adobe Illustrator. The results that can be achieved with Illustrator are greatly dependent on how you combine techniques, and that is learned only through experience. In this book, I have compiled all my knowledge acquired through years of using Adobe Illustrator. There are certain subjects that are discussed in great depth, others that are less emphasized, and even certain features of the program that are not mentioned at all.

I have chosen not to discuss those subjects that are easily learned by simply reading the manual accompanying the program. My main objective in this book is to give you the benefit of what I have learned over the years, coupled with just enough background information so that you can follow the text without any prior knowledge of Illustrator. Some sections will still sound a lot like the manual, because it is necessary for you to learn the basics before reading the advanced sections.

Even if you are an experienced Illustrator user, I suggest you do not skip all of the basic discussion. All of the advanced techniques and explanations are directly related to the basic concepts that are described in great detail. As you read about something you already know, you might discover a new way of looking at it.

I've written this book from an artist's point of view, with just a bit of mathematical background to logically explain how Adobe Illustrator interprets your commands. The main focus is not to simply take you through all the tools and show you how they work, but also to explain why those tools behave as they do. The first step to becoming an expert in Adobe Illustrator is to gain an understanding of the logic behind how the program works. Once you've accomplished that, using Adobe Illustrator will become as easy as using that old Number 2 pencil.

Technically, Adobe Illustrator is a complex piece of software. You'll must not only master its technical aspects, but also learn how to implement that knowledge when you are facing a blank document page. This is one of the main questions I will try to address in this book. All the technical aspects of the program will be introduced by relating them to *path construction* and *manipulation;* which are the core of Adobe Illustrator. All images consist of paths; once you understand how those paths are constructed and manipulated, everything else will become elementary. First, however, you must learn to interpret what you see into how you will create it in Adobe Illustrator. There are very specific procedures that must be followed to translate what's in your head—or in front of your eyes—into the image you render with the tools provided. This will be another aspect stressed in this book.

Chapter 2 is designed to help you associate how paths constructed in Adobe Illustrator can be related to *real-life* objects and professional fields. By comparing Adobe Illustrator's basic concepts to what you already know from everyday life, you may become less intimidated about the program's logic.

Chapters 1 and 3 through 10 are quite technical but will provide you with the knowledge necessary to use the program. The information in these chapters is presented in a very detail-oriented format: The discussions are not only about how to use certain tools, but also why they behave as they do, the most efficient way to use those tools, and what happens when you use them in a different way. Every possible result of every variation is addressed at some point. This is done with path creation and manipulation as the basis of all discussions.

The final chapters concentrate on interpreting what you need to render into how to construct it with Adobe Illustrator. Breaking down an image into its parts in order to translate them into Adobe Illustrator's paths, and the most efficient way to create those paths will be discussed.

Adobe Illustrator can be a very challenging program when you first start to use it. To people unfamiliar with its terminology and logic, it is almost like learning another language. I have tried to translate the program's concepts into terms that can be easily followed, and to use detailed explanations and clear, visual examples. By doing so, I hope that you will learn to use—and abuse—this program's features to their full potential and beyond.

1 *What You Need to Know*

This book is designed for individuals who are—or want to be—in the computer graphics field and have some basic knowledge of the Macintosh computer system. *Basic knowledge* is a broad term that does not mean that you have to be a power user; although you must know how the Macintosh system operates. You should be familiar with turning on the computer; opening, closing, and saving files; running applications; and you should know your way around the desktop.

One of the best features of Macintosh computers is the consistency between software programs. For example, the File and Edit menus are standard in every application. The File menu usually contains New, Open, Close, Save, Print, and Quit options; and the Edit menu includes Undo, Cut, Copy, Paste, and Clear options. You should be familiar with these functions.

Another standard function in the Macintosh operating system is *selecting,* which is used to perform every function. To activate a window, it must be selected. Files and folders must be selected before they are opened, closed, copied, or moved; and—in a program—an object or text has to be selected before anything can be done to it or any of its attributes changed. Selecting is done either by clicking on the desired object with the cursor or dragging across it.

Here is a quick review of some of the Macintosh system's terms and functions that you will need to know to successfully use this book.

The Cursor

The cursor is a small graphic on your screen that moves in the same direction as your mouse or other input device. The cursor will appear as varying graphics, depending on which tool is in use at that time, where the cursor is on the screen, what key—if any—is being pressed, and what action the computer is carrying out. For instance, choosing the *Eyedropper tool* from the toolbox in Illustrator will turn the cursor into the eyedropper icon; moving the cursor off the active window will turn the icon into an arrow. Holding down the **Option** key while the cursor is in the active window will turn the eyedropper into a paint bucket, and while the computer is processing an operation the cursor becomes a watch icon.

Clicking and Dragging

All the operations on the Macintosh computer are done with a combination of clicking, dragging, and holding down certain keyboard keys. A *single click* is achieved by pressing and releasing the mouse button in one step at a specific location on the screen. The result of clicking will differ—like the cursor's appearance—depending on which tool is selected, where the cursor is on the screen, and which keys are pressed.

Double-clicking involves pressing and releasing the mouse button twice quickly in the same location. This will, in most cases, produce a different result than clicking once, even if the combination of tools and keys is the same. The speed at which the mouse button has to be double-clicked can be adjusted in the Mouse option of the Control Panels accessed through the Apple Menu.

Dragging, sometimes referred to as *click and drag,* is defined as moving the mouse while the button is pressed. Moving the mouse without pressing the button will only move the cursor around the screen. The results of dragging will vary based on the combination of the chosen tool, the location, and pressed keys.

Windows

Most of the work in the Macintosh is done in a *window.* Opening, closing, resizing, and moving around within windows should be part of your basic knowledge. Figure 1.1 shows a standard Macintosh window and its components.

Close box: Clicking on this box in an active window will close that window.

Title bar: The title of the window appears in this bar. Clicking and dragging the title bar will allow you to move the whole window around the screen.

Optimal Size box: Clicking on this box will toggle between the current and the optimal size of the active window.

Resize box: Clicking and dragging this box will enable you to manually change the window's size.

Scroll bar: Clicking here will allow you to move through the document in the active window quickly.

Scroll arrow: Clicking here will move you through the document in the active window slowly.

Scroll box: Clicking and dragging this box will allow you to move through the document manually.

Dialog Boxes

Dialog boxes serve two main functions: to provide information and to request information. One type of dialog box is designed to give you information, such as a warning stating the consequences of the function you are about to perform, or a question to determine if you are sure you want to perform this function. If you are trying to execute a command that is impossible or impractical, a dialog box may appear telling you so, and it may give you an explanation or alternative. Other types of dialog boxes require information from you, such as how far you want to move an object or what typeface you want to use. These dialog boxes will have some or all of the following: text fields that can be edited with your specifications, check boxes where the information is provided by selecting or deselecting a combination of different check boxes, and radio buttons that are clicked to select a specific choice one at a time. Figure 1.2 shows a typical dialog box and its components.

The following terms are commonly used with the Macintosh and will be mentioned in this book.

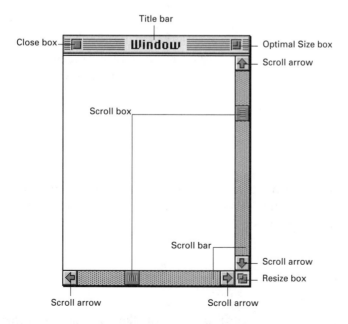

Figure 1.1 Standard Macintosh window.

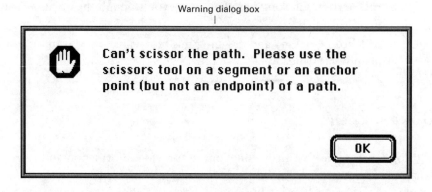

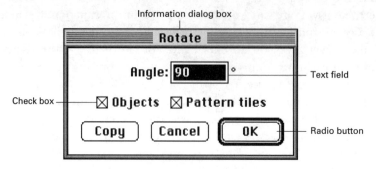

Figure 1.2 *Examples of dialog boxes.*

RAM

Random Access Memory is the memory the computer needs in order to perform any operation. For example, if you are trying to scale an image, the computer uses its RAM to perform that function. The more complex the image, the more RAM necessary to execute the function.

Hard Drive Memory

This is the memory a computer uses to store all files and applications, and this is where you will save your files. Again, the more complex an image, the more memory required on the hard drive to store it.

Subjects Relating Solely to Adobe Illustrator

The following definitions are related to the Adobe Illustrator program. These terms are important to the subjects discussed throughout the book and are mentioned repeatedly. Since their definitions will not be discussed in detail every time, familiarize yourself with them before reading the rest of the chapters.

Constrain

This term is used mainly in combination with the transform tool functions. To constrain a path transformation means to restrict its scaling, rotation, shearing, reflection, and movement relative to the Constrain Angle option set in the general preferences dialog box.

In Illustrator, the Option key is used as the constrain key. Holding down the Option key while manually performing any of the transform operations, will restrict the transformation of that object. For instance, if the Option key is held down while manually scaling an object, the object will be restricted to uniform, horizontal, or vertical scale only. Holding down the Option key while an object is being manually moved, rotated, sheared, or reflected will constrain the angle of these transformations to 45-degree increments relative to the Constrain Angle option set in the General Preferences dialog box. The default Constrain Angle option is set to 0 degrees. This means that if an object is manually rotated while the **Option** key is held down, the angles available for the rotation will be 45 degrees, 90 degrees, 135 degrees, 180 degrees, 225 degrees, 270 degrees, and 315 degrees. If the constrain angle is changed to 10 degrees, the object can be rotated only on 55 degrees, 100 degrees, 145 degrees, 190 degrees, 235 degrees, 280 degrees, and 325 degrees when the **Option** key is held down. To access the Constrain Angle option, go to the File menu and choose **Preferences > General.**

Multiple and Toggle Selection

In Illustrator, the Option key also functions to select multiple objects and to toggle between selecting and deselecting objects. The Option key is used in combination with the selection tools to select multiple anchor points, line segments, and paths one at a time. Holding down the **Option** key will also toggle between selecting and deselecting anchor points, line segments, and paths, while leaving other selected objects unaffected.

Duplicating with the Option key

In Illustrator, the Option key can be used to make duplicates of anchor points, line segments, and paths. Performing any of the transform functions manually while holding down the **Option** key will create a duplicate of the object being transformed, while leaving the original unaffected.

Duplicating with the Repeat Transform Function

Duplicates of anchor points, line segments, and paths can be made by choosing the Repeat Transform function under the Arrange menu after an object has been transformed. For example, if an object has been scaled 50 percent, choosing Repeat Transform immediately after will create a duplicate of the originally scaled object and scale it once again by 50 percent using the same focal point. The Repeat Transform can be used as many times as desired, and the duplicate will be transformed every time using the same settings.

Undo

Use this command immediately after performing an erroneous function to undo that function. Multiple functions can be undone by choosing the Undo command several times from the Edit menu, or by pressing **Command + Z**. The number of Undo levels can be set in the General Preferences dialog box.

Redo

Choose Redo under the Edit menu, or press **Command + Option + Z** to redo the undone function.

Select All

Choose Select All from the Edit menu, or press **Command + A** to select all the objects on the document page, provided they are not locked or hidden.

Select None

Choose Select None from the Edit menu, or press **Command + Option + A** to deselect all selected objects on the document page.

Paste in Front

Choose the Paste in Front command under the Edit menu, or press **Command + F** to paste objects copied to the clipboard on top of any selected objects. If no objects are selected, the Paste in Front command will paste the copied objects on top of the current layer. An important aspect of this command is that objects are pasted in the exact same location from which they were copied. This extends to copying and pasting objects between different Illustrator documents.

Paste in Back

Choose the Paste in Back command under the Edit menu, or press **Command + B** to paste the copied objects in back of selected objects or in back of a current layer if no objects are selected. The objects are pasted in the exact same location from which they were copied, even between different Illustrator documents.

Bring to Front

Choose the Bring to Front command under the Arrange menu, or press **Command + =** to bring the selected object or objects to the frontmost layer in the document.

Send to Back

Choose the Send to Back command under the Arrange menu, or press **Command + –** to send the selected object or objects to the backmost layer in the document.

Lock

Choose the Lock command under the Arrange menu, or press **Command + 1** to lock the selected objects so that they cannot be selected or manipulated in any way. Multiple objects can be added to other already locked objects without affecting them. Holding down the **Option** key while choosing Lock from the Arrange menu or pressing **Command + Option + 1** will lock all the objects not selected.

Unlock All

Choose Unlock All from the Arrange menu, or press **Command + 2** to unlock all the locked objects at the same time regardless of the order in which they were locked. Unlocking objects automatically selects them.

Hide

Choosing the Hide command under the Arrange menu, or pressing **Command + 3** performs a function similar to the Lock command except that objects are also hidden from the screen. Holding down the **Option** key while choosing Hide from the Arrange menu, or pressing **Command + Option + 3** will hide all the unselected objects.

Show All

Choose the Show All command under the Arrange menu, or press **Command + 4** to show all the hidden objects on your screen, regardless of the order in which they were hidden. When previously hidden objects reappear on your screen, they are automatically selected.

Preview

Choose the Preview command under the View menu, or press **Command + Y** to see the paint style attributes of the objects in your document. In Illustrator, documents are set to Preview mode as a default.

Artwork

Choose the Artwork command under the View menu, or press **Command + E** to display all the objects in your document without any paint style attributes. This is a very important function, because it allows you to see whole paths of every object on the page. In Preview mode, certain sections of objects may not be visible when underneath another object filled with a paint style. Artwork mode will display all objects in full, regardless of their layering and paint style. It is very important to go back and forth between the Artwork and Preview modes while working on an image. Selecting and performing certain functions with objects can be more or less difficult, depending on the mode chosen. Throughout the book, examples are shown in either Artwork or Preview mode to achieve the best clarity of a particular function.

$\mathcal{2}$ *Lines and Curves in Real Life*

Why We Need to Draw Straight Lines and Curves

In almost every profession where 2-dimensional renderings or 3-dimensional objects are created, straight lines and curves are used. Whether painting a landscape or making a dining room table, you will need to use straight lines and curves. Almost everything created in nature or by humans will include those two basic elements. As people involved in the visual communications field, we must also acquire the ability to make other people see the same straight lines and curves as we see them. This fact dictates that we not take these two very important visual elements for granted. Even though an artist can choose to represent something with only straight lines or curves, to make a certain point or accomplish a specific goal, the need to eventually create both elements cannot be entirely avoided.

Computers are the perfect tools to combine these two elements. The ease with which most programs create straight lines and curves gives one the ability to communicate any shape without compromising its straightness or curvature. In the visual communication field today, we have almost reached a point where anything—real or imagined—may be rendered on a computer with infinite detail and then manipulated in an unlimited number of ways. How much control we have over this vast visual bombardment—and how well we can represent it—will depend on how well we interpret what we see. Straight lines and curves are what we are left with after breaking down what we see into its most basic elements.

Before you can draw a curve or straight line segment, you must first understand the structure of the curve or straight line and how to distinguish between the two. Knowing when one should be drawn instead of the other is just as important as knowing how to draw them. You will not be able to draw a straight line or curve unless you are first able to visualize it in your head. This is not an easy thing to do, especially if you are not specifically trained to recognize these elements. The distinctions between a straight line and a curve (other than their definitions) may not always be clear, because a great deal depends on not only what you are looking at, but also how you interpret it. For example, when we look at a wheel, we can confidently say that it is round. However, with a little artistic license we can choose to represent it as a square; and by placing it in the right context (under a car), we can make others recognize it as a wheel.

The cubist art movement, in part, took objects curvilinear by nature and represented them with straight lines and sharp edges. These are extreme cases, where what we see is not necessarily what we will depict in our work. Everything that you see must, in some way, be interpreted before it is rendered, even if you are trying to achieve a realistic representation.

When trying to achieve realism in your rendering, you must analyze what you are seeing and divide it into its most basic elements. This is a standard exercise when learning how to draw. In a beginner-level drawing class, the first thing one learns is to draw a human figure using simple geometric shapes. The head, for example, would be represented by a sphere; the nose by a pyramid; and the neck, arms, and legs by various shaped tubes (see Figure 2.1). As virtually everything can be broken down into these simple shapes, you can allow yourself to see the underlying structure of objects and figures without being overwhelmed by the details.

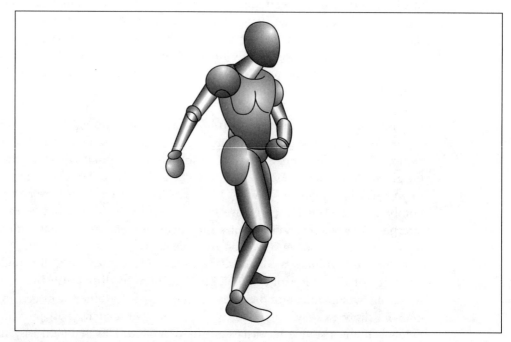

Figure 2.1 Human figure rendered using simple geometric shapes.

We will take this idea one step further and look at it on a 2-dimensional level. Just as all 3-dimensional objects are basically comprised of cubes, spheres, cones, pyramids, and tubes, so 2-dimensional objects are made of rectangles, ovals, and triangles. Breaking this down even further, we get straight lines and curved lines. As Adobe Illustrator is a 2-dimensional drawing program, these will be the elements that we will concentrate on observing and re-creating.

Adobe Illustrator is also an object-oriented program, which means that everything rendered in this program will be composed of flat shapes of various forms combined like a collage. You might think of working in Illustrator as constructing an image by cutting different pieces of colored paper and arranging them on a page in various combinations. When you look at a wheel, you interpret it as a circle, so you will cut a circle out of a piece of paper. If you are looking at a 3-dimensional box, you interpret it as a number of different colored squares, so you will cut them out and arrange them at various angles. This is exactly the procedure you will use to create images in Illustrator. Once you have learned how to draw various shapes with the tools provided in this program, you will be able to render almost anything.

Teaching you how to draw objects with Illustrator, and which tools to use, are the main objectives of this book. However, it is just as important—and maybe more difficult—to learn to interpret what you see into how it will be represented with the tools provided by Adobe Illustrator.

Deconstructing the Object

Deciding what object to draw when rendering a wheel is not that difficult: The main shape is round, so the object must be a circle. What if you are drawing the whole car? On a road? Next to a house? With trees in the yard and clouds in the sky? What objects will you need to draw to gain a realistic representation of this scene? You cannot simply describe this image as being round or square; it has to be deconstructed into simpler geometric shapes, such as circles, squares, rectangles, and ovals. These shapes, which can be created automatically in Illustrator, are just a part of the breakdown process. Images must then be simplified even further, into straight lines and curves. In Illustrator, these images are created by combining straight line segments and curved line segments. Each one of these segments must be thought through and analyzed before you begin to create it, because in an object-oriented program, you need to supply the computer with the information regarding how a segment should look before the program can draw it for you. Learning where one straight or curved line segment ends and the other begins, as you are tracing the contour of an object, will be the main discussion in this and later chapters. From this book you will also learn how those objects may be combined to represent specific images.

As mentioned earlier, what you draw has a great deal to do with how you interpret it. One of the main factors in interpreting what you see is ascertaining how much detail you wish to represent. For instance, let us look at that wheel again. If you look

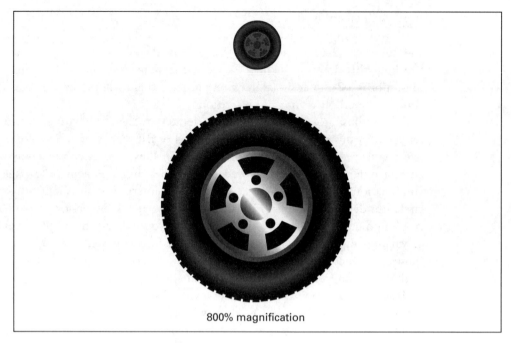

800% magnification

Figure 2.2 *Different magnifications of a wheel.*

at the wheel from a distance, it looks like a circle; but if we magnify it, we begin to see more shapes (see Figure 2.2). In the magnification, we no longer see just a circle, but many lines—straight and curved, and of various lengths and angles. All of this information must be communicated to the program in order for it to render what you want.

Once you have made the decision about how much detail to represent, you must decide which is the most efficient way to combine curved and straight line segments to depict those details. To help you better understand how the combination of those two basic elements is used to construct an image, let's look at how they are combined in real life and how other tools are used to represent them.

Lines and Curves in Nature vs. Man-Made

To be able to dissect the things you see into their most basic elements, you must train your eye to see those elements in regular, everyday objects. Everything we see around us is either natural or artificial. In nature, perfectly straight lines and smooth curves are not found as easily as they are in synthetic objects. This naturally lends itself to the realization that, with an object-oriented program, realistic representation of natural objects is more difficult than of those that are man-made.

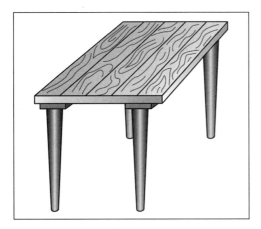

Figure 2.3 *A table.*

For instance, look at a table. You could say that it is made up of various geometric shapes (see Figure 2.3), primarily because that is exactly how the table was created. A carpenter used tools to make straight and curved lines and combine them into shapes that make up a table. In nature it is more difficult to break things down into such basic geometric shapes, so you must interpret natural objects as man-made objects first.

People have been trying to represent nature with available tools since cave art. How closely the man-made object or rendering mimics its natural counterpart depends on how that person interprets the image and the tools they use—the range is virtually infinite. A horse, a natural object, can be depicted so abstractly as to become unrecognizable. On the other hand, it can be sculpted so realistically that only a very close inspection will reveal that it is not real. However, abstract interpretation does not apply to our discussion, so we will focus on realism.

One of nature's most difficult objects to represent realistically is our own geography. This is a perfect example of how one image, interpreted realistically, can have millions of variations, depending on the scale in which it is being represented. A specific section of land can be rendered using a few lines and curves if looked at from a great distance, or with hundreds of thousands of lines and curves if viewed up close. It is also interesting to note that a certain geographical area can never be represented in perfect realism (as can the statue of a horse), but instead must always be interpreted with varying degrees of detail due to the size of its original scale. Maps are created in many mediums, from 3-dimensional sculpture to 2-dimensional drawings. Two-dimensional maps are good subjects for analyzing how a combination of lines and curves can be used to depict their outlines.

Detail

The amount of detail with which a map is to be represented will, for the most part, dictate in what medium it will need to be depicted. For instance, a painting of a map can have only as much detail as the smallest brush and largest canvas will allow. A sculpted map, on the other hand, will have as much detail as the smallest carving tool will allow. The computers of today, however, have extended the boundaries of detail almost indefinitely. This allows the computer artist to decide just how much detail to use. Taking this to a not entirely unattainable extreme, on the computer, one can create—to scale—a planet with an ant crawling on it. How then can we decide how much detail our drawings should have? Even with the limitations of computer memory and our time, the choices are endless.

A good way to train your eyes and brain to see and interpret the amount of detail you wish to depict is to examine how others interpret what they see and how they use the tools available to them to represent it.

Tools Used to Create Lines and Curves

Fine art perhaps has the greatest variety of tools available to create lines and curves. Since almost anything can be considered fine art, almost any tool available can be used to create it.

Painters use brushes to make lines and curves. The variety of those lines and curves depends on the size and shape of those brushes (see Figure 2.4). Both lines and curves are created by a continuous stroke of the artist's hand: The longer the artist keeps the brush on the canvas while moving his or her hand, the longer that line or curve will be. The direction in which the artist moves will also dictate the direction of those lines and curves. Some tools in computer drawing programs use a similar technique for rendering, but the similarity ends there. On the computer, you can make the canvas as large as a building and the brush as small as a speck of dust, thereby eliminating the limits of detail that a traditional painting has.

A sculptor uses a mallet and a chisel to create 3-dimensional lines and curves (see Figure 2.5). Like a painter, the sculptor controls the shape of lines and curves by choosing different size chisels and striking them with a mallet at varying forces. A sculptor has somewhat less control over the shape of lines and curves, because more instruments are involved in the process. Filing and sanding are then used to achieve more precise straight and curved lines.

Adobe Illustrator has tools that can create lines and curves quickly to get a general outline of an object, but then you must return to those outlines and fine-tune them with other tools to achieve the desired result.

A potter uses one of the oldest art tools that can be directly mimicked by some rendering programs; this tool is the throwing wheel. Potters use their hands to sculpt a 2-dimensional curved line, and the wheel rotates it around an axis to create a perfectly symmetrical 3-dimensional object (see Figure 2.6).

Carpenters use the same principle with the lathe (see Figure 2.7). This tool has even greater control over the shape of curves and lines. Precise instruments are used to establish the specific angles and distances for the carving tools while the object spins

Figure 2.4 *Brushes and their strokes.*

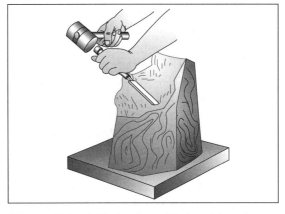

Figure 2.5 *A block of wood being chiseled.*

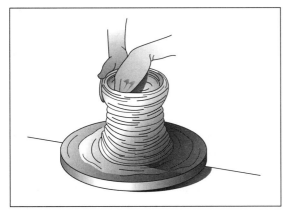

Figure 2.6 *A potter's wheel.*

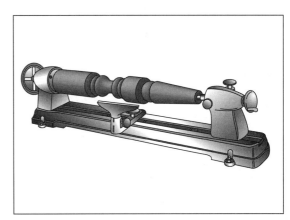

Figure 2.7 *A lathe.*

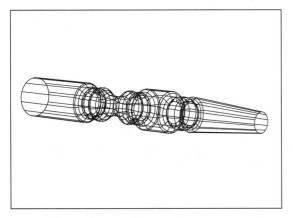

Figure 2.8 *A lathe in a 3D computer program.*

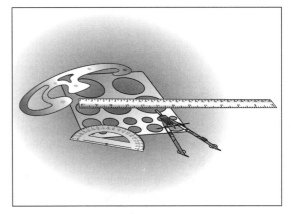

Figure 2.9 *Measuring tools.*

around an axis. Even more control is achieved by being able to adjust the contour of a lathed object to the finest detail. The unsteadiness of the human hand is eliminated, as is any distortion in the contour of the final product.

The lathe is exactly what some computer programs use to create objects (see Figure 2.8). Even though Illustrator does not have a lathe tool, it creates similar effects with the Reflect and Rotate tools.

The Architecture, Industrial Design, and Drafting industries use tools that are perhaps most closely related to tools in object-oriented software programs. In fact, some of the first applications of computer-rendered images were used primarily in those fields. These fields combine art with math and science, much as computers are doing now. Imagination and drawing skills are used in combination with mathematical formulas and theories of physics. Drawing a line no longer means moving a brush across the canvas, or striking a chisel with a mallet.

The length of a line can be measured by rulers, the angle of a line established with protractors, and various circle and curve templates can be used to create perfect outlines and contours (see Figure 2.9). All of this adds up to a great deal of preparation before the actual rendering could take place. Analyzing how long a line should be and at what angle; at what point the direction of that line will change; if it will be sharp or smooth; and in what direction the curve travels and how its slope changes over its duration are only some of the questions that must be answered before the image can be rendered.

Object-oriented programs such as Illustrator work on similar principles. Where does a straight or curved line segment begin and end? At what angle is it and what is its slope? You must provide the program with this information. To help you, the software provides you with tools similar to those used in drafting. Rulers, angle measurements, and various circle and rectangle templates are just a few. The shape of a computer-generated curve does not have to depend on how steady your hand is (although it still could), but instead on the information you provide to the program regarding how the curve should look. The only thing left to chance is how you combine those lines and curves to create the rendering that you want.

Dividing Shapes into Lines and Curves

First let's look at how an image is broken down into straight lines. If we analyze a single 2-dimensional image, such as a five-point star (see Figure 2.10), we can say that it is made up of straight lines. The next step is to identify where each line begins and ends, and its angle. Usually, a line segment will begin and end at a corner. In the case of the star, it is fairly simple to determine where the corners are. Each outer point of the star is a corner, as is each inner point. We can then divide the star shape into ten straight lines and ten corners. This is all the information you have to tell the program to create this image. The angle of the line segments and their length will be calculated

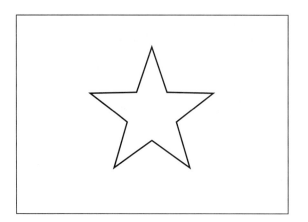

Figure 2.10 *Simple 2-dimensional image.*

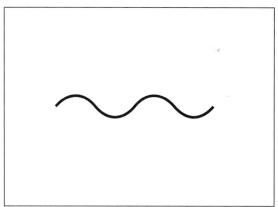

Figure 2.11 *Simple wave shape.*

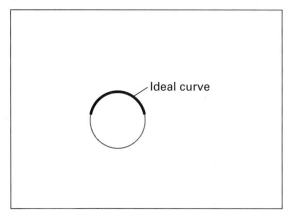

Figure 2.12 *Ideal curve.*

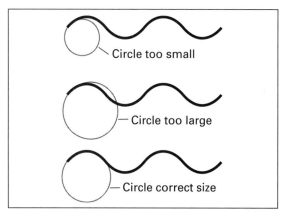

Figure 2.13 *Using a circle to establish an ideal curve within an outline.*

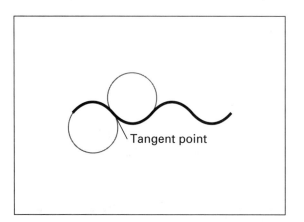

Figure 2.14 *Draw the next circle tangent to the first one.*

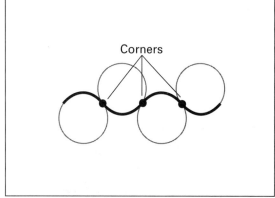

Figure 2.15 *Using tangent circles to divide an outline into ideal curves.*

automatically when you identify the star's corners. The locations of the corners are communicated to the program by placing anchor points (see Chapter 3) at those corners.

Breaking down a shape that is composed of curves is not quite as obvious, mainly because a continuous smooth curve may not have any defined corners to signify the beginning or end of a segment. Instead, it is up to you to figure out where a curved line segment ends and the other one begins, according to how they are constructed in Illustrator.

For example, let us look at a simple wave shape (see Figure 2.11). This shape cannot be drawn in Illustrator with one line segment. Therefore, it must be broken down into simpler curved line segments. The variety of curved line segments that you can create in Illustrator is vast. There are, however, curved line segments that are more or less efficient than others. One of the most efficient curved line segments is the *ideal curve* (Chapter 7). The simplest way to identify an ideal curve is by comparing it to a section of a circle. Any section of a circle that is less than a semicircle is an ideal curve (see Figure 2.12). With this in mind, let's divide the wave shape into ideal curves.

Begin by drawing a circle to match as much of the curved outline as possible, without intersecting it (see Figure 2.13). A second circle should also match as much of the curved outline as possible, starting at the point where the first circle left off. The two circles will be considered tangent at that point (see Figure 2.14). Continue until you have outlined the whole wave shape with circles (see Figure 2.15). The points where the circles touch are the *corners* that divide the shape into line segments.

In cases where a continuous curve travels in the direction of the circle a distance that is longer than a semicircle, the corner must be placed before a semicircle is reached. In Figure 2.16, the S curve is outlined using three circles. If the corners are identified only by where the circles touch, then the shape may be broken down into three segments. The segment along the largest circle is an ideal curve because it is smaller than a semicircle. The other two segments are larger than a semicircle. Those

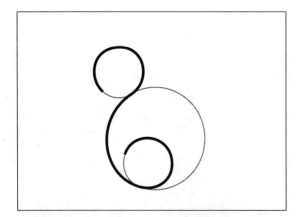

Figure 2.16 *Using circles to divide an S-curve outline.*

Figure 2.17 *Ideal curve segments.*

two segments must be divided in half to create segments that are ideal curves (see Figure 2.17). This is precisely the technique that you would use to identify where the anchor points should be placed along a continuous smooth curved shape when creating paths in Illustrator.

Using circles of varying diameters, and the corner rule, you can break down any shape into straight and curved line segments. Once you have learned how to combine straight and curved line segments into paths, you will be able to lay out those paths to create illustrations. Chapters 12 and 13 will discuss how those paths are arranged to achieve a desired rendering.

Beziér Curves

To help you better understand what you are drawing and how to manipulate it, this chapter will discuss some of the more technical aspects of curves.

The curves that are created using object-based programs like Adobe Illustrator are called *Beziér* (Bez-ee-ay) curves. These curves are named for Pierre Beziér whose work involved developing mechanical cutting devices for Renault (the car manufacturer) in France in the early 1970s. Renault used Beziér curves to streamline the process of controlling the devices that were used to cut car bodies. Prior to Beziér's work, car-body designers used traditional tools, such as French curves, lathes, and sweeps, to render the car body parts at different stages of development. By the time a small scale drawing had been translated into a master model, small discrepancies had accumulated, resulting in an impairment of the final product. The Beziér curves allowed the computer to describe any shape curve with four points—two anchor points and two direction points—which led to a perfect duplication of curves on any scale. The integrity of the originally constructed outlines was kept perfectly constant through all the stages of production.

PostScript Language

This is why Beziér curves are so easily applied to *PostScript* language. PostScript is the foundation upon which most object-oriented programs are built. The main feature of object-based programs is that the structure and resolution of an object or a shape is kept constant at any scale and can be duplicated infinitely without alteration.

The creation of Beziér curves with PostScript language takes place *behind the scenes* of the Adobe Illustrator program. Most computer artists never see, nor care to see, how that is done. Creating shapes or paths in Illustrator by typing in commands in PostScript requires a thorough knowledge of the PostScript language. To give you an idea of how it works, imagine an 8 1/2" × 11" page divided into a grid of 72 sections per inch. To draw a straight line, you would have to specify the coordinates for two anchor points on that grid. The bottom left of the page is a 0, 0 coordinate. To draw a line that is 3 inches long horizontally and starts six inches from the left side of the page and four inches from the bottom, you must input the first anchor point coordinates as 288, 432 ($72 \times 4, 72 \times 6$) and the second anchor point coordinates as 504, 432 ($72 \times 7, 72 \times 6$).

The first operation in most PostScript graphics routines is to save the current graphic state **gsave**. This operation will allow you to alter the existing graphic state while saving the original values that might be used in other routines. When you have completed a routine, the original graphic state is restored **grestore**. In most cases, the first and last lines of a routine or program are **gsave** and **grestore**.

The two most basic positioning commands in PostScript are **moveto** and **lineto**. The **moveto** command tells the computer where to place a specific point, and the **lineto** command specifies to which point the last point is connected. The command that actually creates a path between those points is **newpath**.

The PostScript language also operates in *post fix notation*–you first identify the objects you want to use, then you say what you want to do with them. For example, to add 3 and 4, you write (3 4 add) instead of (3+4).

You now have enough information to draw a horizontal line across the page. This is the PostScript language program to write to execute that graphic:

gsave + 288 432 moveto + newpath + 504 432 lineto + stroke + grestore

Making a PostScript program for a curved line segment requires specifying the coordinates for four points: two anchor points for the beginning and the end of a segment, and two direction points to describe the shape of the curve.

The PostScript language was written with the graphic artist in mind. It uses a way of describing images that is modeled after the graphic arts. This makes the use of PostScript-based programs somewhat easier for a graphic artist than programs based on other languages. If you are interested in learning more about PostScript language, there are books available and some art schools offer classes.

Bitmap vs. Object-Oriented Programs

Not all drawing programs are object-oriented. There are also a great variety of *bitmap* programs; Adobe Photoshop is the leader of bitmap-based applications. Originating as a photo retouching and manipulation software, Photoshop quickly became the most popular illustration program as well. A very powerful and intuitive interface makes it a primary choice with graphic artists. There are, however, some downsides to using a bitmap program. The file size and memory required to run and fully utilize these applications is overwhelming. Unlike object-oriented programs, the size and resolution of a bitmap image directly relates to the amount of memory it consumes. From personal experience, an image created with a bitmap program can be as large as 20 to

50 megabytes, while most of the images created with an object-oriented program will not exceed 5 megabytes and are rarely larger than 1 or 2 megabytes. This also directly relates to the amount of RAM (Random Access Memory) needed to work with an image. Adobe Illustrator can run on 4 or 5 megabytes of RAM and handle a fairly complex illustration. Adobe Photoshop, on the other hand, may need 8 to 16 megabytes of RAM to open and manipulate a complex image at a high resolution.

The advantage of a bitmap program like Photoshop is that it is more intuitive than object-oriented programs. Using Adobe Photoshop is more like using traditional artists' tools, which makes it more inviting and user-friendly. You can choose an airbrush from the toolbox and drag it across the screen to create an airbrush-looking stroke. The size and density of the stroke can be specified in the Airbrush dialog box. The shape of the stroke will directly relate to the movement of the mouse with your hand. Using a pressure-sensitive tablet will vary the density of the stroke, according to the pressure you apply with the pen—much like a real airbrush. Most image creation with object-based programs, however, involves drawing paths with tools that do not rely on the movement of your hand. To emulate an airbrush stroke in Illustrator can require drawing a number of paths and blending them (see Chapter 12). This is not nearly as intuitive or easy as dragging an Airbrush tool across the screen.

It is difficult to compare the two programs based only on the images and effects that can be achieved by either one. Some graphic artists use a combination of both programs to utilize the more powerful features of each. There are, however, some basic technical differences that can be compared.

As mentioned earlier, the resolution of a bitmapped image will relate directly to its size. An image created with an object-oriented program is resolution-independent. This means that if you draw a curved line at a certain size, manipulating the scale of that line will not affect its resolution, because the computer recognizes this curved line as one solid object described by a formula. Changing the size of that object does not change the formula and therefore keeps the object at the same resolution. However, in a bitmap program a curved line is described to the computer as a number of small squares, or *pixels*. When the line is enlarged, so are the pixels, making the image coarser. The resolution is defined as a number of pixels per inch. The smaller the number of pixels per inch, the lower the resolution. When the pixels are enlarged, there will be fewer of them per inch. Figure 2.18 shows an object-based curved line and a bitmapped curved line at different scales.

A large amount of memory is required for bitmap programs because every individual pixel must be examined to identify its attributes before constructing the image. An object-based program looks at an object as a whole, no matter how many pixels it takes up on the screen.

The manipulation of the shapes of objects in an object-oriented program, although less intuitive, is faster and more precise. Once an object is drawn in a bitmap program, to alter its outline, pixels have to either be added or removed. This is done by using the program's *eraser* or *white paint*. The pixels that are located in the incorrect spots

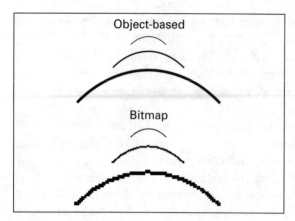

Figure 2.18 *Comparing object-based and bitmap curves.*

Figure 2.19 *Manipulating shapes in a bitmap program.*

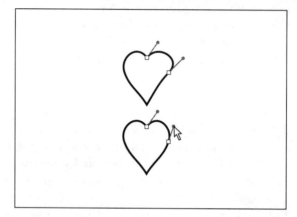

Figure 2.20 *Manipulating shapes in an object-based program.*

must be deleted or covered up and new ones must be created (see Figure 2.19). This is a somewhat intuitive exercise because it mimics traditional artists' methods.

In an object-oriented program, a shape is comprised of straight and curved segments. Straight segments can be moved by dragging them in the desired direction, and curved segments are manipulated by changing the position of four points (two anchor points and two direction points). This allows you more precise control over the shape of an object (see Figure 2.20). Editing shapes by changing the position of their points is anything but intuitive to an artist. Part of what this book will do is explain the logic behind how object-oriented programs operate, and how to master their tools so that using them will become as natural as using a pencil or paint brush.

3 *Points*

In order to follow and execute some of the examples in this chapter, you may need to construct a simple path using the Pen tool. Refer to the "Pen Tool" section in Chapter 5 to learn how to construct a simple path with straight line segments.

Definition

A *point* is the most basic element in a drawing program. It has neither dimension nor area, and therefore cannot be previewed or printed. To create a single point, choose the Pen tool from the toolbox and click the mouse anywhere on the document page (see Figure 3.1). A point's primary applications are: to describe the beginning and end of a line segment or curve; to connect line segments to each other—thereby creating paths; and to identify the center of an object (see Figure 3.2 a, b, c).

Center Points vs. Stray Points

When a point is not part of a line segment or path, it is either a *center point* or a *stray point.* Center points indicate the exact center of a path; you may choose to make the center point visible or not in the Attributes dialog box accessed through the Objects menu (Figure 3.3). Ovals and rectangles created automatically will have the center point shown as a default. All other paths, however, will not have the center point shown unless otherwise specified in the Attributes dialog box.

Stray points result when—with the Pen tool selected—the mouse button is clicked on the document page. If that point is then not connected to another point by a line

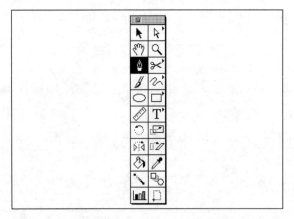

Figure 3.1 *The Pen tool.*

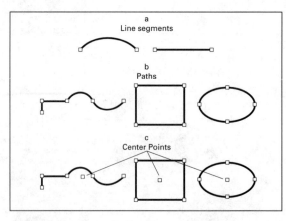

Figure 3.2 *Point's primary applications.*

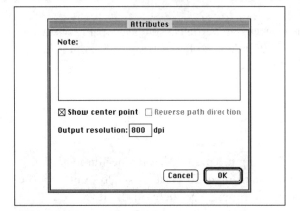

Figure 3.3 *Objects Attributes dialog box.*

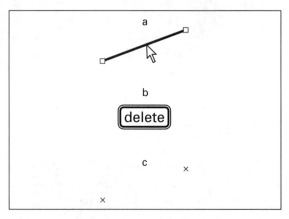

Figure 3.4 *One way to create stray points.*

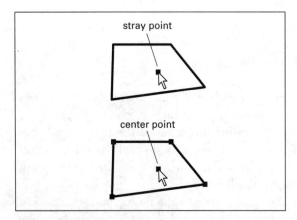

Figure 3.5 *Distinguishing between center and stray points.*

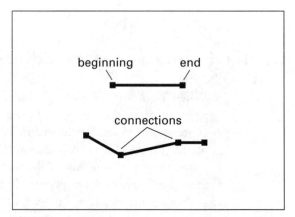

Figure 3.6 *Anchor points.*

segment, or if you delete all line segments that are attached to a point without deleting that point (see Figure 3.4 a, b, c), you will have a stray point. Since stray points serve no purpose other than to take up memory, all stray points should be deleted from your document; you can do this by choosing the *Select Stray Points* filter and pressing the **Delete** key. Both stray and center points are represented by an (x) when not selected. To determine if a point is a center point or a stray point, without using the filter, click on it with a selection tool. If no other points become selected, then it is a stray point. If other points do become selected, then the point is the center point of a path (see Figure 3.5).

Anchor Points vs. End Points

There are two types of anchor points that relate to drawing paths: *regular anchor points* and *end points*. As you read more about line segments and paths, the difference between these two types of anchor points—and your ability to distinguish between them—will become clearer. For now, we will discuss some of the more obvious differences.

Anchor points serve two purposes: They identify the beginning and end of a line segment, and they serve as connections between those line segments to create paths (see Figure 3.6). End points describe the beginning and end of a line segment or path, but do not connect line segments to each other (see Figure 3.7). A regular anchor point joins only two line segments and, therefore, cannot be connected to any other line segment or path (see Figure 3.8). End points have only one line segment connected to them, so they can be joined to other line segments or paths (see Figure 3.9). You can also start, or end, a path at the end point of an existing path in order to combine the two paths (see Figure 3.10 a, b). Joining a line segment or path to an end point will then make that point a regular anchor point.

Aside from noting whether a point has one or two line segments connected to it, there are no other visual hints to discern an anchor point from an end point. In many cases, even that visual distinction is not obvious. It is very important to understand the difference between these two types of points, as there are many other operations that will specifically involve a particular point type. Later in the book, you will come across instances where this topic is brought up again and your understanding of anchor points and end points will be reinforced.

Smooth vs. Corner Points

Anchor points can either be *smooth* or *corner* points. Both types connect one line segment to another. A corner point can connect two curved line segments, two straight line segments, or a curved and a straight line segment (see Figure 3.11). A smooth point, however, only connects two curved line segments where it is necessary for the transition from the first curve to the second to be perfectly smooth (see Figure 3.12).

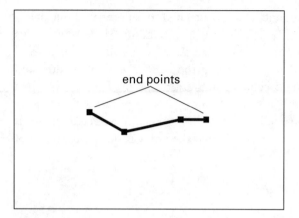

Figure 3.7 *End points.*

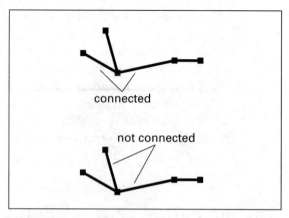

Figure 3.8 *Anchor points can connect only two line segments.*

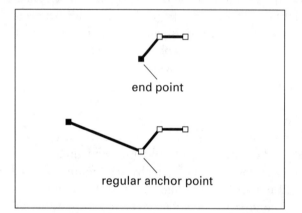

Figure 3.9 *End point becomes a regular anchor point when another line segment is connected to it.*

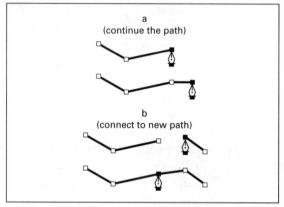

Figure 3.10 *Line segments can be continued from or connected to end points.*

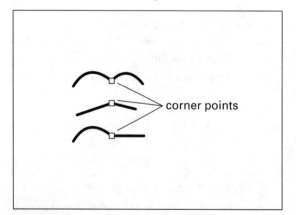

Figure 3.11 *Corner points.*

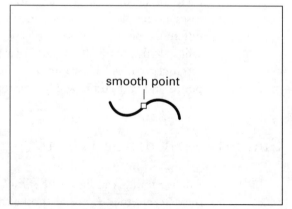

Figure 3.12 *Smooth point.*

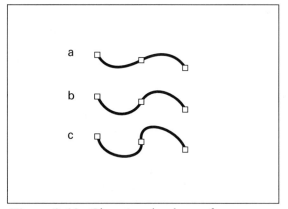

Figure 3.13 *Changing the shape of a curve will affect the shape of a curve connected to it by a smooth point.*

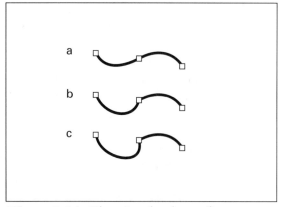

Figure 3.14 *Changing the shape of a curve will not affect the shape of a curve connected to it by a corner point.*

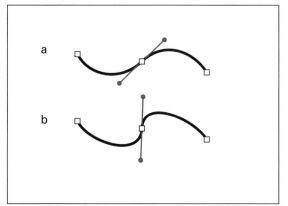

Figure 3.15 *Determining the point type by changing the angle of a direction handle.*

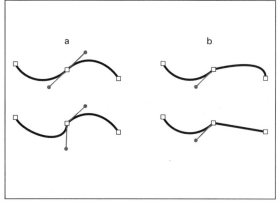

Figure 3.16 *Determining the point type by changing the angle of a direction handle.*

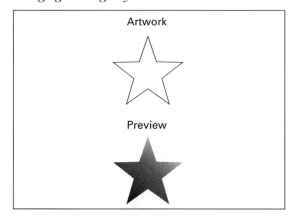

Figure 3.17 *Unselected object.*

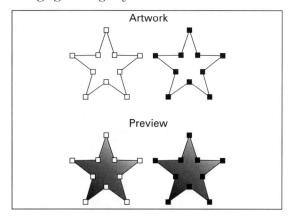

Figure 3.18 *Selected objects.*

When two consecutive curves flow smoothly, one into the other, the transition is kept unvaried by a constant alignment between the two curves. Therefore, if the shape of one curve is altered, the shape of the second curve will automatically change as well (see Figure 3.13 a, b, c). A corner point is used when two connected curved or straight line segments do not require a smooth transition; changing the shape of one line segment will not affect the other (see Figure 3.14 a, b, c)

To determine whether a point is a smooth or corner point, grab a *direction handle* and change its angle. If the direction handle on the other side of the same point has also changed its angle, then the point is a smooth point (see Figure 3.15 a, b). If the direction handle on the other side of the same point has not changed its angle, or there is no other direction handle, then the point is a corner point (see Figure 3.16 a, b).

Understanding the difference between corner and smooth points requires a thorough knowledge of direction handles and how they affect the curves; you may wish to refer to this section after you have covered those subjects in later chapters.

Selecting Single Points

When an anchor or end point is not selected, it cannot be seen in either *Artwork* or *Preview mode* (see Figure 3.17). However, unselected center and stray points will be represented with an X, regardless of the View mode. When a point is selected, it is displayed as a solid or hollow square (see Figure 3.18): A solid square means that a point is *directly* selected and can be manipulated using any of the editing features. *Moving, Rotating, Scaling, Copying,* and so on will affect only the directly selected points. A hollow square represents a point that is not directly—*indirectly*—selected and cannot be manipulated by most tools.

To directly select a point, choose the Direct Selection tool from the toolbox—the cursor will become a hollow arrow (see Figure 3.19). Click the mouse button with the tip of the arrow precisely on the point that you wish to select (see Figure 3.20). You can also directly select a point by selecting its surrounding area with a *marque.* With the Direct Selection tool, click and drag the mouse in a diagonal motion across the anchor point (see Figure 3.21); a dashed rectangle will be created. This is called a *marque.* Make sure that the point you wish to select is inside that rectangle. When you release the mouse button, the marque will disappear and the point will be selected.

Selecting a point indirectly is somewhat more obscure. In a path, when any line segment or anchor point is directly selected, all other points in that path will be indirectly selected.

Selecting Multiple Points

Directly selecting two or more points can be done by using the Shift key. Choose the Direct Selection tool from the toolbox and, while holding down the **Shift** key, click,

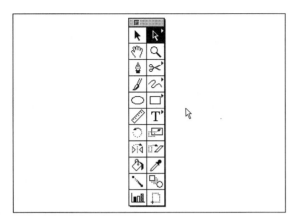

Figure 3.19 *Direct Selection tool.*

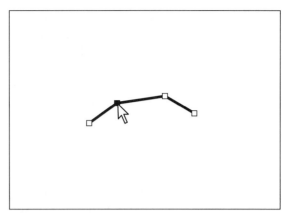

Figure 3.20 *Directly selecting an anchor point.*

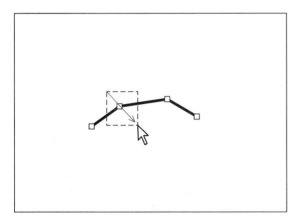

Figure 3.21 *Directly selecting an anchor point with a marque.*

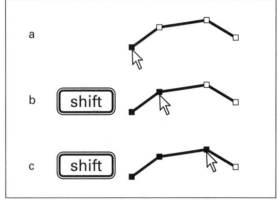

Figure 3.22 *Directly selecting multiple anchor points.*

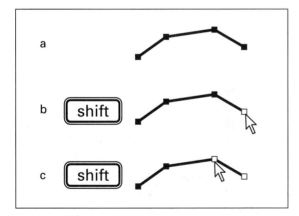

Figure 3.23 *Toggle selection.*

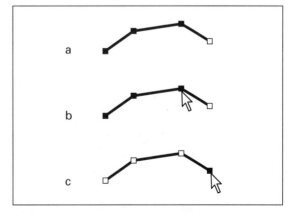

Figure 3.24 *Effects of the Direct Selection tool without the Shift key.*

one point at a time, on all the points you wish to select (see Figure 3.22 a, b, c). Holding down the **Shift** key turns the Selection tool into a *toggle* selection. Clicking on any point will either select or deselect it without affecting any of the other previously selected points (see Figure 3.23 a, b, c). If you use the Selection tool without the Shift key, clicking on an already selected point will have no effect, while clicking on a nonselected point will select that point and deselect all other points already selected (see Figure 3.24 a, b, c).

Selecting multiple points can also be done by using the marque, although the technique is a bit tricky. Since a marque can be created only in a shape of a rectangle, the area that is affected by the marque is harder to control. To select multiple points using a marque, click and drag the marque around the desired points (see Figure 3.25). This becomes more difficult when the point you want to select is near points you do not wish to select; selecting undesired points is often unavoidable (see Figure 3.26 a, b). To correct this, choose the direction in which you drag the marque and its size carefully. Start from a different location and create the smallest marque possible (see Figure 3.27 a, b). If you still have undesired points selected, use the Shift key methods previously described to deselect them (see Figure 3.28).

Manipulating Points

Manipulating points primarily involves using the editing features. These are: *Moving, Copying, Cutting, Deleting, Pasting, Scaling, Rotating, Shearing,* and *Reflecting.* The points we will be working with are mainly anchor and end points. Manipulating these points in any way will directly affect the line segments and paths that are attached to them. Your understanding of some of the editing techniques will be improved once you have read Chapter 4 "Line Segments," and Chapter 5 "Paths."

Moving

To manipulate a point in any way, it must be directly selected. After selecting a point or points, place the cursor on one of the selected points and drag the mouse in the direction you want those points to move (see Figure 3.29 a, b, c). While dragging, you will see both the original points you selected and the points you are moving. When you have finished moving the selected points, release the mouse button and the original points will disappear, leaving only the moved ones. Hold down the **Shift** key while dragging to constrain the movement of the selected points to 45-degree angle increments (see Figure 3.30 a-h). Holding down the **Option** key while dragging creates duplicates of the moved points and line segments attached to them, leaving the original shape unaffected (see Figure 3.31 a, b, c).

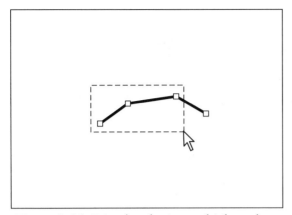

Figure 3.25 *Directly selecting multiple anchor points with a marque.*

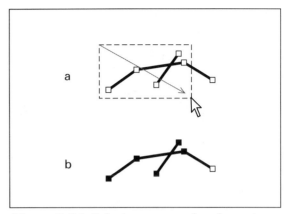

Figure 3.26 *Selecting unwanted anchor points is sometimes unavoidable.*

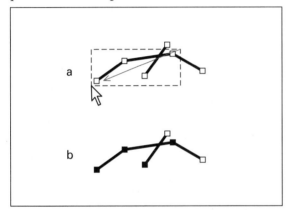

Figure 3.27 *Choose the marque selection area more carefully.*

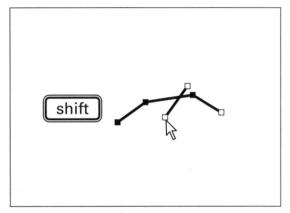

Figure 3.28 *Deselect unwanted points using the Shift key.*

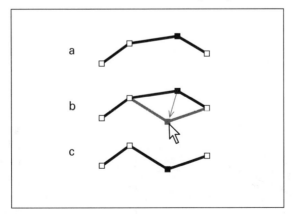

Figure 3.29 *Moving an anchor point.*

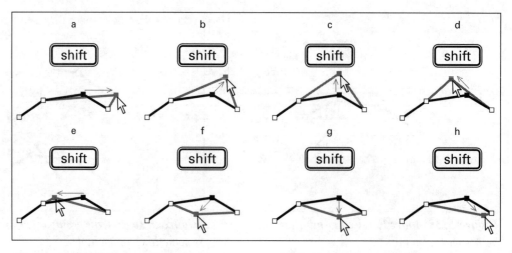

Figure 3.30 *Shift key constrains movement to 45-degree angle increments.*

Even though there are various measuring tools available to you, moving points a precise distance by dragging can be difficult. To move selected points an exact distance on a specific angle, hold down the **Option** key and click the Regular Selection tool (solid arrow) or select Move from the Arrange menu; the Move dialog box will appear. In this box, you can input a specific distance and direction relative to the orientation of the X and Y axes.

Entering a positive horizontal distance will move the selected points to the right, while a negative horizontal distance will move points to the left. A positive vertical distance moves points up, while a negative vertical distance will move them down. Entering a distance and an angle will automatically calculate the horizontal and vertical entries. If you enter the horizontal and vertical distances, the angle will be automatically calculated.

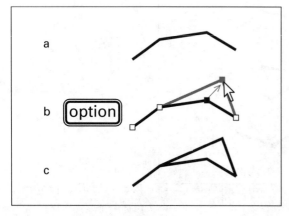

Figure 3.31 *Option key creates a duplicate of a moved object.*

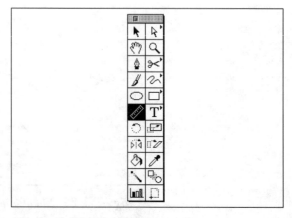

Figure 3.32 *The Measure tool.*

You can use the Measure tool (see Figure 3.32) to measure the distance you want the selected points to move. Immediately after measuring, select the Move dialog box. The measurement results will be automatically entered in the Horizontal, Vertical, and Angle boxes. Click **OK** for the move to take place, or **Copy** to create a duplicate of the moved points. To read more about how to use the Measure tool, read Chapter 9, the "Smooth Transitions between Curved and Straight Line Segments" section.

Cut, Copy, Paste, and Delete

After directly selecting a point or points, you can cut, copy, or delete them from your document. To delete points, press the **Delete** key or choose Clear from the Edit menu. Deleting points erases them from your screen completely. Cutting points will also erase them from the screen, but will keep a duplicate in the *clipboard* for temporary storage. To cut, press **Command + X** or go to the Edit menu and choose Cut. Pressing **Command + C**, or choosing Copy from the Edit menu, will result in a duplicate copy of the selected points and store them in the clipboard, while leaving the original points intact on the screen (see Figure 3.33 a-d).

The points that were cut or copied can now be pasted back into the document by pressing **Command + V** or by choosing Paste from the Edit menu. Keep in mind that the clipboard can hold only the most recently cut or copied object. If the points that you have cut or copied were part of a path, pasting them back into the document will not connect them to their original path. A separate path consisting of the points stored in the clipboard will be created and placed in the middle of your screen (see Figure 3.34 a, b, c).

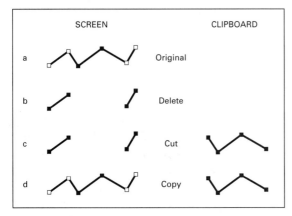

Figure 3.33 *What you see on the screen and what is in the clipboard as you perform different functions.*

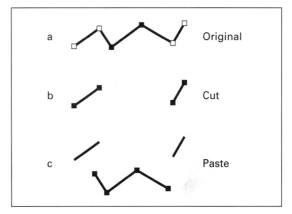

Figure 3.34 *The pasted object does not get connected to the path it was cut from.*

The Four Transform Tools

The effects of the four Transform tools are somewhat diminished when applied to a single anchor point of a path. The result is similar to simply moving that point to a different location, thereby altering the shape of the path. The effects of the Transform tools are more evident when multiple anchor points or whole paths are selected as discussed in Chapters 4 and 5.

The use of the four Transform tools—*Rotate, Scale, Reflect,* and *Shear*—involves choosing an *axis* or a *focal point.* Selecting the right spot for the focal point is an important step and should be thought through carefully. Drastically diverse effects are achieved by placing the focal point in different spots. This will be discussed in greater detail in Chapters 4 and 5.

Rotate

To rotate a point, directly select those points and choose the Rotate tool from the toolbox (see Figure 3.35). The pointer will turn into a plus (+) sign when you move into the active window. Now you need to decide where to place the focal point to establish the axis of rotation. For now, just follow the example (see Figure 3.36) and click to establish the focal point as shown. The plus sign will turn into an arrowhead to indicate that the selected point is ready to be rotated. Hold down the mouse button and drag the mouse in a circular motion around the chosen axis. The selected point will rotate around the axis (see Figure 3.37). To get more control over the rotation, begin dragging further away from the axis of rotation. While dragging, you will see both the original path and the path that is being altered by the rotation of its anchor point or points. When you are finished rotating, release the mouse button and the original path will no longer be seen, leaving only the newly altered path. Holding down the **Shift** key while rotating will constrain the angle of rotation to 45-degree increments (see Figure 3.38 a-h).

If you wish to create a duplicate of the rotated point without affecting the original, hold down the **Option** key while rotating (see Figure 3.39).

Rotating a point by a specific amount requires inputting the angle of rotation into the Rotate dialog box. To access the Rotate dialog box, hold down the **Option** key while clicking to establish the focal point (see Figure 3.40). After you have input the information, click **OK** for the rotation to occur, or **Copy** to duplicate the rotating point.

Scale

Scaling objects also involves choosing a focal point or point of origin from which an object can become reduced or enlarged. Select the point to be scaled, and choose the

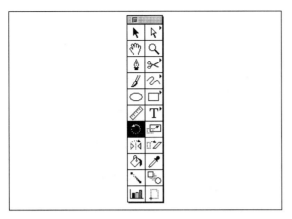

Figure 3.35 *The Rotate tool.*

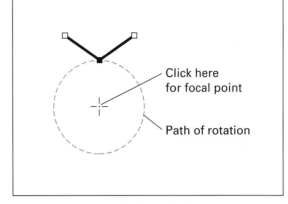

Figure 3.36 *Establishing the focal point.*

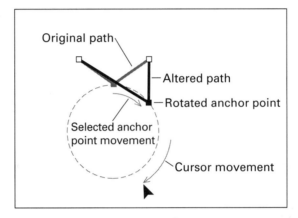

Figure 3.37 *Rotating an object.*

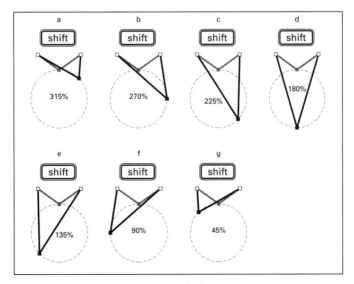

Figure 3.38 *Shift key constrains rotation to 45-degree angle increments.*

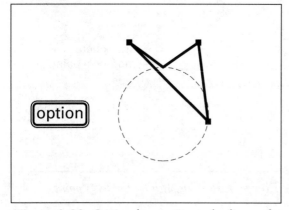

Figure 3.39 *Option key creates a duplicate of a rotated object.*

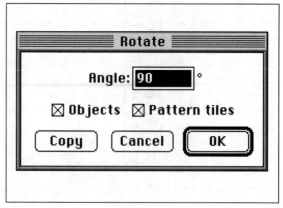

Figure 3.40 *Rotate dialog box.*

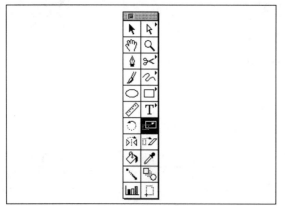

Figure 3.41 *The Scale tool.*

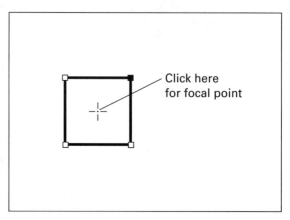

Figure 3.42 *Establishing the focal point.*

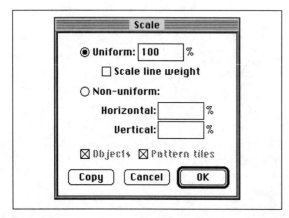

Figure 3.43 *Scale dialog box.*

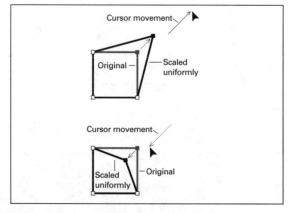

Figure 3.44 *Scaling an object.*

Scale tool from the toolbox (see Figure 3.41). If you wish to enter precise percentages for scaling, hold down the **Option** key while clicking to establish a point of origin. Follow the example for the placement of the point of origin (see Figure 3.42); the Scale dialog box will then appear on the screen. Enter a uniform scale percentage or vertical and horizontal percentages separately for a non-uniform scale (see Figure 3.43), click **OK** or **Copy**.

To scale an object freehand, *do not* hold down the **Option** key while clicking to establish the point of origin. The plus sign will change to an arrowhead to indicate that the selected point is ready for scaling. Drag the mouse away from or toward the point of origin to scale the object (see Figure 3.44). As with the Rotate tool, the further away you start dragging the mouse from the focal point, the more control you will have over the scaling.

Holding down the **Shift** key while dragging the mouse will constrain the horizontal, vertical, or uniform scale (see Figure 3.45). Holding down the **Option** key while dragging the mouse will make a duplicate of the scaled object without affecting the original.

Reflect

Select a point to be reflected and choose the Reflect tool from the toolbox (see Figure 3.46). The pointer will turn into a plus sign (+) after you move it into the active window. If you want to reflect the selected point by dragging, click the mouse button on the spot that you want to become the focal point (see Figure 3.47); the pointer will change to an arrowhead to indicate that the object is ready to be reflected. Drag the arrowhead cursor around the focal point to establish the angle of the *axis of reflection*. The axis of reflection is an imaginary line between the focal point and the arrowhead (see Figure 3.48). The further away from the focal point you begin dragging, the greater control over the angle of the axis of reflection you will have. While dragging, both the original selection and the reflected counterpart will be visible on the screen. When you release the mouse button, the original selection is deleted, leaving the reflected object.

To enter a precise angle of reflection into the Reflect dialog box, hold down the **Option** key as you click the mouse button on the spot that you want to become the focal point. Click the **OK** button for the reflection take place, or the **Copy** button if you want a duplicate of the reflected object (see Figure 3.49).

Shear

The Shear tool is used to slant a selected object on an angle. The effects of this tool are best demonstrated by using whole objects. (Read Chapters 4 and 5 to further explore

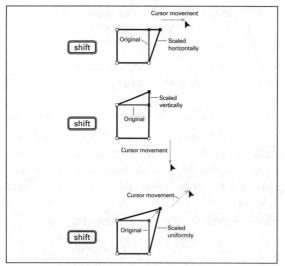

Figure 3.45 *Shift key constrains to horizontal, vertical, or uniform scale.*

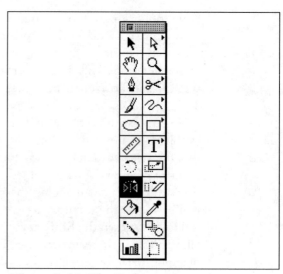

Figure 3.46 *The Reflect tool.*

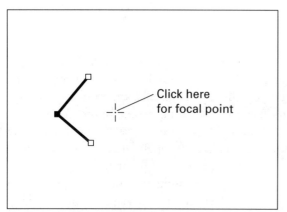

Figure 3.47 *Establishing the focal point.*

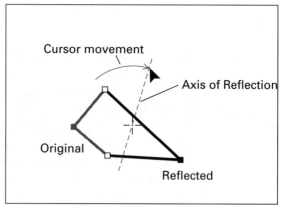

Figure 3.48 *Reflecting an object.*

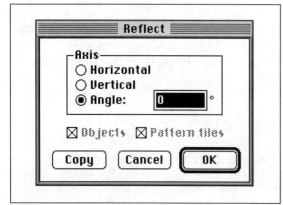

Figure 3.49 *Reflect dialog box.*

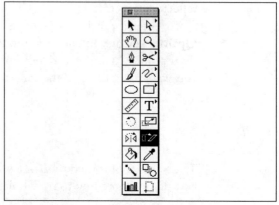

Figure 3.50 *The Shear tool.*

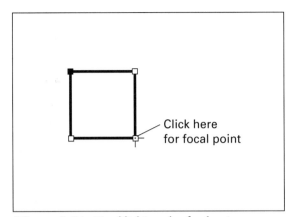

Figure 3.51 *Establishing the focal point.*

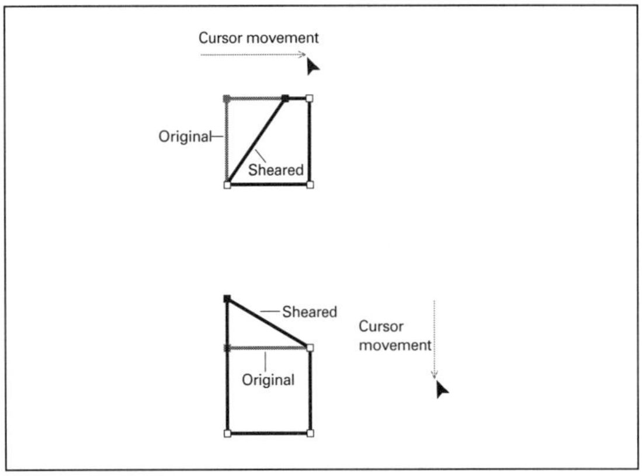

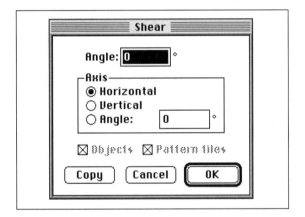

Figure 3.52 *Shearing an object.*

Figure 3.53 *Shear dialog box.*

the Shear tool.) Select the point to be sheared, and choose the Shear tool from the toolbox (see Figure 3.50). The cursor will turn into a plus sign when you move it into the active window. If you want to shear the selected point by dragging, click the mouse button on the spot that you want to be the focal point (see Figure 3.51); the cursor will turn into an arrowhead to indicate that the selected points are ready for shearing. Drag the arrowhead pointer back and forth in a horizontal or vertical motion (see Figure 3.52). The further away from the focal point you start dragging, the more control over the shear you will have. While dragging, both the original selection and the sheared counterpart will be visible on the screen. When you release the mouse button, the original selection is deleted, leaving only the sheared object.

To enter the precise angle of shearing in the Shear dialog box, hold down the **Option** key as you click on the spot that you want to be the focal point. Click the **OK** button for the shear to take place, or the **Copy** button if you wish to make a sheared duplicate (see Figure 3.53).

4 *Line Segments*

Definition

Line segments are created by connecting two points (see Figure 4.1). A line segment can be a curved or straight line (see Figure 4.2). The length of a straight line segment depends on the distance between its two anchor points. The length of a curved line segment varies with its slope (see Figure 4.3). Every object created in Adobe Illustrator is made up of a combination of curved and straight line segments.

Drawing a Line Segment

To draw a straight line segment, select the Pen tool from the toolbox (see Figure 4.4). When you move into the active window, the cursor will turn into a Pen tool with an (x) on the lower right of it to indicate that it is ready to start drawing (see Figure 4.5). Click the mouse button in the active document window to create the first anchor point (see Figure 4.6). The (x) next to the Pen tool icon will disappear, indicating that the line segment is under construction. Next, click the pointer in the spot where you want the line segment to end. The program will automatically draw a straight line between the two points (see Figure 4.7). To create a curved line segment, refer to Chapter 6, "Curves."

Straight vs. Curved

The difference between a straight and curved line segment is not always easily discernible. For example, a curved line segment that has a very shallow slope (see

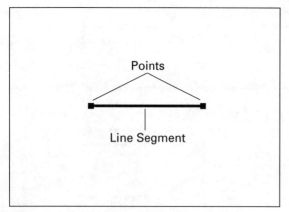

Figure 4.1 *Line segment.*

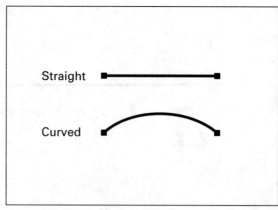

Figure 4.2 *Curved and straight line segments.*

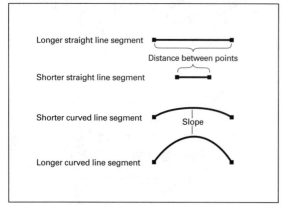

Figure 4.3 *Length of line segments.*

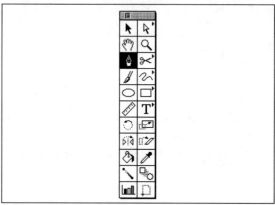

Figure 4.4 *The Pen tool.*

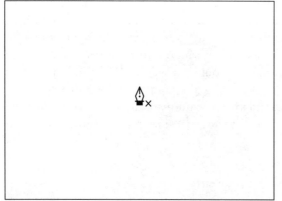

Figure 4.5 *Cursor turns into a Pen tool icon with an (x) next to it.*

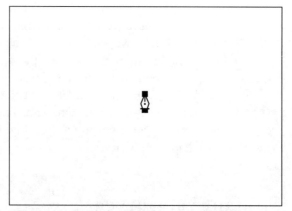

Figure 4.6 *Click to create an anchor point.*

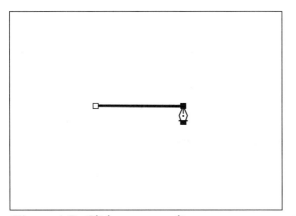

Figure 4.7 *Click to create a line segment.*

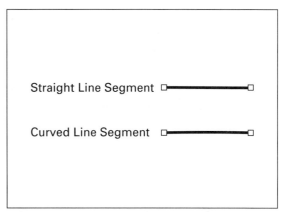

Figure 4.8 *Subtle difference between curved and straight line segments.*

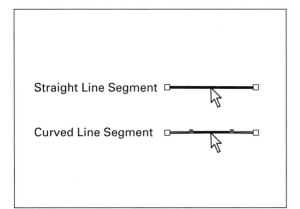

Figure 4.9 *Select to determine whether a line segment is curved or straight.*

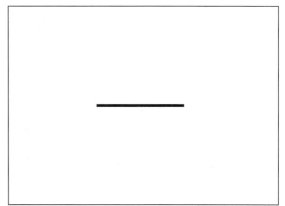

Figure 4.10 *Unselected line segment.*

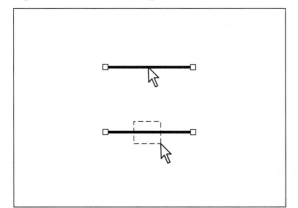

Figure 4.11 *Selecting a line segment without directly selecting its points.*

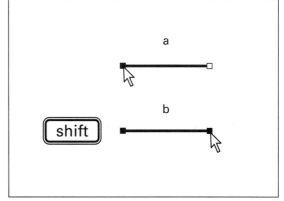

Figure 4.12 *Selecting both points of a line segment using the Shift key.*

Chapter 6) can sometimes look like a straight line (see Figure 4.8). You can determine if a line segment is straight or curved by clicking on the actual line segment with the Direct Selection tool. A curved line segment will have at least one direction handle appear at its points. If a line segment is straight, no direction handle will appear (see Figure 4.9). A selected straight line segment can be affected by the Transform and Edit tools even if its points are not directly selected. The effects of the Transform and Edit tools on a selected curved line segment are not as evident if its points are not directly selected. To learn about how the Transform and Edit features in Illustrator affect curved line segments, read Chapter 1.

Selecting Single Line Segments

In this section, only straight line segments will be discussed. (To learn how to select a curved line segment, see Chapter 6, "Curves.") When a line segment is not selected, its points are not visible (see Figure 4.10). To select a straight line segment, click directly on the line segment with the Direct Selection tool, or drag a marque around a section of it (see Figure 4.11). The points of the line segment will be shown as hollow squares to indicate that the line segment is selected. With a straight line segment, direct or indirect selection of its points (see Chapter 3) will make no difference in the effect of the Edit and Transform tools. The Cut, Copy, and Delete functions are the only editing features that will affect directly selected points differently than points that are indirectly selected. To select a line segment with its points directly selected, click on the first point with the Direct Selection tool, hold down the **Shift** button, and click on the second point (see Figure 4.12 a, b). You can also directly select points of a line segment by dragging a marque around the entire line segment (see Figure 4.13); both points of the line segment will be shown as solid squares. When you directly select points of a line segment, you are indirectly selecting the line segment immediately preceding or following that selected segment. This will affect the indirectly selected line segment when you cut, copy, or delete the directly selected line segment. There will be further discussion of this topic in the "Manipulating Line Segments" section later in this chapter.

Selecting Multiple Line Segments

Selecting multiple line segments within a path can be done by using the Shift key. Choose the Direct Selection tool from the toolbox; press the **Shift** key and click, one line segment at a time, with the Direct Selection Tool, on all the line segments that you wish to select (see Figure 4.14 a, b). Visually, there will be no difference between a path that has one segment selected and a path that has multiple segments selected. You will recall that the Shift key turns the selection tool into a toggle selection. Clicking

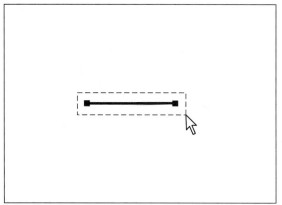

Figure 4.13 *Selecting both points of a line segment using the marque.*

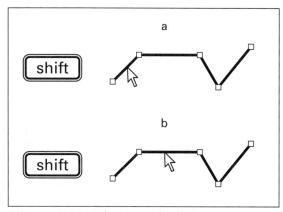

Figure 4.14 *Selecting multiple line segments using the Shift key.*

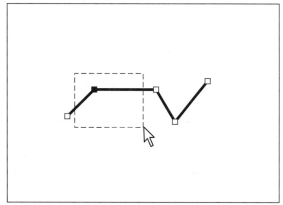

Figure 4.15 *Selecting multiple line segments using the marque.*

on any line segment will either select or deselect it without affecting any of the other line segments. Using the selection tool without the Shift key will have no effect on an already selected line segment. Clicking on a nonselected line segment, without the Shift key, will select that line segment while deselecting other already selected line segments. This applies to both clicking and marque selection.

You can also select multiple line segments by dragging a marque around all the line segments you wish to select. If undesired line segments become selected, hold down the **Shift** key and deselect them. Selecting in this way will directly select the points that fall within the marque area (see Figure 4.15). The consequences of this selection were mentioned earlier and will be discussed again in the next section.

Manipulating Line Segments

Moving, copying, cutting, deleting, pasting, scaling, rotating, shearing, and reflecting are the ways in which a line segment can be manipulated. However, before any of these editing features take effect, a line segment must be selected. A line segment can be selected with its points directly or indirectly selected (see previous section). Of the available editing tools, only Cut, Copy, Delete, and Paste will act differently based on how the points are selected. The functions of the other editing tools will not be affected by the type of selection.

Move

To move a straight line segment, select it either by clicking with a selection tool, or by dragging a marque around it. Once the line segment has been selected, place the cursor on it and drag the mouse in the direction that you want the line segment to move (see Figure 4.16). Keep in mind that moving a line segment that is part of a larger path will also affect any line segments immediately preceding or following the selected line segment, altering the shape of that path (see Figure 4.17). While dragging, you will see both the original line segment and an image of the one you are moving. When you have completed the move, release the mouse button and the original line segment will disappear, leaving only the moved segment. Holding down the **Shift** key while dragging will constrain the movement of the line segment to 45-degree angle increments. Holding down the **Option** key while dragging creates a duplicate of the selected line segment and any line segments attached to it, while leaving the original path unaffected.

Moving a line segment a precise distance by dragging can be difficult, even with the various measuring tools provided in the program. To move selected line segments an exact distance on a specific angle, hold down the **Option** key and click on the regular selection tool (solid arrow), or select Move from the Edit menu. The Move dialog box will appear and allow you to input a specific distance and angle for the move. In the dialog box, click **OK** for the move to take place, or **Copy** to create a duplicate of the selected line segment.

Cut, Copy, Paste, and Delete

A selected line segment may be cut, copied, or deleted from a document. To delete a selected line segment, press the Delete key or choose Clear from the Edit menu. If the anchor point or points of a selected line segment within a larger path are directly selected, then the line segments attached to the selected line will also be deleted (see

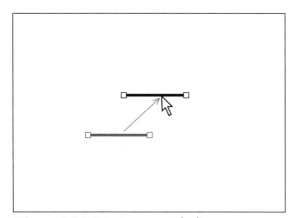

Figure 4.16 *Moving a straight line segment.*

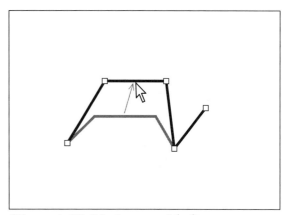

Figure 4.17 *Moving a straight line segment attached to other line segments.*

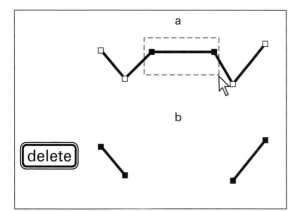

Figure 4.18 *Deleting a line segment when its points are directly selected.*

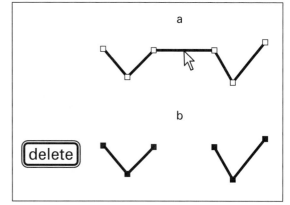

Figure 4.19 *Deleting a line segment when its points are not directly selected.*

Figure 4.18 a, b). If, on the other hand, the anchor points of that same line segment are not directly selected, only that line segment will be deleted (see Figure 4.19 a, b).

Deleting line segments will erase them from your document completely. Cutting line segments will also erase them from the screen, but will keep a duplicate in the clipboard for temporary storage. To cut a selected line segment, press **Command + X** or go to the Edit menu and select Cut. If the anchor points of a line segment that is part of a path are directly selected, the line segments attached to the selected line segment will also be cut (see Figure 4.20 a, b). Only the selected line segment will be cut if its anchor points are not directly selected (see Figure 4.21 a, b).

Pressing **Command + C** or choosing Copy from the Edit menu will result in a duplication of the selected line segment in the clipboard, while leaving the original line segment intact on the screen (see Figure 4.22 a, b). Copying will affect directly and indirectly selected anchor points of a line segment in the same manner that cutting and deleting do.

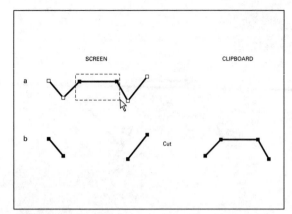

Figure 4.20 *What you see on the screen and what is in the clipboard when a line segment, with its points directly selected, is cut.*

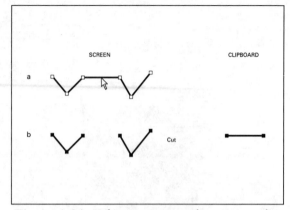

Figure 4.21 *What you see on the screen and what is in the clipboard when a line segment, with its points not directly selected, is cut.*

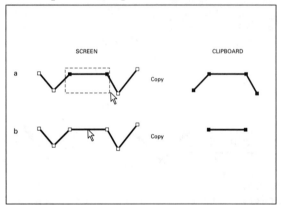

Figure 4.22 *What you see on the screen and what is in the clipboard when a line segment, with its points directly and not directly selected, is copied.*

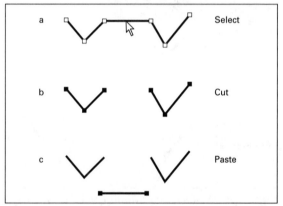

Figure 4.23 *Pasting a line segment after it has been cut from a path.*

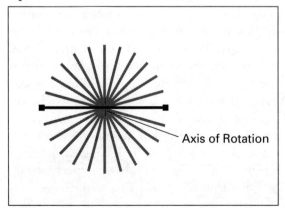

Figure 4.24 *Axis of rotation near the center of a line segment.*

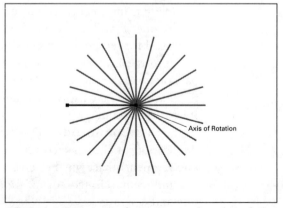

Figure 4.25 *Axis of rotation at the edge of a line segment.*

Line segments that were cut or copied can be pasted back into the document by pressing **Command** + **V** or by going to the Edit menu and choosing Paste. Keep in mind that the clipboard can hold only the most recently cut or copied objects. If the line segment that was cut or copied was part of a path, pasting it back into the document will not connect it to the path that it was cut or copied from. Instead, a separate path consisting of the line segment or segments stored in the clipboard will be created and placed in the middle of your screen (see Figure 4.23 a, b, c).

The Four Transform Tools

The four Transform tools—*Rotate, Scale, Reflect,* and *Shear*—are essentially used to manipulate line segments in the same way as they are used to manipulate points. There are, however, some distinct differences. These differences, plus some techniques on improving your skills with these tools, will be discussed next.

Rotate

As with all editing functions, to rotate a line segment, you will need to select it. The Rotate tool's performance will not be affected by the direct or indirect selection of a line segment's anchor point. After choosing the Rotate tool from the toolbox, the pointer will turn into a plus sign when moved into the active window. At this time, you must choose a place for the focal point or the axis of rotation. The axis of rotation will determine the point around which the line segment will rotate; this point can be placed anywhere on the document. You are now faced with an infinite number of possible locations for the axis of rotation.

To narrow down these possibilities, you must first decide what you want the selected line segment to do. For instance, if you wish for the line segment to rotate around its center, click to establish the axis of rotation near the center of the line segment (see Figure 4.24). To have the line segment rotating around one of its points, click with the Rotate tool at that point to establish the axis of rotation (see Figure 4.25). If you decide to rotate the line segment around an area away from the line segment, click there to establish the axis. The further away from the selected line segment you place the axis of rotation, the greater the radius of the rotation will be (see Figure 4.26 a, b).

Once the axis of rotation has been established, the plus sign will turn into an arrowhead, indicating that the selected line segment is now ready to be rotated. Hold down the mouse button and drag the cursor in a circular motion around the chosen axis; the selected line segment will rotate around the axis as you drag (see Figure 4.27). To get more control over the rotating object, begin dragging further away from the axis of rotation. While dragging, you will see both the original selected line segment and the line segment that is being rotated. Once you have finished rotating, release the

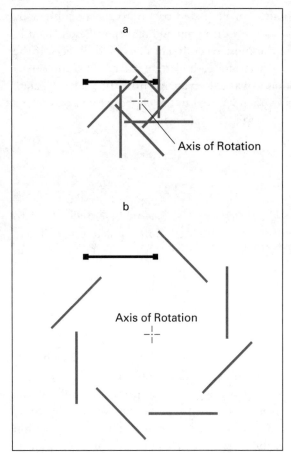

Figure 4.26 *Axis of rotation away from a line segment.*

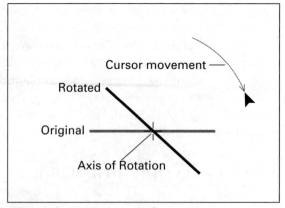

Figure 4.27 *Rotating a line segment.*

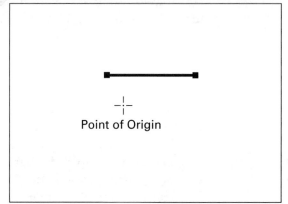

Figure 4.28 *Establishing the point of origin.*

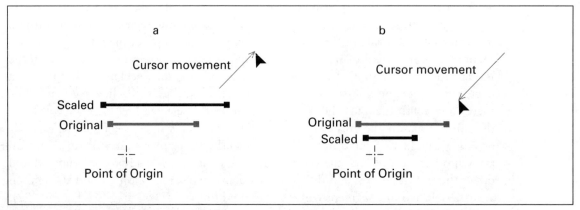

Figure 4.29 *Scaling a line segment.*

mouse button and the original line segment will disappear, leaving only the newly rotated line segment.

To rotate a line segment by a specific amount requires inputting the angle of rotation into the Rotate dialog box. To access this dialog box, hold down the **Option** key while clicking to establish the axis of rotation. After inputting the desired angle, click **OK** for the rotate to occur, or **Copy** to duplicate the rotated line segment.

Scale

Scaling single or multiple line segments can also be described as moving the points away from or toward the focal point or the point of origin. The further two points in a line segment move away from the focal point and each other, the longer that line segment becomes, and vice versa. That is why, when scaling, where you place the point of origin is very important. The effects of the Scale tool, and the location of the point of origin, will be discussed in more depth in Chapter 5.

First, select the line segment to be scaled and choose the Scale tool from the toolbox. The cursor will become a plus sign when moved into the active window to indicate that the point of origin needs to be specified. Click where you want to establish the point of origin (see Figure 4.28). The plus sign will change to an arrowhead to indicate that the selected line segment is ready for scaling. Drag the mouse away or toward the point of origin to scale the object (see Figure 4.29 a, b); start dragging further away from the point of origin to get more control over scaling.

You can enter precise vertical, horizontal, and uniform percentages for scaling in the Scale dialog box. To bring up the Scale dialog box, hold down the **Option** key while clicking to establish the point of origin. After entering the desired percentages, click **OK** for the scaling to take place, or **Copy** to create a duplicate of the scaled object.

Reflect

To reflect a selected line segment, choose the Reflect tool from the toolbox. The cursor will turn into a plus sign when you move it into the active window. If you want to reflect the selection by dragging, click the mouse button on the spot that will be the focal point. The pointer will change to an arrowhead to indicate that the object is ready to be reflected.

Move the arrowhead cursor away from the focal point and click the mouse button. The axis of reflection will be established by the imaginary line that intersects the focal point and the spot where the arrowhead was clicked. The distance between the focal point and the arrowhead will have no effect on the axis of reflection. As you click to establish the axis of reflection, the line segment will be reflected (see Figure 4.30).

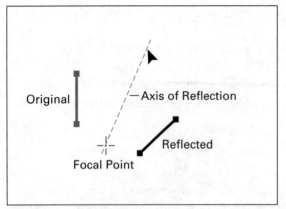

Figure 4.30 *Reflecting a line segment without manually varying the axis of reflection.*

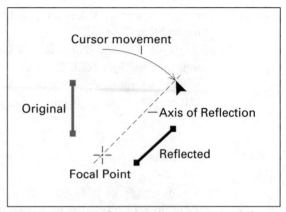

Figure 4.31 *Reflecting a line segment while manually varying the axis of reflection.*

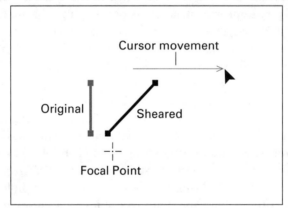

Figure 4.32 *Shearing a line segment.*

To vary the axis of reflection while the line segment is being reflected, click to establish the focal point, and drag the mouse in a circular motion around that focal point. This will change the axis of reflection as you drag. In this case, the further from the focal point you start dragging, the more control over the angle of the axis of reflection you will have. While dragging, both the original line segment and the reflected counterpart will be visible on the screen (see Figure 4.31). When you release the mouse button, the original selection is deleted, leaving the reflected line segment.

You can enter a precise angle for the axis of reflection into the Reflect dialog box. Hold down the **Option** key as you click the mouse button on the screen to establish the focal point. Select either the vertical or horizontal, or enter an angle for the axis of reflection. Click **OK** for the reflection to occur, or **Copy** to reflect a duplicate.

Shear

Shearing an object requires you to select not only the focal point and the angle of shearing, but also the angle of the axis of shearing. This makes shearing objects by dragging much trickier, since you are trying to establish two angles with one move.

Select the line segment to be sheared, and choose the Shear tool from the toolbox. The cursor will become a plus sign when you move it into the active window. After you click to establish the focal point, the pointer will turn into an arrowhead to indicate that the selected line segment is ready for shearing. Drag the arrowhead to establish the angle of shearing and the angle of the axis of shearing. While dragging, you will see both the original segment and the one you are shearing (see Figure 4.32). Even though dragging further away from the focal point will give you somewhat greater control, shearing an object by hand can produce some unexpected results (see Chapter 5).

Using the Shear dialog box to shear an object is a better option. Hold down the **Option** key while clicking to establish the focal point; this will bring up the Shear dialog box. Select either the horizontal or vertical axis and the angle of shearing. You can also input a specific angle for the axis as well as the shear angle. Click **OK** for the shear to take place, or the **Copy** button to create a duplicate of the sheared object.

The effects of the Shear tool are best demonstrated when using whole objects or paths. The discussion of the effects of the placement of the focal point, and the selection of angles of the axis of shearing, and the angle of shearing, will be dealt with in greater detail in the next chapter.

5 *Paths*

Definition

In Adobe Illustrator, a path can consist of only one point. Two points that are connected with a line segment are also considered a path. However, for our purposes, we will deal only with paths that are made up of two or more connected line segments. These line segments can be curved, straight, or a combination of both. The discussion of curves will come later; for now, we will concentrate on paths comprised of straight line segments.

Open vs. Closed

Paths can either be *open* or *closed*. The difference between these two varieties of paths is important to understand, but not always easy to recognize. Certain commands and techniques can be applied to only one type of path. Operations such as *cutting with the scissors, blending, masking, painting, compounding, joining,* and many others will act differently, depending on whether they are being applied to an open or a closed path.

The first and most obvious visual hint to recognizing a path as open or closed is the presence of end points (see Figure 5.1). An open path has a definite beginning and end marked by end points; while a closed path has no end points, as it consists only of regular anchor points (see Figure 5.2). Sometimes, this visual difference is not present. For instance, an unselected path painted with a *fill* (see the "Painting Paths" section later in this chapter) will look the same in the Preview mode whether it is closed or open (see Figure 5.3). The program automatically fills an open path with specified color, gradient, or pattern to the boundary of its line segments and an imaginary straight line between its end points. In other words, instead of letting the fill color *spill* out of the

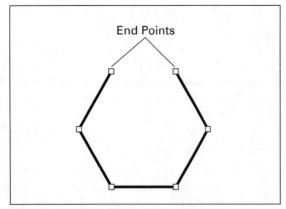

Figure 5.1 *Open path has end points.*

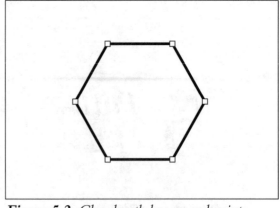

Figure 5.2 *Closed path has no end points.*

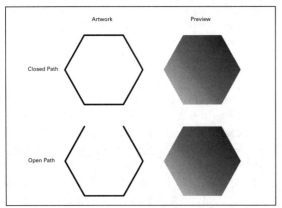

Figure 5.3 *Artwork and Preview modes of open and closed paths.*

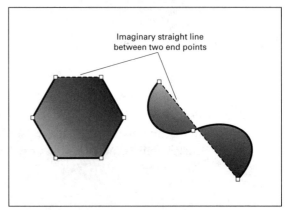

Figure 5.4 *Open paths get filled up to the imaginary straight line between the end points.*

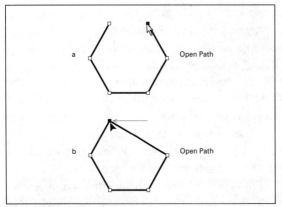

Figure 5.5 *Positioning two end points directly on top of each other.*

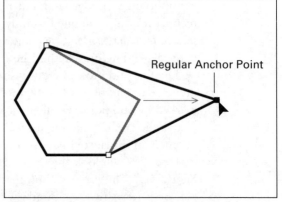

Figure 5.6 *Moving a point to determine whether it is an anchor or an end point.*

gap of the open path onto the surrounding area, like bitmap programs tend to do, Illustrator assumes a straight line between the two end points and fills the path up to that line (see Figure 5.4). In this case, to determine whether a path is open or closed, you must select it. Once selected, the path displays its points and line segments so that end points are easily recognized and a path can be determined as closed or open.

There is another case in which the visual distinction between an open and a closed path is vague. An end point can be moved close to or onto another end point to give an open path the illusion of being closed (see Figure 5.5 a, b). Even though this path may look closed in all views, and no matter how it is painted, it is an open path. It still has the two end points that make it an open path, but since they are right next to or on top of each other, it seems like they are one regular anchor point. In this case, determining what kind of path it is becomes difficult, since selecting the path will not produce any more hints to whether it is open or closed.

If you have done the actual move shown in Figure 5.5 yourself, then you know the path is open even though it appears closed. On the other hand, if you had just walked into the room and saw this path on the computer screen, you would have no way of knowing whether it was open or closed. This can also happen inadvertently while you are working if you are not paying close attention to the construction of the path.

Even if you cannot see an actual difference, there are several ways to determine whether a path is open or closed. Click and drag any of the points in the path with the Direct Selection tool; if both line segments that seem to be connected to that point move with it, then that particular point is not an end point (see Figure 5.6). Undo the move by pressing **Command + Z** or by choosing Undo from the Edit menu, for the path to return to its original shape. Repeat these steps for all other points in the path. When you click and drag on a point and only one of the connected line segments moves with it, then that point is an end point and the path is an open path (see Figure 5.7).

Unfortunately, this process is not efficient when the path you are working with has a large number of points. Unless you get lucky and discover an end point right away, it can take a very long time to check every point on a path. In this case, the only way to find out if a path is open or closed is to try to complete a function that is specific to open or closed paths. Various dialog boxes will appear to let you know that you are trying to affect a wrong type of path. When that happens you can open or close the path with a variety of options. Different techniques regarding the opening and closing of paths will be discussed later in the book in Chapters 9 and 11.

Creating Paths

Paths can be created in many different ways with the Illustrator drawing tools. These tools are: the *Pen tool, Brush tool, Freehand tool, Auto Trace tool,* the *Oval* and *Rectangle tools,* and the *Polygon* and *Star filters*. Of these tools, only the Pen and Freehand tools are capable of drawing both open and closed paths. All the other tools create closed paths only.

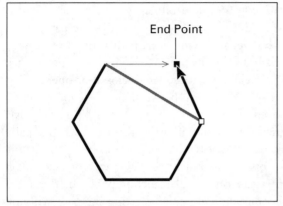

Figure 5.7 *If a point separates from one of the line segments, it is an end point.*

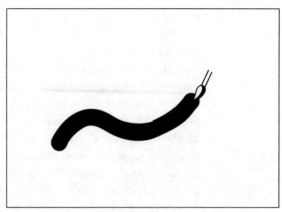

Figure 5.8 *Brush stroke.*

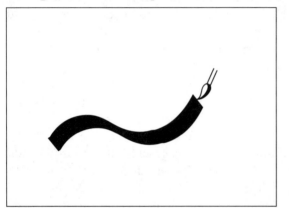

Figure 5.9 *Calligraphic brush stroke.*

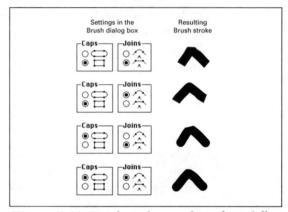

Figure 5.10 *Brush strokes resulting from different Caps and Joins settings.*

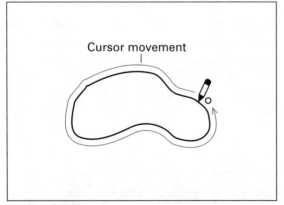

Figure 5.11 *Closing a Freehand path.*

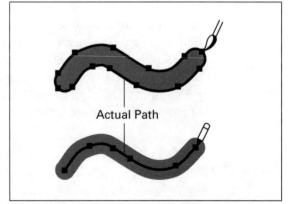

Figure 5.12 *Freehand and Brush paths.*

Brush Tool

To create a path using the Brush tool, select it from the toolbox—the pointer will turn into a brush when you move into the active window. Drag the mouse or other input device in a motion that will determine the shape you want to create on-screen (see Figure 5.8). The width of the brush path is specified in the Brush dialog box. To bring up the Brush dialog box, double-click on the Brush tool in the toolbox. Enter the desired width of the brush path, or choose the *calligraphic angle.* Entering a calligraphic angle will vary the thickness of the brush path as you drag (see Figure 5.9). If you are using a pressure-sensitive drawing pad, select the Variable Width brush option and specify minimum and maximum path widths. Different *caps* and *joins* can be selected unless you are using a calligraph brush style. The effect of the Caps and Joins options are shown in Figure 5.10.

Freehand Tool

The only similarity between the Freehand and Brush tools is that they both create paths while you are dragging the mouse or another input device, and the shapes of those paths are directly related to the movements of your hand. The main difference in the Freehand tool is that the path it draws is an open path. This also means that the width of the path drawn by the Freehand tool cannot be specified. To draw a closed path with the Freehand tool, you must return to the exact spot where you started to draw the Freehand path and release the mouse button while it is on top of the first end point. The pencil icon will have a (0) to the lower right of it, indicating that it is positioned directly on top of the first end point (see Figure 5.11).

Another way of describing this is that the Brush tool draws two lines that are a set distance from each other, relative to the information input in the Brush dialog box. The Freehand tool, however, draws only one line that can be painted with a stroke (see Figure 5.12) to give it width (see the Painting Paths section later in this Chapter).

To use the Freehand tool, select it from the toolbox; the cursor will become a *pencil* when moved into the active window. Drag the mouse or another input device in the motion of the shape you want to create on the screen. As you drag, the pencil will draw a dotted line that will turn into a regular path when you release the mouse button (see Figure 5.13 a, b). The dotted line can be erased while you are dragging by holding down the **Command** key and dragging back over the line. While the Command key is pressed, the pencil will turn into an eraser (see Figure 5.14 a, b).

Both the Brush and Freehand tools respond to variations in the movement of your hand. Even if you have a very steady hand, your drawings can be far from smooth. For

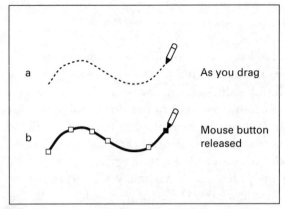

Figure 5.13 *Creating a Freehand path.*

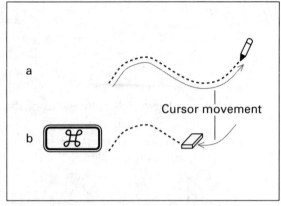

Figure 5.14 *Erasing a Freehand path.*

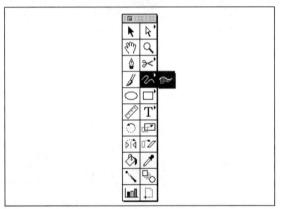

Figure 5.15 *The Auto Trace tool.*

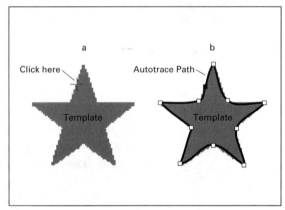

Figure 5.16 *Autotracing a Template.*

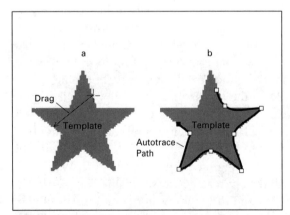

Figure 5.17 *Autotracing a portion of a Template.*

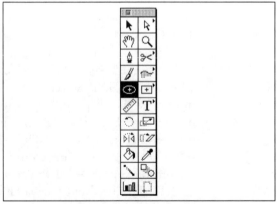

Figure 5.18 *The Oval tool.*

the best drawing results, use the Pen tool. You can set the *freehand tolerance level* to reduce or increase its sensitivity by choosing Preferences > General from the File menu or by pressing **Command** + **K**. The default setting for the freehand tolerance level is 2 *pixels,* which means that a variation of 2 pixels in the movement of the cursor will not affect the freehand line.

Auto Trace Tool

The Auto Trace tool automatically traces the outlines of a template (see Chapter 10). To use the Auto Trace tool, click on the Freehand tool and drag to the right to get the Auto Trace tool (see Figure 5.15). Click near the edge of a template to indicate a starting point. A path will be drawn (see Figure 5.16 a, b), producing a continuous line along a template until it comes back to the original starting point to close the path. If you do not wish for the Auto Trace tool to close the path, drag across from the starting point to the desired ending point (see Figure 5.17 a, b).

As with the Freehand tool, the paths created using the Auto Trace tool are not precise. You can set the *autotrace tolerance level* in General Preferences. This will give you somewhat greater control over the autotraced path, but the best results are still achieved by using the Pen tool.

Oval Tool

The Oval tool is used when you need to create perfect ovals or circles. All ovals are created with four curved line segments connected by four smooth points with one center point. Ovals can be drawn from the center outward, or from edge to edge. To change from a Center Oval tool to an Edge-to-Edge Oval tool—or vice versa— double-click on the Oval tool in the toolbox, or hold down the **Option** key while drawing an oval.

To draw an oval from the center, make sure that the (+) sign in the Oval tool icon is in the center (see Figure 5.18); if it is not, double-click on the Oval tool or hold down the **Option** key. Click where you want the center of the oval to be and drag in any direction away from the center; an oval will be created (see Figure 5.19). While you are dragging, the oval will change shape relative to the direction of the drag. When the oval is the size and shape that you want, release the mouse button—the oval will remain in that shape.

To create a perfect circle, hold down the **Shift** key while dragging away from the center. The circle will get larger as you drag further away from the center, and smaller as you drag closer to the center (see Figure 5.20 a, b). When the circle is the right size, release the mouse button first and then the **Shift** key. Releasing the **Shift** key *before* the mouse button will create an oval.

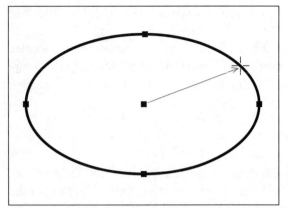

Figure 5.19 *Creating an oval from the center.*

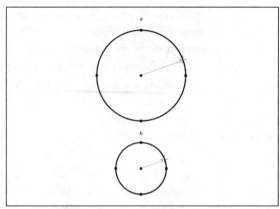

Figure 5.20 *Creating a circle from the center.*

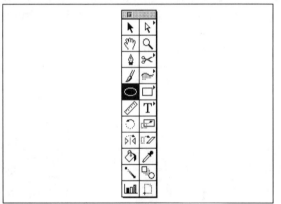

Figure 5.21 *The Oval edge-to-edge tool.*

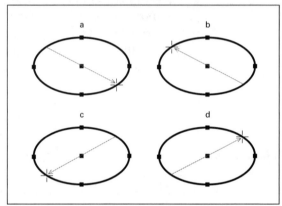

Figure 5.22 *Creating an oval edge-to-edge.*

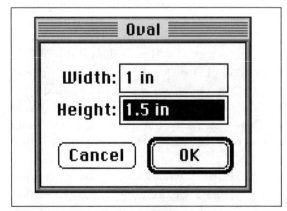

Figure 5.23 *The Oval dialog box.*

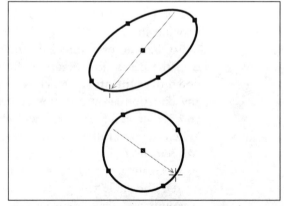

Figure 5.24 *Constrain angle set to 30 degrees.*

To draw an oval from edge to edge, make sure that there is no (+) sign on the Oval tool icon (see Figure 5.21); if not, double-click on the Oval tool or hold down the **Option** key. Click where you want one edge of the oval to be and drag diagonally (see Figure 5.22 a-d). While you are dragging, the oval will change shape relative to the direction of the drag. Release the mouse button to finish the oval. Follow the same procedure while holding down the **Shift** key to create a circle from edge to edge.

You can also create an oval from the center or edge to edge by entering the precise amount into the Oval dialog box (see Figure 5.23). To bring up this dialog box, click with the Oval tool in the document where you want the oval to start. The dialog box will appear. Entering the same values in the width and the height will result in a circle. Click **OK** for the oval to be created. An oval can be rotated using the Rotate tool. To create an oval already on an angle, set the Constrain Angle option in the General Preferences menu to the desired degree. Once you have changed these settings, all subsequent ovals will automatically be created on that angle (see Figure 5.24). The Constrain Angle option has no effect on circles, because rotating a circle has no effect on its appearance.

Rectangle Tool

The Rectangle tool is used to create a perfect rectangle or a square. All rectangles are created with four straight line segments connected by four corner points with one center point. Like circles and ovals, rectangles can be drawn from the center or from edge to edge. To change from a Center Rectangle tool to an Edge-to-Edge Rectangle tool, or vice versa, double-click on the Rectangle tool in the tool palette, or hold down the **Option** key while drawing a rectangle.

To draw a rectangle from the center, make sure that the (+) sign in the Rectangle tool icon is in the center (see Figure 5.25); if not, double-click on the Rectangle tool or hold down the **Option** key. Click where you want the center of the rectangle to be and drag in any direction away from the center (see Figure 5.26).

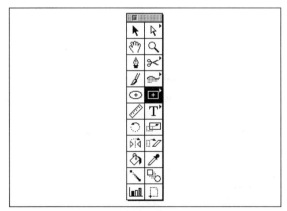

Figure 5.25 *The Rectangle tool.*

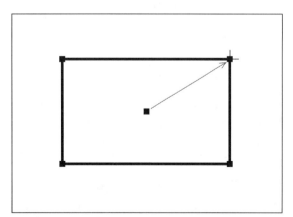

Figure 5.26 *Creating a rectangle from the center.*

While you are dragging, the rectangle will change shape relative to the direction of the drag. Dragging further away from the center in a horizontal direction—rather than a vertical—will result in a long, flat rectangle. Dragging more on the vertical than the horizontal will result in a narrow, tall rectangle (see Figure 5.27). When the rectangle is the size and shape you want, release the mouse button.

To create a perfect square, hold down the **Shift** key while dragging. When making squares, you will see that the square will become larger as you drag the mouse away from the center and smaller as you drag closer to it (see Figure 5.28 a, b). When the square is the right size, release the mouse button first and then the **Shift** key. Releasing the **Shift** key *before* the mouse button will result in a rectangle.

To draw a rectangle from edge to edge, make sure that there is no (+) sign on the Rectangle tool icon (see Figure 5.29); if not, double-click on the Rectangle tool or hold down the **Option** key. Click where you want one edge of the rectangle to be and drag diagonally (see Figure 5.30 a-d). While you are dragging, the rectangle will change shape relative to the direction of the drag. Release the mouse button to finish the rectangle. To create an edge-to-edge square, follow the same procedure while holding down the **Shift** key.

You can also create a rectangle, from the center or edge to edge, by entering the precise amount into the Rectangle dialog box. To bring up this dialog box, click in the document with the Rectangle tool at the point where you want the rectangle to begin. The dialog box will appear (see Figure 5.31). Enter the desired measurements for the rectangle—entering the same values in the width and height boxes will result in a square. Click **OK** for the rectangle to be created. Although you can rotate the rectangle using the Rotate tool, to draw a rectangle that is already angled, set the Constrain Angle option in the General Preferences settings to the desired degrees. All rectangles and squares that are drawn from then on will be tilted to that angle (see Figure 5.32).

Rounded Corner Rectangle Tool

You can also create rectangles with rounded corners. *Rounded corner rectangles* consist of four straight line segments and four curved line segments that are exactly quarter circles (see Figure 5.33).

To create a rounded corner rectangle, click on the regular Rectangle tool and drag to the right to get the Rounded Corner Rectangle tool (see Figure 5.34). If the Rounded Corner Rectangle tool has a plus (+) sign in the center, the rounded corner rectangle will be drawn from the center; if there is no (+) sign, it will be drawn edge to edge. Proceed with the same steps as for a sharp corner rectangle.

When a rounded corner rectangle is drawn from edge to edge, the origin point that you pick to start it from is not the actual edge of the rectangle as it is with a sharp corner rectangle. This is simply because a rounded corner rectangle has no actual

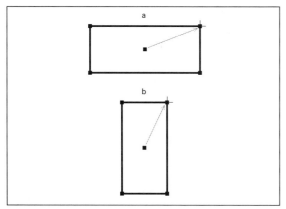

Figure 5.27 *Creating various shaped rectangles by changing the direction of the drag.*

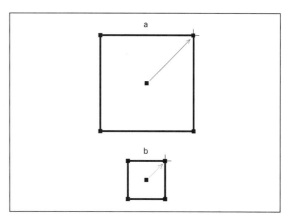

Figure 5.28 *Creating a square from the center.*

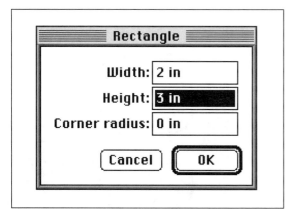

Figure 5.29 *The Rectangle edge-to-edge tool.*

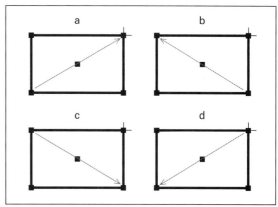

Figure 5.30 *Creating a rectangle edge-to-edge.*

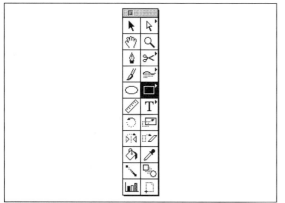

Figure 5.31 *The Rectangle dialog box.*

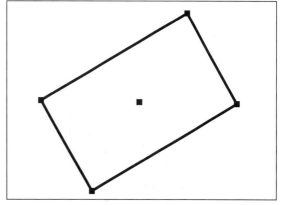

Figure 5.32 *Constrain angle set to 30 degrees.*

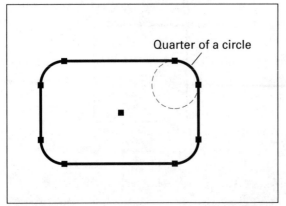

Figure 5.33 *A rounded corner of a rectangle is a quarter circle.*

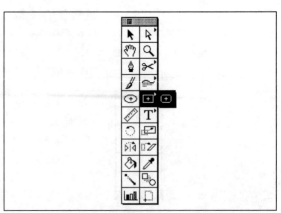

Figure 5.34 *The Rounded Corner Rectangle tool.*

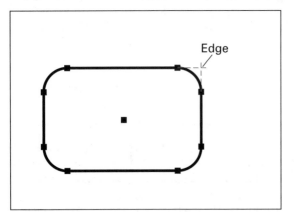

Figure 5.35 *Determining the edge of a rounded corner rectangle.*

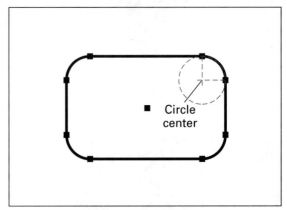

Figure 5.36 *Determining the corner radius.*

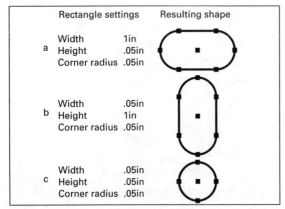

Figure 5.37 *Creating rounded corner rectangles with two sides and no sides.*

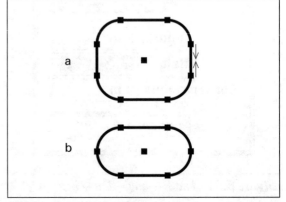

Figure 5.38 *What happens to the rounded corner rectangle side.*

edges. The edges of a round corner rectangle are determined by the *corner radius* of that rectangle. This is an imaginary edge where the two adjacent sides of a rectangle would intersect if they were to extend past the rounded corner (see Figure 5.35). This distance is equal to the corner radius assigned to that rectangle. A *radius* is the distance between the center of a circle and its edge. To find the center of the circle, which makes up a rounded corner, draw two perpendicular lines, one from each anchor point where the rounded corner and the straight side meet (see Figure 5.36). The intersection of the two lines is the center point of the rounded corner. The distance from that center point to anywhere along the rounded corner is the corner radius.

In Illustrator, the default corner radius is 12 points. You can change this by typing in a different amount in the Rectangle dialog box or in the General Preferences. If the corner radius is greater than one half of either the width or the length of the rectangle, then that side of the rectangle will be perfectly rounded with no straight lines. Entering a corner radius greater than half of both the width and the length of the rectangle will result in a circle (see Figure 5.37 a, b, c).

Creating circles in this way is not exactly the same as creating them with the Oval tool. Even though the shape may look similar to one drawn by the Oval tool, there is one distinct difference in the way the path is created. The straight line segments that are created from the flat sides of the rectangle are not eliminated when the corner radius is greater than half of either side. The line segment and its connecting points still exist in this path but with a length of 0. The two points that describe the ends of the straight line segment and connect it to the curved line segments of the rounded corners are simply placed one right on top of the other (see Figure 5.38 a, b). If you select one of those points with the Direct Selection tool and drag it in any direction, you will see the straight line segment that is *hidden* there (see Figure 5.39 a, b). This means that the two curved line segments that make up the rounded corners are not connected together with a smooth point, as they would be with an oval. Instead, they are connected by a corner point, a straight line, and another corner point (see Figure 5.40 a, b).

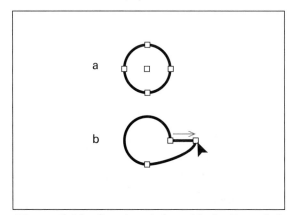

Figure 5.39 *Creating circles with the Rounded Corner Rectangle tool creates extra line segments.*

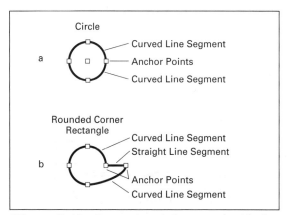

Figure 5.40 *Comparing circles created with the Oval tool and the Rounded Corner Rectangle tool.*

The quality and efficiency of a path is diminished in these cases. Recognizing and avoiding such instances is a crucial part of becoming a path expert. Later chapters will more closely examine the consequences, and prevention, of inefficient paths.

The Polygon and Star Filters

To create a *polygon,* choose Create Polygon from the Filters menu, and the Create Polygon box will appear (see Figure 5.41). Enter the information for the number of sides and radius length, and click **OK**. The radius of a polygon is determined by the distance from its center point to one of its path points (see Figure 5.42). The number of sides can be as few as 3 (a triangle) and as many as 4,000 (a circle). Creating a circle with a Polygon tool is not efficient. Even though the shape may look like a circle, it is actually many straight lines connected by corner points (see Figure 5.43).

To create a star, select Create Stars from the Filters menu. A Create Stars dialog box will appear (see Figure 5.44). Here, you need to enter two radii lengths and a number of star points. The number of star points is actually half the number of corner anchor points in the path (see Figure 5.45). The first radius is for the inner corner points of the star, and the second radius is for the outer points (see Figure 5.46). Entering the same value for both radii will result in a polygon with twice as many sides as the number of star points specified. Entering a first radius greater than the second will invert the star (see Figure 5.47); this will, however, have no effect on a star with an even number of points. The minimum number of star points is 3 and the maximum is 4,000.

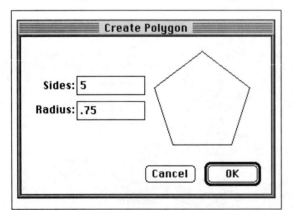

Figure 5.41 *The Create Polygon dialog box.*

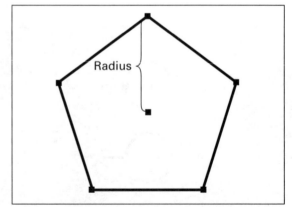

Figure 5.42 *Polygon radius.*

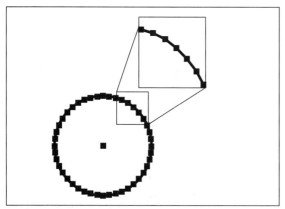

Figure 5.43 *Magnification of a section of a circle created with the Polygon tool.*

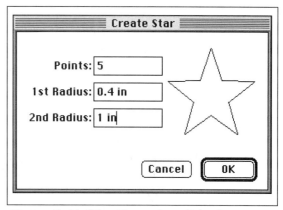

Figure 5.44 *The Create Star dialog box.*

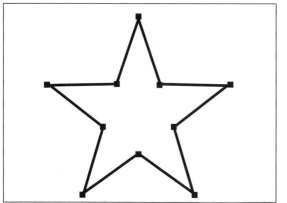

Figure 5.45 *5 Star points = 10 Anchor points.*

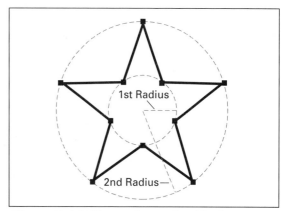

Figure 5.46 *First and second radii of a star.*

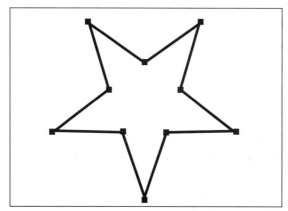

Figure 5.47 *Reverse star.*

The Pen Tool

Using the Pen tool, you can create all of the paths discussed earlier, plus much more. The Pen tool can be used to create almost any shape imaginable with a combination of straight and curved line segments. In this section, however, we will discuss creating paths with only straight line segments using the Pen tool. To see how curved line segments are created, read Chapters 6 and 7.

The Pen tool is the core of the Illustrator program, as it gives you the most control over the path you are creating. This tool is also, unfortunately, the most difficult to learn. Once you understand how the Pen tool works, you'll have a better understanding of how many of the other tools work, and PostScript in general.

One of the most important facts to remember about the Pen tool is that—before you start drawing—you must first imagine what the path will look like. Since the tool works by connecting anchor points with line segments, you must decide where those points should go. And because you do not actually see the line segment until you find a place for its beginning and ending anchor points, you must find the proper placement for those points by imagining how the line segment will look like once those points have been placed. *Templates* are an essential part of creating paths in Illustrator. If you have difficulty drawing freehand with traditional artist's tools, using the Pen tool to create images without a template will be almost impossible. To learn how to create and use templates, read Chapter 10.

For now, though, we are dealing only with drawing paths with straight line segments. Drawing paths with curved line segments or a combination of curved and straight line segments requires much more input from the user than just placement of anchor points.

When you are creating a path with straight line segments, all you have to look for is where the path changes direction. As long as a path is going in a straight line, it can be drawn with one line segment. As soon as it changes direction, that is where you need to place an anchor point (see Figure 5.48 a, b). In other words, you must place an anchor point in the beginning and end of every straight line; two consecutive lines share the anchor point that connects them. Do not place anchor points on a line segment if it is not changing direction at that point. This is not an efficient way of drawing and will alter the straightness of that segment (see Figure 5.49).

To create a path with straight line segments using the Pen tool, choose it from the toolbox. The cursor will turn into a pen with an (x) in the lower right of it when you move into the active window. Click where you want your first line segment to begin and release the mouse button. The first point will be created and the Pen tool cursor will no longer display an (x), indicating that the path construction is in progress. Next, move the Pen cursor to the spot where you want the line segment to end, and click the mouse button. A line segment will automatically be drawn between the two points (see Figure 5.50). Holding down the **Shift** key while creating straight line segments will constrain these line segments to vertical, horizontal, or 45-degree angles. To con-

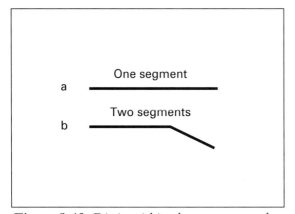

Figure 5.48 *Distinguishing between one and multiple line segments.*

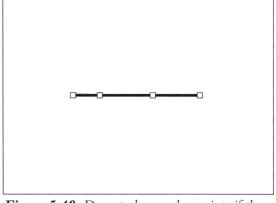

Figure 5.49 *Do not place anchor points if the outline does not change direction.*

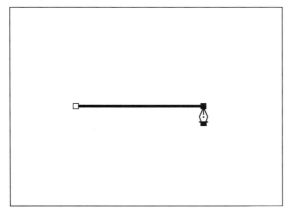

Figure 5.50 *Creating a straight line segment.*

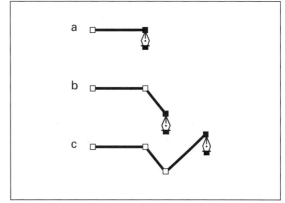

Figure 5.51 *Creating multiple straight line segments.*

tinue drawing a path with multiple straight line segments, click the mouse button in every location where a line should change direction. Each time you click to establish an anchor point, a new line segment will be drawn to that point from the previous one (see Figure 5.51 a, b, c).

All the line segments of the drawn path will be connected together as long as you continue to make new anchor points. To stop drawing a path, you can follow one of two procedures: If you wish to end an open path, after placing your last anchor point, choose any selection tool from the toolbox and click anywhere in the active window. The next point you create with the Pen tool will then begin a new path.

If you are drawing multiple open paths, it could become tiresome to constantly return to the toolbox for a selection tool. To avoid this, you can turn the cursor into the selection tool last used by pressing the Command key while working with any other tool.

To end a closed path, position the Pen tool cursor directly on top of the first end point of the path. The Pen tool cursor will then display a (o) in the lower right corner of it. Click the mouse button to close the path (see Figure 5.52). If you click while the circle is not displayed, the path will not be closed. To learn more about closing paths, read Chapters 9 and 11.

Selecting Paths

Selecting paths involves using a combination of the selecting methods discussed in earlier sections. A path that is not selected will not show its anchor points, while a directly selected path will show all anchor points in that path as solid squares (see Figure 5.53). If any of the anchor points are displayed as hollow squares, the path is indirectly selected.

Selecting one or more line segments or points within a path will indirectly select that path. To do so, choose the Direct Selection tool from the toolbox and click on— or drag a marque around—any part of the outline of the path (see Figure 5.54 a, b). This type of selection is used to adjust individual points, line segments, and series of points on the path. Even though a portion of the path is selected, certain actions will still affect the entire path. Most attributes of the Object and Arrange menus will affect the whole path even if only a part of it is selected. These attributes include *Paint Style, Masking, Compound Paths, Hiding, Locking, Grouping, Bring to Front,* and *Send to Back.*

To directly select a path, choose either the Regular Selection tool (solid arrow) or the Group Selection tool (hollow arrow with a +) from the toolbox (see Figure 5.55). Click on or drag a marque around any part of the outline of the path (see Figure 5.56). All of the points of that path will then be shown as solid squares to indicate that the path is directly selected. A direct selection will allow for all of the Transform and Edit tools to affect the whole path. An entire path can also be directly selected by using the Direct Selection tool and dragging a marque around the whole path, or by holding down the **Shift** key and selecting all the points one by one until all points are selected (see Figure 5.57).

All of these selecting methods can be used in both the Artwork and Preview modes. In Preview mode you can also select a path by clicking on the inside of the path if it is filled with a *color, gradient,* or *pattern* (see Figure 5.58). To choose this option, go to General Preferences and select Area Selection.

Grouping Paths

Multiple paths may be grouped together to form *clusters.* Those clusters can be grouped to other groups of objects. Multiple grouped clusters of objects can be

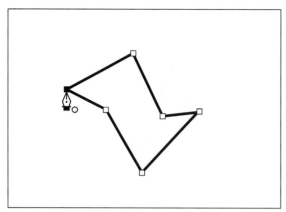

Figure 5.52 *Closing a path.*

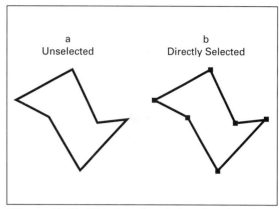

Figure 5.53 *Unselected and directly selected paths.*

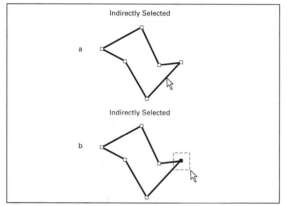

Figure 5.54 *Indirectly selected paths.*

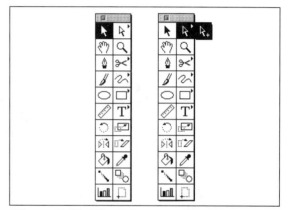

Figure 5.55 *The Selection tools.*

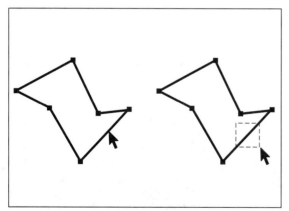

Figure 5.56 *Directly selecting a path.*

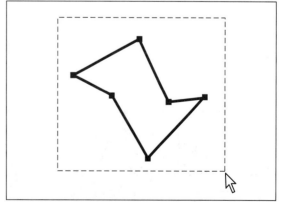

Figure 5.57 *Directly selecting a path with the Direct Selection tool marque.*

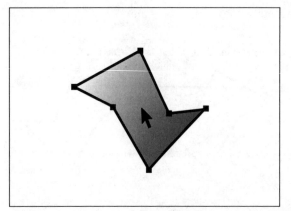

Figure 5.58 *Area select in Preview mode.*

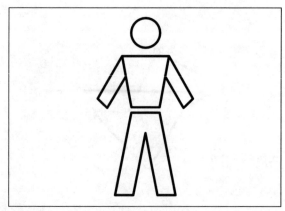

Figure 5.59 *A drawing made up of a number of paths.*

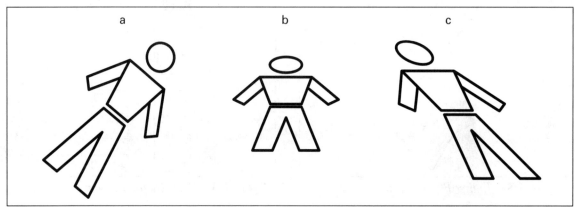

Figure 5.60 *Manipulating a group of objects.*

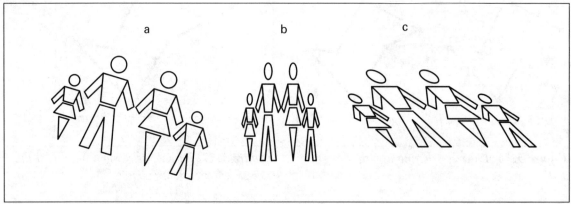

Figure 5.61 *Manipulating a group of groups of objects.*

grouped with as many other multiple clusters of objects as necessary. This kind of grouping hierarchy allows you much greater control over how you select objects.

For example, if you have a drawing which is made up of a number of objects or paths (see Figure 5.59) and you need to manipulate the whole drawing without altering the individual objects within that drawing, grouping it prior to the editing will let you accomplish this task faster and easier (see Figure 5.60 a, b, c).

This function also allows you to group a number of drawings together to form larger groups and manipulate them as one (see Figure 5.61 a, b, c). To Group objects, select all objects or groups of objects to be part of the group, and choose Group from the Arrange menu—or press **Command + G**. An object need not be directly selected to be grouped. Since you cannot group parts of objects, selecting any part of an object will group the whole object.

Due to the increased amount of control over the selection of objects gained by grouping them, some features in Illustrator mimic grouping after their application. These features are *masking* and *compound paths*. The *blending* function actually does the grouping for you. These topics will be discussed in Chapter 12.

Selecting Grouped Objects

The most beneficial aspect of grouping objects is that you can choose how to select them from a variety of available methods.

To select a whole group, choose the Regular Selection tool (solid arrow) from the toolbox and click, or drag a marque, on any part of an object within a group (see Figure 5.62). All of the points on all of the objects in that group will be shown as solid squares to indicate that the whole group is selected.

You can also select grouped objects by the hierarchy of the grouping. This is useful when you have groups of objects grouped together and you need to select only some of the groups within the larger group. For instance, if you have a grouped scene that consists of a number of grouped drawings (see Figure 5.63) and you want to select only one drawing within that scene, you would use the hierarchy selection methods.

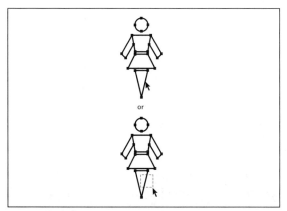

Figure 5.62 *Selecting a group of objects.*

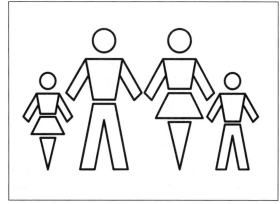

Figure 5.63 *A group of groups of objects.*

To select one group of objects within another group, choose the Group Selection tool (hollow arrow with a +) from the toolbox. Clicking once on a path within the group you want to select will select only that path (see Figure 5.64). Clicking on the same path the second time will select the first group of which that object is a part (see Figure 5.65). Clicking a third time on any of the selected objects will select the next group of which the first group is part, and so on.

This type of selection technique does not work with a marque. Using a marque with the Group Selection tool on a group of objects will select only those objects that fall into the marque area (see Figure 5.66). Dragging a marque around an already selected object a second time will not have any effect.

Holding down the **Shift** key will turn the Group Selection tool into a toggle selection. Clicking on an already selected object will deselect it, and clicking on nonselected objects will select them one by one.

The Direct Selection tool (hollow arrow) is used to select individual points and line segments within a group of objects. Choose the Direct Selection tool from the toolbox and click on a point or line segment. Clicking on a point will make it a solid square, indicating that it is directly selected, while other points of that path will be visible as hollow squares, indicating that the path is indirectly selected (see Figure 5.67). Clicking on a curved line segment will show that segment's direction handles, indicating that the line segment is directly selected, while all the points of that path will show up as hollow squares, indicating that it is indirectly selected. Hint: If you are not sure if a particular straight line segment is selected, hit the **Delete** key. The segment that disappears is the selected one. Immediately after deleting, undo the delete by pressing **Command + Z** or choosing Undo from the Edit menu. The segment will still be selected when it returns to the screen.

Manipulating Paths

To manipulate an entire path, it must be directly selected; once this is done, it can be manipulated and transformed using all the edit and transform options available in the program. The four Transform tools and the options in the Edit menu affect the whole path in the same way as they do a line segment. (Manipulating portions of a path will produce somewhat different results.) Using a combination of these features on a whole path or portion of a path, allows you unlimited control over its shape. Advanced features such as *masks, compounds,* and *blending* will be discussed in Chapter 12.

Move

A path may be moved as a whole or in parts. While moving the path as a whole will not alter its shape—only its position on the page—moving sections of a path will change the shape of the path.

Figure 5.64 *Selecting a single object within groups.*

Figure 5.65 *Selecting a group of objects within larger groups.*

Figure 5.66 *Marque selection within groups.*

Figure 5.67 *Single point selection within groups.*

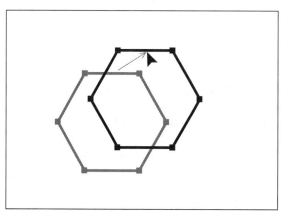

Figure 5.68 *Moving an object.*

To move a whole path, it must be directly selected, which means that every anchor point on that path must appear as a solid square. Choose either the Regular or the Group Selection tool from the toolbox, and click on the outline of the path or drag a marque around a section of it.

All the anchor points should be solid, indicating that the whole path is selected. You can use any of the selection tools to move the path; simply click and drag the path to the new location (see Figure 5.68). While dragging, you will see both the original path and the one you are moving. When you have finished the move, release the mouse button and the original path will disappear, leaving only the path that was moved.

Holding down the **Shift** key while dragging will constrain the movement of the path to 45-degree angle increments; while holding down the **Option** key during the move will create a duplicate of the moved path, leaving the original path unaffected. A path can also be moved with the aid of the Move dialog box. After selecting the path, hold down the **Option** key and click on the Regular Selection tool (solid arrow) in the toolbox, or choose Move from the Edit menu. The Move dialog box will appear, allowing you to input the angle and the distance you want the path to move. Once you have done so, click **OK** for the move to occur, or **Copy** to move a duplicate of the selected path.

Moving Sections of a Path

If only a portion of a path is selected, executing a Move command will alter the shape of that path. You can select parts of a path with the Direct Selection tool. If you wish to adjust the shape of the path point by point, directly select only the anchor point you want to move. Once an anchor point has been directly selected, it can be moved either by dragging it with the Direct Selection tool or by inputting the angle and the distance in the Move dialog box. The line segment or segments attached to that anchor point will then change their angle and length, altering the shape of the path (see Figure 5.69). While dragging, you will see both the original path shape and the shape of the path being altered. After releasing the mouse button, the original path will disappear, leaving only the newly altered path. Holding down the **Option** key will create a duplicate of the moved anchor point and the line segments attached to it, leaving the original path unaltered. The duplicated anchor point and segment will not be attached to the original path (see Figure 5.70).

Multiple, nonconsecutive anchor points may be moved simultaneously. Select the anchor points you wish to move by clicking directly on each one with the Direct Selection tool while holding down the **Shift** key. Once the desired anchor points have been selected, dragging any one point will move them all in the same direction (see Figure 5.71). While dragging, you will see both the original path and the shape of the path being altered, but only the newly altered path will remain after the mouse button is released.

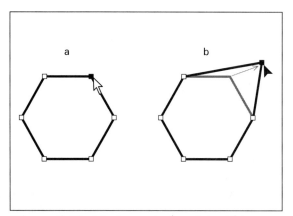

Figure 5.69 *Moving a single point within a path.*

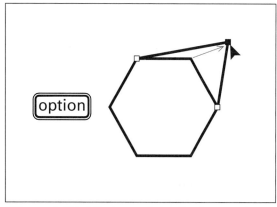

Figure 5.70 *Moving and duplicating a point within a path.*

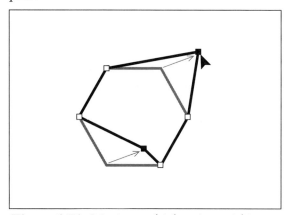

Figure 5.71 *Moving multiple points within a path.*

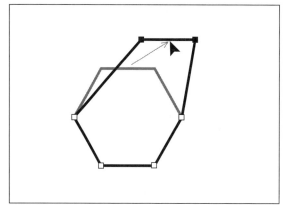

Figure 5.72 *Moving a line segment within a path.*

To move whole line segments of a path, directly select those segments or their anchor points. Both anchor points of a line segment must be directly selected to move the segment as a whole. The Move feature works the same whether the line segments have their points directly selected or not. Once a line segment or segments are selected, drag them with the Direct Selection tool or use the Move dialog box. Moving a line segment will not affect the length or angle of that line segment, but the length and angle of the line segments attached to it will be altered (see Figure 5.72). While dragging, you will see both the original and altered path shapes. After releasing the mouse, only the altered path will remain.

Cut, Copy, Paste, and Delete

To delete a whole path, directly select it and press the **Delete** key, or choose Clear from the Edit menu. Deleting a path will erase it from your document. Cutting a path will also erase it from the screen, but will keep a duplicate in the clipboard for temporary storage. To cut, directly select a path and press **Command** + **X**, or choose Cut from the Edit menu. Pressing **Command** + **C** or going to the Edit menu and choosing Copy will result in a duplicate of the selected path being placed in the clipboard, while leaving the original path unaffected. Selecting a part of a path and performing the Clear, Cut, or Copy commands will affect only the portion of the path that is directly selected.

Paths that were cut or copied can be pasted back into the document by pressing **Command** + **V** or by choosing Paste from the Edit menu. Keep in mind that the clipboard can hold only the most recently cut or copied path. Paths stored in the clipboard will be pasted in the middle of the screen. To paste the path in the exact spot from which it was copied or cut, choose Paste in Front or Paste in Back from the Edit menu, or hit **Command** + **F** or **Command** + **B**. Pasting in front or in back places the object in front of or behind currently selected objects on the screen. This is a good way of changing the layering of objects within a document.

Be cautious when using the Paste in Front and Paste in Back commands. If the object you are pasting is the same shape as the one you are pasting in front or in back of, there will be no visual differences on the screen to indicate that there is more than one object in the same spot. You may end up with multiple unwanted objects in your document if you do not pay close attention to where and how many times you are pasting. The Paste in Front and Paste in Back features will be discussed in greater detail in Chapter 13.

The Four Transform Tools

Rotate a Whole Path

Whole or parts of paths may be rotated, scaled, reflected, or sheared. To rotate a whole path, it must be directly selected. When you choose the Rotate tool from the toolbox, the pointer will turn into a plus sign when moved into an active window. After clicking to establish the axis of rotation (see Figure 5.73), the plus sign will turn into an arrowhead to indicate that the selected path is ready to be rotated. Move away from the axis of rotation for more control, and hold down the mouse button and drag the cursor in a circular motion around the axis of rotation.

The selected path will rotate around the axis of rotation as you drag (see Figure 5.74). While dragging, you will see both the originally selected path and the path being rotated. When you are finished rotating, release the mouse button and the original path will disappear, leaving only the rotated one.

You may also rotate a path by inputting a specific angle in the Rotate dialog box. To bring up this dialog box, hold down the **Option** key while clicking to establish the

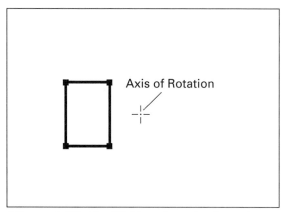

Figure 5.73 *Establishing the axis of rotation.*

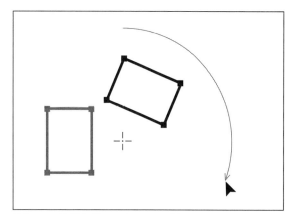

Figure 5.74 *Rotating an object.*

axis of rotation. If you wish for the path to be rotated around its center on a specific angle, do not establish the axis of rotation. Double-clicking on the Rotate tool in the toolbox will automatically establish an axis of rotation in the center of a path and bring up the Rotate dialog box. Enter the desired angle and click **OK** or **Copy**.

Paths created using the Rectangle and Oval tools will automatically be drawn with a center point, but paths created with any other tool will not have a visible center point. If you wish to see the center point of any path, select Show Center Point from the Attributes dialog box under the Object menu.

Rotating Sections of a Path

If a section of a path is directly selected, only that section will be affected by the Rotate tool. This can produce some interesting effects. To rotate a section of a path, directly select the line segment or segments to be rotated by clicking on them with the Direct Selection tool or dragging the marque around them. Choose the Rotate tool and click to establish the axis of rotation. Rotate by dragging or inputting the angle in the Rotate dialog box, as mentioned previously; only the selected section will rotate. This technique will prove useful in many situations; do the following exercise to learn one of its applications.

Draw a path similar to the one shown in Figure 5.75 using the methods described in Chapter 5 in the "Pen Tool" section; this path could represent an arm with a pointing finger. Make sure that all the anchor points in this path are positioned exactly as shown. To rotate the arm at the elbow—to change the direction in which the finger is pointing—select the lower portion of the arm, including the hand and up to but not including the elbow. This is best done using the marque with the Direct Selection tool (see Figure 5.76). The directly selected portion will have its anchor points shown as solid squares, while all other points will appear as hollow squares (see Figure 5.77).

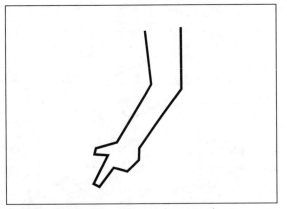

Figure 5.75 *Draw this path using the Pen tool.*

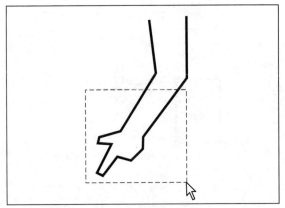

Figure 5.76 *Select a portion of a path using the Direct Selection tool marque.*

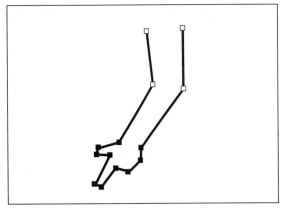

Figure 5.77 *Directly selected points within a path.*

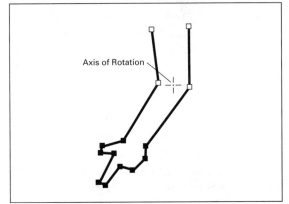

Figure 5.78 *Establish the axis of rotation.*

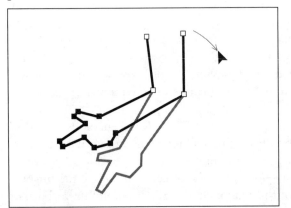

Figure 5.79 *Rotate the selected portion of the path.*

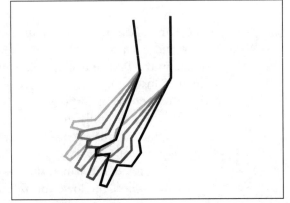

Figure 5.80 *Using Repeat Transform.*

Choose the Rotate tool from the toolbox and click to establish the axis of rotation, as shown (see Figure 5.78). Move the cursor away from the axis of rotation and start dragging in a circular motion. The arm will appear to be rotating at the elbow (see Figure 5.79). When the arm is in the position you want, release the mouse button and the new position will be in effect. Hold down the **Option** key and rotate the arm a few degrees, and then press **Command + D** (repeat transform) a few times. This effect can be used to represent movement (see Figure 5.80).

Scaling a Whole Path

As mentioned in Chapter 4, scaling objects that consist of straight line segments can be explained as moving the points of those objects closer to or further away from the focal point or point of origin. This technique can be applied to achieve a variety of effects.

To scale an entire path, directly select that path and choose the Scale tool from the toolbox. The point will turn into a plus (+) when moved into the active window. Click to establish the point of origin (see Figure 5.81) and the plus sign will become an arrowhead to indicate that the selected path is ready to be scaled. Drag the cursor away from or toward the point of origin, and the path will become larger or smaller (see Figure 5.82 a, b). Holding down the **Shift** key while dragging will constrain the path to uniform, horizontal, or vertical scale (see Figure 5.83 a, b, c). Be aware that if, while you drag, the arrowhead crosses the imaginary horizontal or vertical line stretching from the point of origin, the selected object will be reflected (see Figure 5.84 a, b). This, however, is not an efficient way of reflecting objects; the Reflect tool should be used to best reflect an object (see the "Reflecting Paths" section in this chapter).

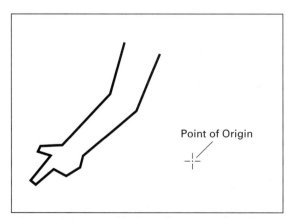

Figure 5.81 *Establishing the point of origin.*

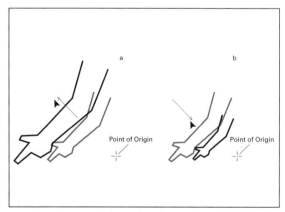

Figure 5.82 *Scaling the object.*

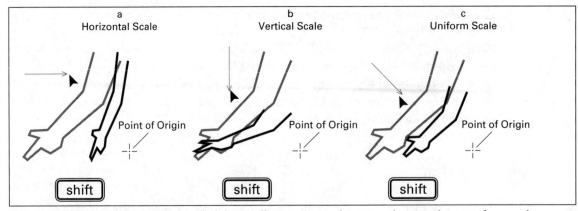

Figure 5.83 Holding down the Shift key will constrain to horizontal, vertical, or uniform scale.

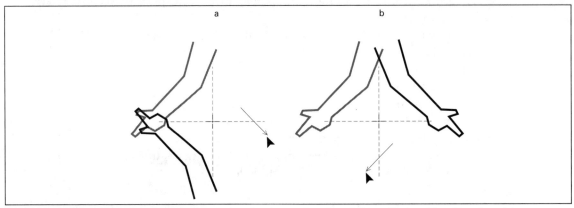

Figure 5.84 Dragging across the vertical or horizontal axis, while scaling, will reflect the object.

If a path must be scaled by a specific amount, hold down the **Option** key while clicking to establish the point of origin, and the Scale dialog box will appear. If you wish for the path to be scaled from its center by a specific amount, do not establish a point of origin. The point of origin will be automatically chosen as the center of the path, and the Scale dialog box will appear when you double-click on the Scale tool in the toolbox. Enter a percentage for uniform scale, or horizontal and vertical scale separately for a non-uniform scale, and click **OK** or **Copy**.

Scaling Sections of Paths

The Scale tool can be used to alter paths in many ways. The next few examples will show how to transform drawings by using only the Scale tool. Simple drawings have been used so that you can create them easily with the techniques discussed so far.

Create a simple drawing representing a graphic male figure, as shown in Figure 5.85, by using the Oval tool for a head and the Pen tool for the body. Be sure that all the anchor points in the body path are positioned exactly as shown. You can use the drawing in this book to create a template to use as a guide (see Chapter 10). The oval path representing the head and the path representing the body should be aligned by their centers. If they are not, select both paths and choose Filter > Objects > Align Objects; an Align Objects dialog box will appear. Choose Center in the Horizontal column and None in the Vertical column before clicking **OK**. It is important to have the head and body paths aligned perfectly, because, for this example, we will use the center point of the circle (head) path as our point of origin.

Select the four anchor points, as shown in Figure 5.86, and choose the Scale tool from the toolbox. Hold down the **Option** key and click on the center point of the circle (head) path to establish the point of origin (see Figure 5.87). When the Scale dialog box appears, enter **100%** in the Horizontal textfield, **65%** in the Vertical field, and press **OK**. Your drawing should now look like Figure 5.88. Select the anchor point, as shown in Figure 5.89, choose the Scale tool, hold down the **Option** key, and click to establish the point of origin as you did before. Enter **100%** in the Horizontal textfield, **200%** in the Vertical field, and click **OK**. Your drawing should now begin to resemble a graphic female figure (see Figure 5.90). For the final touch, select the two anchor points, as shown in Figure 5.91, and choose the Scale tool. Hold down the **Option** key and click to establish the point of origin, as before, then enter **65%** in the Horizontal field and **100%** in the Vertical. The final result in Figure 5.92 has been transformed from the original drawing by using only the Scale tool. This exercise is an example of using the Scale tool at its most basic level to alter drawings. With some imagination, you can find many other ways to utilize the Scale tool.

The next example also uses the Scale tool to alter drawings. Create the drawing shown in Figure 5.93 using the Pen tool and placing the anchor points exactly as shown. This graphic can be used to represent a mouth. Once you learn how to create more complex paths, you can apply the same techniques to much more realistic drawings.

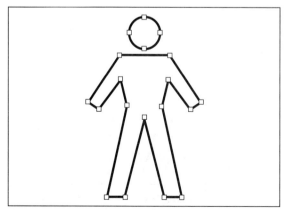

Figure 5.85 *Graphic drawing of a male figure.*

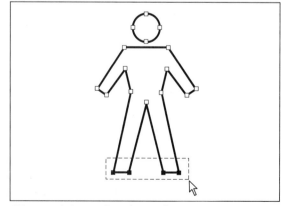

Figure 5.86 *Select the anchor points, as shown.*

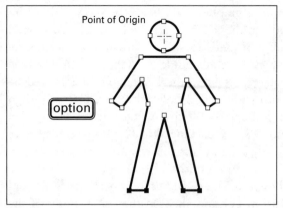

Figure 5.87 *Establishing the point of origin, as shown.*

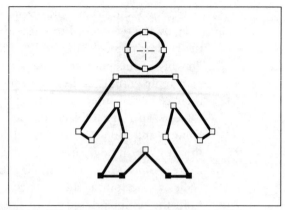

Figure 5.88 *Resulting image after scaling.*

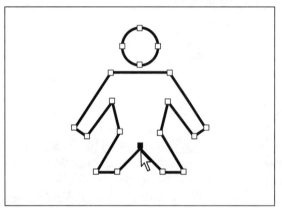

Figure 5.89 *Select the anchor point, as shown.*

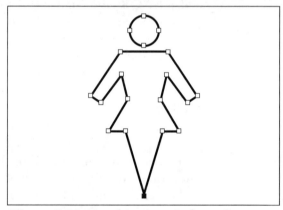

Figure 5.90 *Resulting image after scaling.*

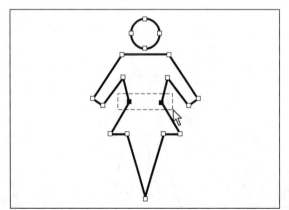

Figure 5.91 *Select the anchor points, as shown.*

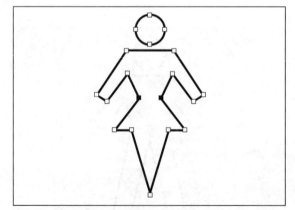

Figure 5.92 *Result is a graphic drawing of a female figure.*

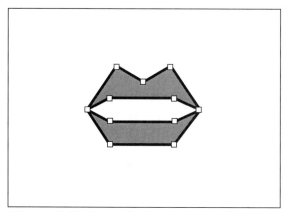

Figure 5.93 *Draw the lips image, as shown.*

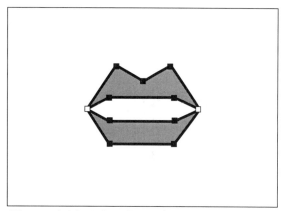

Figure 5.94 *Select the anchor points, as shown.*

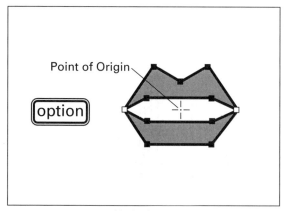

Figure 5.95 *Establish the point of origin, as shown.*

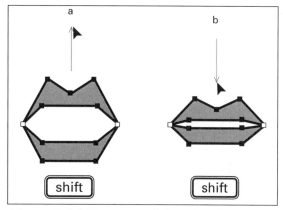

Figure 5.96 *Drag up and down, as shown.*

Select the points of the drawing, as shown in Figure 5.94, and choose the Scale tool from the toolbox. Hold down the **Option** key and click to establish the point of origin, as shown in Figure 5.95. Move away from the point of origin and drag up and down in a vertical motion while holding down the **Shift** key (see Figure 5.96 a, b). The mouth will appear to be opening and closing. You can duplicate this drawing in different poses and use them to show stages of speech.

Another useful application of the Scale tool is to create a true one-point perspective. Create the drawing shown in Figure 5.97 to represent an architectural column. Select the entire drawing (see Figure 5.98) and choose the Scale tool from the toolbox. Click to establish the point of origin, as shown in Figure 5.99. This will be your *vanishing* point. Move the cursor to the opposite side of the column drawing and drag the mouse toward the origin point while holding down the **Option** and **Shift** keys (see Figure 5.100). Release the mouse button and then the **Option** and **Shift** keys. The uniform scaled column is now duplicated relative to the vanishing-point perspective. Choose Repeat Transform from the Edit menu or press **Command + D** three times. The column repeats maintaining the same perspective (see Figure 5.101).

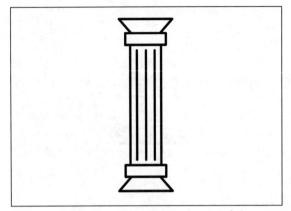

Figure 5.97 *Graphic representing a column.*

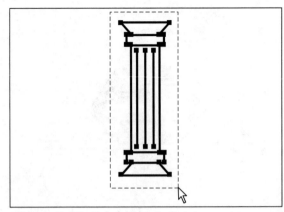

Figure 5.98 *Select the whole image.*

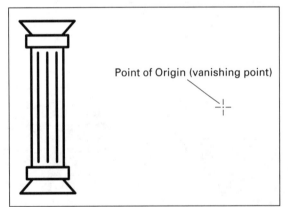

Figure 5.99 *Establish the point of origin, as shown.*

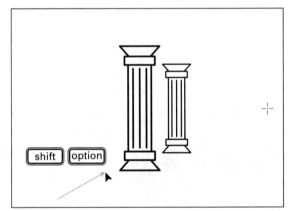

Figure 5.100 *Drag while holding down the Shift and Option keys to create a scaled duplicate.*

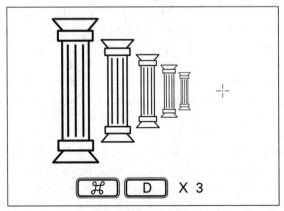

Figure 5.101 *Press Command+D three times.*

The same technique can be used to create 3-dimensional objects and type. For this example, we will use the Create Star filter. Choose Create Star Filter from the Filters menu and input the settings, as shown in Figure 5.102. Get the Scale tool from the toolbox and click to establish the point of origin, as shown in Figure 5.103. Move the cursor to the opposite side of the star and drag the mouse toward the origin point while holding down the **Option** and **Shift** keys (see Figure 5.104). Release the mouse button and then the **Option** and **Shift** keys. From the Objects menu, choose Guides and then Make from the submenu. The smaller star will now be represented by a dashed line, indicating that it is a guide (see Figure 5.105). You may now use the corresponding points of the two stars to create the sides of the star. Figure 5.106 shows the corresponding points of the two stars by number. Each side of the star will be a closed path consisting of four straight line segments and four anchor points.

To use the guides more efficiently, go to the General Preferences menu and make sure that the Snap to Point option is selected. This will enable you to place the points of the sides of the star precisely on top of the star points.

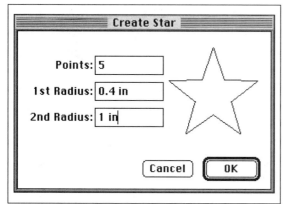

Figure 5.102 *Create a star.*

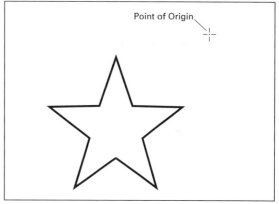

Figure 5.103 *Establish the point of origin, as shown.*

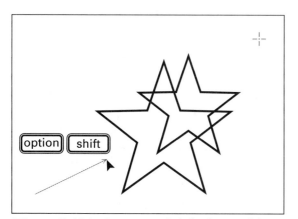

Figure 5.104 *Create a scaled duplicate of the star.*

Figure 5.105 *Make guides from the smaller star path.*

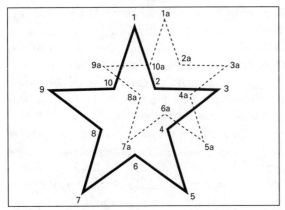

Figure 5.106 *Corresponding points of the two stars.*

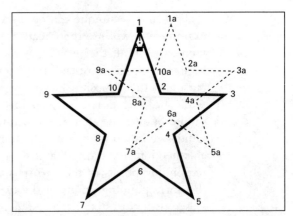

Figure 5.107 *Click with the Pen tool at point 1.*

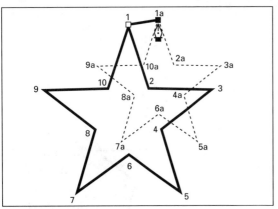

Figure 5.108 *Click at point 1a to create a line segment between points 1 and 1a.*

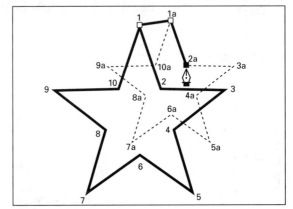

Figure 5.109 *Click at point 2a to create a line segment between points 1a and 2a.*

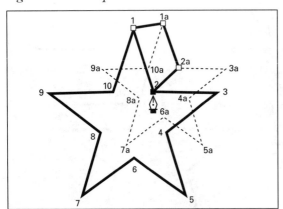

Figure 5.110 *Click at point 2 to create a line segment between points 2a and 2.*

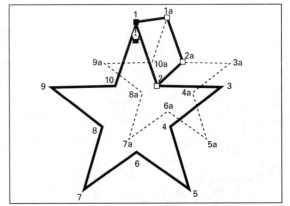

Figure 5.111 *Click at point 1 to create a line segment between points 2 and 1, and close the path.*

To draw the star sides, choose the Pen tool from the toolbox and click on point 1 of the large star (see Figure 5.107). Move the cursor to the corresponding point 1a on the dashed star and click. A line segment will be created between the two points (see Figure 5.108). Next, move the cursor to point 2a on the dashed star, and click. A line segment will be created from point 1a to 2a, connected to the first line segment (see Figure 5.109). Move the cursor to point 2 of the large star, and click (see Figure 5.110). The final click should be on the first end point (1) of the path. This will create a line segment from point 2 to point 1 and thereby close the path (see Figure 5.111). Even though you will not see the last line segment created, it is crucial that you end the path at the beginning end point to ensure that the path is closed.

There are now actually two line segments between points 1 and 2. One belongs to the star and the other to the side you just drew. You will see only one line segment, because the two paths (star and side) are butting up against each other and the two line segments share the same space, one on top of the other.

This occurrence is typical of Illustrator. For this reason, it is important that you keep track of the paths you create and how they overlap—in some cases, there is not enough visual information on the screen to determine where one path ends and the other begins. This will be discussed in greater detail in Chapter 13.

Continuing with our example, create the next star-side path by tracing over points 2 to 2a to 3a to 3 and back to 2 (see Figure 5.112). If this path gets connected to the first one (the points on the first path are shown as hollow squares while you are creating the second path), you have not closed the first path and must start the whole thing over. To learn more about how to create closed paths, read Chapter 12. Continue creating side paths with the Pen tool by tracing over the corresponding points until all the sides are drawn (see Figure 5.113).

Now select the large star and choose Bring to Front from the Arrange menu (see Figure 5.114). Different sides of the 3-dimensional star can be painted with shades of color or gradients to achieve a more realistic look (see the "Painting Paths" and

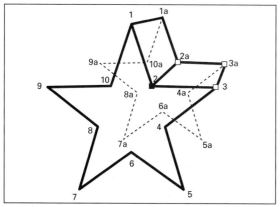

Figure 5.112 *Create a closed path by clicking at points 2 to 2a to 3a and 2 again.*

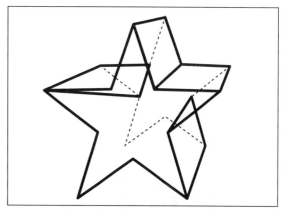

Figure 5.113 *Visible sides of the star are created with four closed paths.*

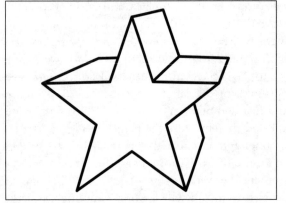

Figure 5.114 *Bring the large star path to the front and paint it with a fill.*

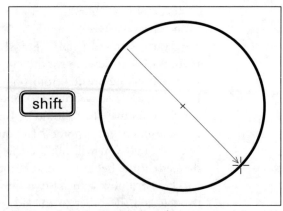

Figure 5.115 *Create a circle.*

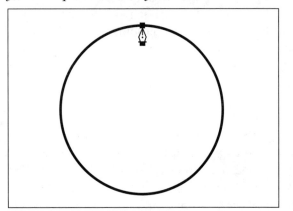

Figure 5.116 *Click with the Pen tool, as shown.*

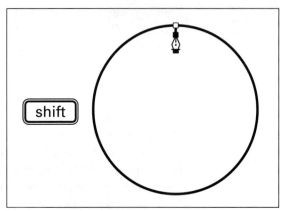

Figure 5.117 *Create a short straight line.*

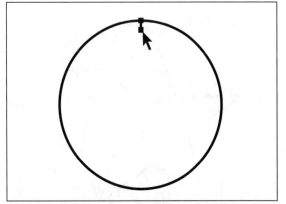

Figure 5.118 *Select the whole line segment.*

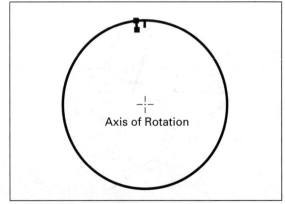

Figure 5.119 *Establish the axis of rotation, as shown.*

"Advanced Path Painting" sections in Chapters 5 and 12, respectively). The same technique can be used to create 3-dimensional type.

The next example will use a combination of the Rotate and Scale tools to create a clock dial. Select Artwork View from the View menu and then choose the Oval tool from the toolbox. Click and drag in the document while holding down the **Shift** key to create a circle. Release the mouse button after the circle is drawn, and then the **Shift** key (see Figure 5.115).

Choose the Pen tool from the toolbox, and click at the top edge of the circle (see Figure 5.116). Move the cursor down a few points. Hold down the **Shift** key to constrain the Pen tool to a vertical line, and click to create a vertical line segment (see Figure 5.117). Next choose the Regular Selection tool (solid arrow) from the toolbox and click on the line segment you just created. The two end points of the line segment will be shown as solid squares to indicate that they are directly selected (see Figure 5.118). Go to the toolbox, choose the Rotate tool, and hold down the **Option** key as you click on the center point of the circle to establish the axis of rotation. The Rotate dialog box will appear; input a 6-degree rotate angle and hit **Copy**. This will rotate a duplicate of the selected line segment 6 degrees relative to the center of the circle (see Figure 5.119). Press **Command + D** immediately after the rotate to continue duplicating the line segment and rotating it 6 degrees. Use the Repeat Transform function (**Command + D**) until the line segment has been duplicated (59 times) around the whole circle (see Figure 5.120).

Mathematical Explanation: We have divided the circle, which is 360 degrees, into 60 divisions (minutes) — 360/60 = 6 degrees.

As a final step, choose the Direct Selection tool from the toolbox and select only the inner points of every fifth line segment around the circle, starting with the topmost line segment (see Figure 5.121). Return to the toolbox and choose the Scale tool, clicking in the center point of the circle to establish a point of origin. Move the cursor to the outside of the circle, hold down the **Shift** key, and start dragging toward

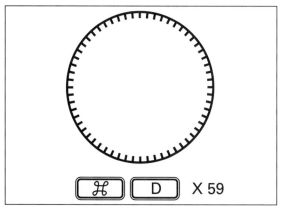

Figure 5.120 *Rotate the line segment by 6 degrees and Repeat Transform 59 times.*

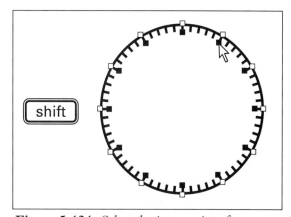

Figure 5.121 *Select the inner point of every fifth line segment.*

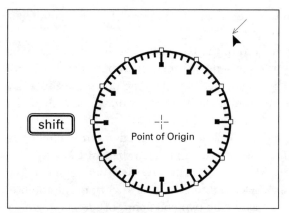

Figure 5.122 *Establish the point of origin at the center of the circle and uniformly scale the selected points.*

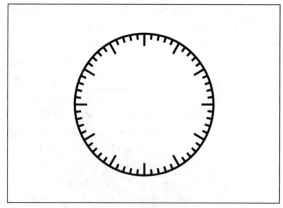

Figure 5.123 *This image can be used to render a clock.*

the center (see Figure 5.122). The selected points of every fifth line segment will move toward the center of the circle, stretching the line segments. Release the mouse button when the line segments are the desired length. The long line segments will represent the hours, and the short line segments the minutes (see Figure 5.123).

The preceding examples demonstrate some of the basic uses of the Scale and Rotate tools. This, in combination with the other transformation tools, will allow you to achieve an unlimited number of effects.

Reflecting Paths

Reflecting a path results in a mirror image of that path. This will be useful when creating symmetrical drawings, as demonstrated later in this section. To reflect a whole path, select it with a Regular Selection tool (solid arrow), choose the Reflect tool from the toolbox, and click in the document to establish the focal point. The cursor will turn into an arrowhead to indicate that the axis of reflection is ready to be established.

Next, move the cursor away from the focal point and click the mouse button. The object will be reflected on the axis of reflection, which is an imaginary line between the first click (focal point) and the second click (arrowhead) (see Figure 5.124). If you wish to vary the axis of reflection while the object is being reflected, drag the arrowhead instead of just clicking it after the focal point has been established. This will change the angle of the axis of reflection while you are dragging. Start dragging further away from the focal point to gain more control over the angle of the axis of reflection. While dragging, you will see both the originally selected path and the one you are reflecting. Release the mouse button when the object is reflected on the desired angle.

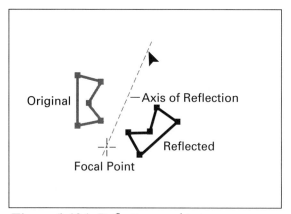

Figure 5.124 *Reflecting an object.*

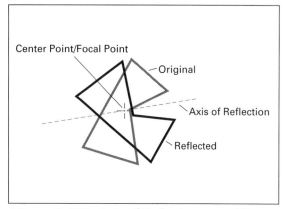

Figure 5.125 *Axis of Reflection set at 10 degrees.*

You may reflect a path on a specific angle of the axis of reflection by inputting it into the Reflect dialog box. Hold down the **Option** key while clicking to establish the focal point, and the Reflect dialog box will appear. Enter the vertical, horizontal, or angled axis, and hit **OK** or **Copy**.

Double-clicking on the Reflect tool after selecting a path will also bring up the Reflect dialog box. The axis of reflection will then be at a specified angle and intersecting the center of the selected path (see Figure 5.125). To see the center point of any path, choose Show Center Point in the Objects Attributes menu.

To reflect a portion of a path, select only the points and the line segment you want to reflect—with the Direct Selection tool (hollow arrow)—and follow the same steps as previously described.

The following example will demonstrate how the Reflect tool can be used to create symmetrical objects. Draw one side of a column, as shown in Figure 5.126, making sure that the two end points align vertically. This can be done in one of two ways:

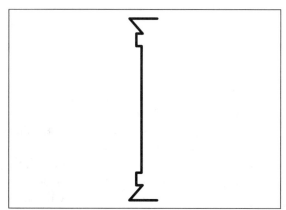

Figure 5.126 *Draw one side of a column.*

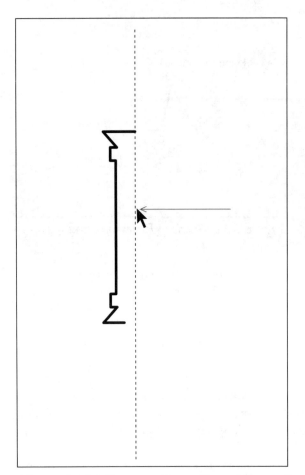

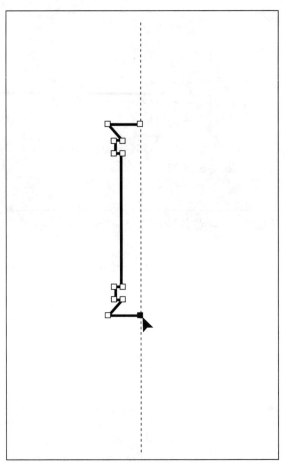

Figure 5.127 *Drag a guide to align with one of the end points.*

Figure 5.128 *Move an end point to align with the guide.*

Press **Command** + **R** or choose Show Rulers from the View menu and click on the vertical ruler and drag it into the document. A dashed vertical guide will appear as you drag; keep dragging the guide until it reaches the end points of the half column (see Figure 5.127). Move the end points with the Direct Selection tool so that they align with the guide (see Figure 5.128).

A second way to align points is by first selecting them with the Direct Selection tool (see Figure 5.129) then choosing Average from the Objects menu—or pressing **Command** + **L**. Click on Vertical Axis and hit **OK**. The points will now be aligned on the vertical axis (see Figure 5.130).

Once you have aligned the two end points, directly select the whole path with the Regular Selection tool (solid arrow). Choose the Reflect tool from the toolbox and click to establish the focal point at one of the end points while holding down the **Option** key (see Figure 5.131). After the Reflect dialog box appears, click on Vertical Axis and hit **Copy**. A reflected duplicate of the left side of the column will be created, and the symmetrical drawing will be completed (see Figure 5.132).

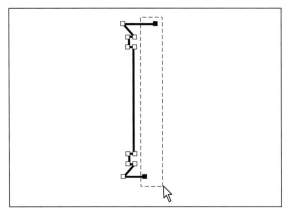

Figure 5.129 *Select both end points.*

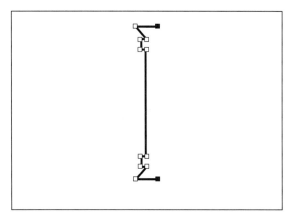

Figure 5.130 *End points averaged on a vertical axis.*

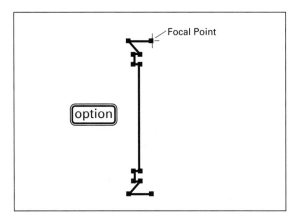

Figure 5.131 *Establish the focal point, as shown.*

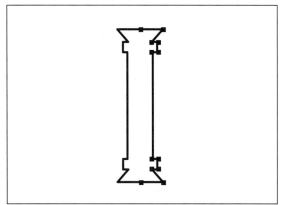

Figure 5.132 *One side of the column is reflected to form the other side.*

The two sides of the column, however, are still two separate open paths that must be joined together to attain one closed path. Chapter 11 explains how to open and close paths by *cutting* and *joining*.

Shearing Paths

The Shear tool is the most difficult transform tool to use freehand. While you are dragging to shear an object, you are supplying the computer with two sets of information. The angle on which you drag establishes the angle of the axis of the shearing, and the distance of the drag establishes the angle of the shear from the axis of shearing. Also keep in mind that if, while dragging, the angle of the shear goes over or under 75 degrees, the object you are shearing will become an unrecognizable mess (see Figure 5.133 a, b).

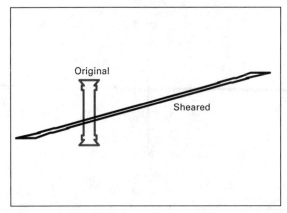

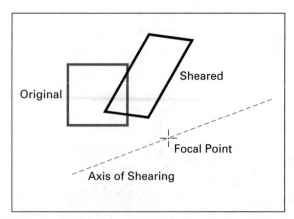

Figure 5.133 *Shear angle set at 75 degrees and shear axis set to Horizontal.*

Figure 5.134 *Shear angle set at 40 degrees and shear axis set at 20 degrees.*

However, if you still wish to shear a path by dragging, select the path to be sheared with the Regular Selection tool (all the points should be shown as solid squares) and choose the Shear tool from the toolbox. Click in the document to establish the focal point, move the cursor away from the focal point, and start dragging. Holding down the **Shift** key will constrain the angle of the axis of shearing to 45-degree increments.

Due to the potential difficulties of shearing in this manner, you will find using the Shear dialog box a much better method. Select the object to be sheared with the Regular Selection tool, and click in the document to establish the focal point while holding down the **Option** key; the Shear dialog box will appear. Enter the angle of shearing and a vertical, horizontal, or angled axis of shearing. The axis of shearing will be established vertically, horizontally, or on the specified angle from the focal point (see Figure 5.134). Click **OK** or **Copy** and the object will be sheared on the specified angle relative to the angle of the axis of shearing. Figure 5.135 shows variations of an

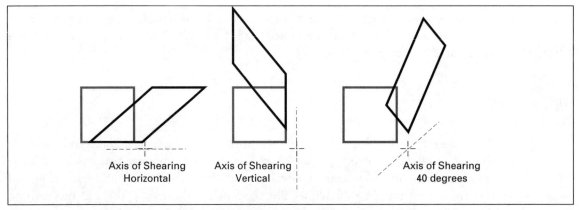

Figure 5.135 *Varied axis of shearing with the angle of shearing set to 50 degrees.*

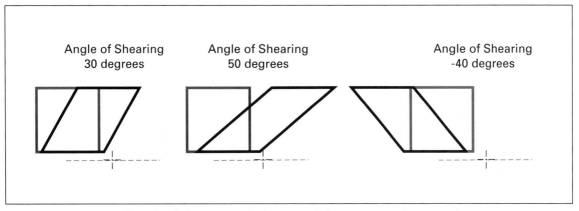

Angle of Shearing
30 degrees

Angle of Shearing
50 degrees

Angle of Shearing
-40 degrees

Figure 5.136 *Varied angle of shearing with the axis of shearing set to horizontal.*

object being sheared 50 degrees with different axis of shearing angles. Figure 5.136 shows variations of an object being sheared on various angles with a horizontal axis of shearing.

If you choose to have the axis of shearing start at the center of the object, double-click on the Shear tool after selecting the object to be sheared. The Shear dialog box will appear and the axis of shearing will be established at the center of the object.

One of the effects that can be achieved with the Shear tool is shadow. Draw a column, as shown in Figure 5.137, select it with the Regular Selection tool, and choose the Shear tool from the toolbox. Click to establish the focal point at the bottom of the column while holding down the **Option** key (see Figure 5.138). The Shear dialog box will appear. Enter a 30-degree shear angle and a horizontal axis. Click **Copy** and a sheared duplicate of the column will be created with the bottom remaining in the original place (see Figure 5.139). Select Send to Back from the Arrange menu. If you *paint* the sheared column with a different fill, an instant shadow will be created (see Figure 5.140).

Figure 5.137 *Drawing of a column.*

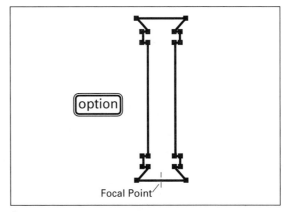

option

Focal Point

Figure 5.138 *Establish the focal point, as shown.*

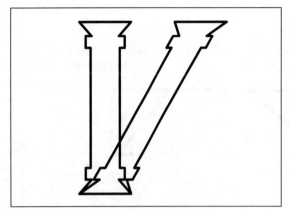

Figure 5.139 *Reflected duplicate.*

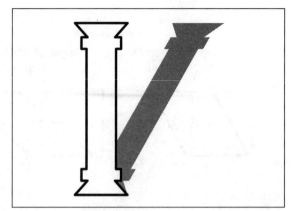

Figure 5.140 *Send the sheared image to the back and fill with a shade of black, while leaving the original column image in the front and filled with white.*

Painting Paths

To paint a path, it must be selected with any of the methods described earlier. Selecting a portion of a path will paint the entire path in the selected Paint Style. After a path is selected, go to the Objects menu and select Paint Style or press **Command + I**; the Paint Style dialog box will appear.

An object can be painted with a *fill* or a *stroke* or both. Fills can be painted with None (transparent), White, Black, a combination of four process colors, or any custom color provided by the program, or created by you. Fills can also be painted with patterns or gradients provided with the program or custom created in the Gradient or Patterns dialog boxes.

Strokes can be painted with everything that the fill can be painted with, except gradients. Stroke thickness can also be specified in the Stroke Weight text field. Choose a solid or dashed stroke by pressing the Solid or Dashed button. Input *dash* and *gap* distances in point units for dashed strokes. Dashes and gaps will then be repeated for the duration of the stroked path. Three different lengths of dash and stroke may be specified for each stroked path.

Caps and *joins* can also be varied for stroked paths. Caps are applied to end points, and joins applied to regular anchor points. Caps and joins may be square, round, beveled, or miter. Different effects of caps and joins are demonstrated in Figure 5.141. The *Miter Join* can be altered by setting the miter limit; the higher the miter limit, the sharper the angle of the join can be.

The *Overprint* option can be applied to both the fill and the stroke. Overprint combines colors and objects that overlap. To see the effects of Overprint, the file must be separated and printed on an offset printer. Not choosing the Overprint option will print the file similar to how it appears on the screen.

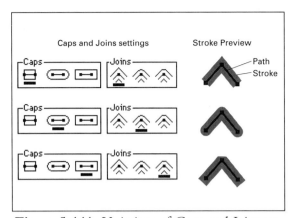

Figure 5.141 *Variations of Caps and Joins settings for Strokes.*

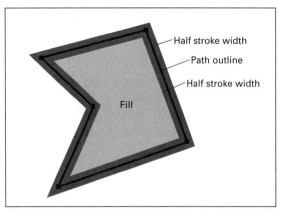

Figure 5.142 *Stroke is drawn on both sides of the path outline.*

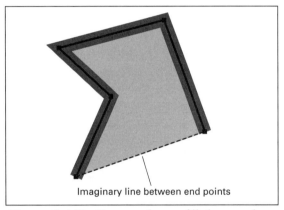

Figure 5.143 *Open paths are filled up to the imaginary line between end points.*

After you have set the desired paint attributes for your object, hit the **Apply** button or check the Auto Apply box to always have the attributes applied automatically thereafter. Both open and closed paths may be painted with any fill or stroke. Closed paths will be filled up to their outline. Strokes are drawn around the outline, with half the width on the inside of the path overlapping the fill and the other half on the outside of the path outline (see Figure 5.142).

Open paths are painted in much the same way except for the opening in the open path. The fill attribute is applied up to an imaginary straight line between the two end points. The stroke is applied only to the existing outline of an open path. The imaginary line between the two end points of an open path will remain without a stroke (see Figure 5.143).

6 *Curves*

Direction Handles

Direction handles consist of a straight line with a small solid circle at the end, called the *direction point* (see Figure 6.1). A direction point should not be confused with any other points discussed in the "Points" section.

Direction handles and points are used to define the structure of a curved line segment. They are not part of the art and will not print. Direction handles are always attached to anchor points, and they describe the direction and incline of the curved line segments between those anchor points. The angle and the length of the direction handle are what determine how a curve will look.

To create a direction handle, you must first create an anchor point. Choose the Pen tool from the toolbox and click in the document to create an anchor point. Without releasing the mouse button, drag in the direction you want the direction handle to be, as far as you want the length of the direction handle to stretch (see Figure 6.2). (How the angle and the length of direction handles affect a curved line segment is discussed in Chapters 7 and 8. Clicking and dragging with the Pen tool will always produce a direction handle, while releasing the mouse button after clicking with the Pen tool will create an anchor point without a direction handle.

If you wish to create a direction handle at an existing anchor point that does not have one, you must use the Pen tool—provided that the anchor point is an end point. Simply click on that end point with the Pen tool and drag out a handle (see Figure 6.3). If an anchor point that is not an end point does not have a direction handle, a *Convert Anchor Point tool* must be used to create a direction handle at that point. This technique is discussed in Chapter 11.

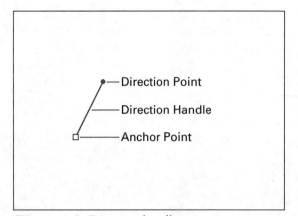

Figure 6.1 *Direction handle.*

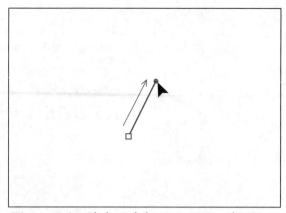

Figure 6.2 *Click and drag to create a direction handle.*

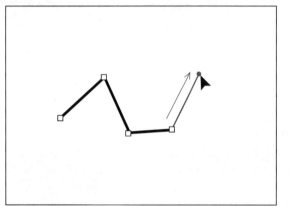

Figure 6.3 *Creating a direction handle at an end point.*

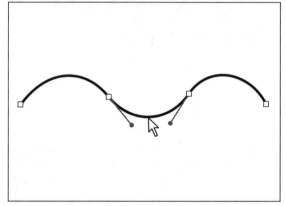

Figure 6.4 *Displaying direction handles of a curved line segment.*

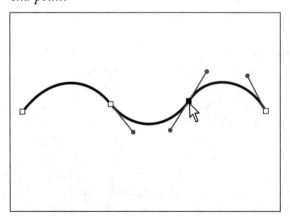

Figure 6.5 *Displaying direction handles at an anchor point.*

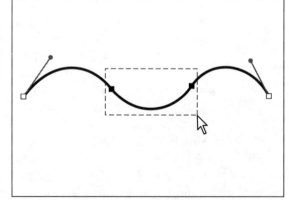

Figure 6.6 *No direction handles are displayed for the curved line segment when both its anchor points are selected.*

Display of Direction Handles

Direction handles will not be visible if the curved line segment they are describing is not selected. Directly selecting an anchor point or a curved line segment between two anchor points will display a handle or handles related to the selected point or line segment.

In a path, selecting a curved line segment will show only a direction handle or handles describing that line segment. Directly selecting an anchor point, however, will show direction handles for both line segments attached to that point.

Choose the Direct Selection tool from the toolbox and click on a curved line segment; direction handles for that line segment will be displayed (see Figure 6.4). Selecting with the Direct Selection tool a single anchor point on a path will display all the direction handles of line segments attached to that anchor point (see Figure 6.5).

If more than one anchor point is selected in a single path, the display of direction handles changes. For instance, selecting two consecutive anchor points in a path will not display the direction handles for the curved line segment between those anchor points (see Figure 6.6). Furthermore, if two or more anchor points in a path made of curved line segments are directly selected, the direction handles belonging to those points will not be displayed. Only the direction handles belonging to the indirectly selected anchor point of a line segment that has its other point directly selected will be displayed (see Figure 6.7).

Not every anchor point has two direction handles; in some cases, an anchor point may have only one. This will be the case if an anchor point connects a curved line segment to a straight line segment, or to two curved line segments and one or both of those line segments have only one direction handle (see Figure 6.8 a, b). Your understanding and control over curves and their direction handles will be improved after reading the following "Curves" sections.

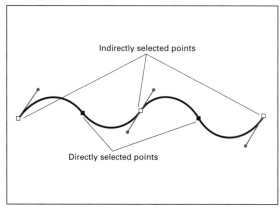

Figure 6.7 *Direction handles are displayed at the indirectly selected anchor points.*

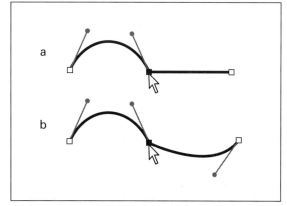

Figure 6.8 *Anchor point with one direction handle.*

Manipulating Direction Handles

Manipulating direction handles to achieve specific results requires a thorough knowledge of how they affect curved line segments. This will be discussed later in the book. The following description is intended to give you a basic idea of—and introduce you to—how direction handles are physically manipulated.

Direction handles may be manipulated by dragging the direction point with any of the selection tools. There is an important distinction that must be made between the initial creation of a direction handle, and editing one that has already been created.

When a direction handle is pulled out from an anchor point with the Pen tool, its length and angle will be altered while you are still dragging with the Pen tool. Once you have released the mouse button, the Pen tool can no longer be used to manipulate the direction handle. Clicking on the direction handle with the Pen tool will result in creating an anchor point. To edit the length or angle of a direction handle, choose the Direct Selection tool from the toolbox and click on a curved line segment or one of its anchor points. The direction handle or handles will be displayed, indicating that they are ready to be manipulated. Click and drag the direction point to alter the length and angle of the direction handle.

Once a direction handle is displayed, any of the selection tools can be used to manipulate it. If the anchor point of the direction handle you are editing is a smooth point, then the second direction handle of that anchor point will change its angle but not its length as you move the first direction handle (see Figure 6.9)

Altering the direction handle of a corner anchor point will not affect the second handle, if there is one. Dragging a direction point directly on top of the anchor point it stems from will result in eliminating the direction handle from the anchor point (see Figure 6.10 a, b).

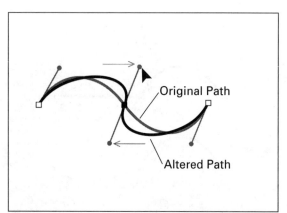

Figure 6.9 *Direction handles at a smooth anchor point.*

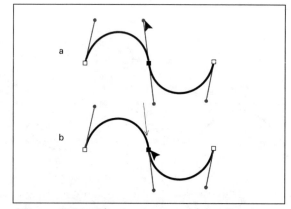

Figure 6.10 *Eliminating one of the direction handles at an anchor point.*

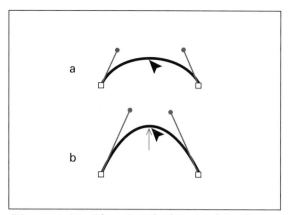

Figure 6.11 *Changing the length of the direction handles by dragging the curve.*

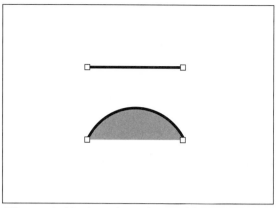

Figure 6.12 *Straight and curved line segments filled with color.*

Direction handles can also be manipulated by dragging the curve itself with the Direct Selection tool. If that curve has two direction handles, both will be affected simultaneously. Only the length of the direction handles will be altered by moving the curve itself. The angle of the direction handles will remain constant (see Figure 6.11 a, b).

Curves

A curved line segment, like a straight line segment, must have two anchor points—but unlike a straight segment, curves involve more data. Simply clicking with the Pen tool to establish beginning and end anchor points for a line segment is not sufficient; the Pen tool must be used to supply Illustrator with more information regarding the appearance of the curved segment.

Dragging a Pen tool produces *direction handles* that tell the program in which direction the curve will travel, how steep it will be, and how those elements are to change over the span of the curve.

A curve may have one or two direction handles; curves with only one direction handle will supply the program with only half the information of a curve with two direction handles. Therefore, the variety of shapes that a curve with two direction handles can be made into is twice that of a curve with only one direction handle. Also, unlike a straight line segment, a single curved line segment may be filled with a paint style. This is because a straight line segment has no area, while a curved line segment does (see Figure 6.12).

The length of a curved line segment does not depend solely on the distance between its anchor points, as it does with straight line segments. The length of the curve's direction handles is more of a factor in determining that curve's length than is the distance between the anchor points. The longer the direction handles, the steeper and longer the curved line segment will be. Shorter direction handles create shallow,

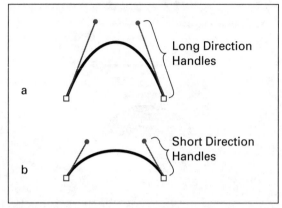

Figure 6.13 *Long curve and short curve.*

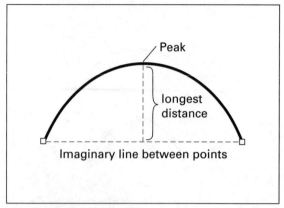

Figure 6.14 *Peak of a curve.*

shorter curves (see Figure 6.13 a, b). The shallowest curve is, of course, a straight line that has no direction handles.

The Peak

A curve's *peak* is the point that is the furthest away from the center of an imaginary straight line between its two anchor points (see Figure 6.14).

The Slope

The *slope* of a curve describes how steep or shallow the curve is. The greater the distance between the imaginary line and the peak of the curve, the steeper the slope. The less the distance, the shallower the curve will be (see Figure 6.15 a, b).

The slope can also be described by comparing the distance between the two anchor points to the length of the curve; the greater the difference, the steeper the slope (see Figure 6.16 a, b). Note that the length of the curve will always be greater than the distance between its two anchor points.

Selection

A curved line segment may be selected with its points directly or indirectly selected. To select a curved line segment without directly selecting its points, choose the Direct Selection tool from the toolbox and click anywhere along the curve, or click and drag a marque around any part of the curved line segment (see Figure 6.17). The direction handles for that curve will be displayed and the anchor points will appear as hollow squares, indicating that the curve is directly selected but the anchor points are not.

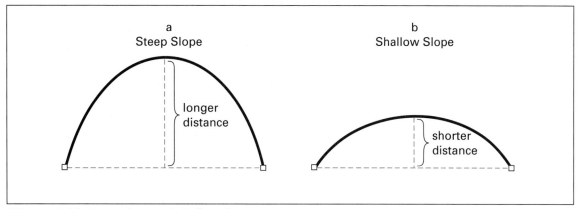

Figure 6.15 *Steep slope and shallow slope.*

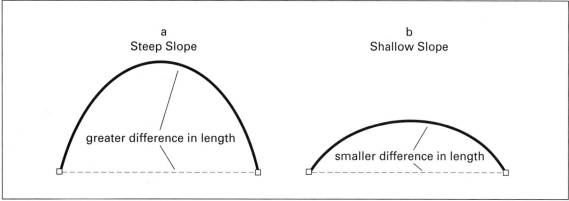

Figure 6.16 *Steep slope and shallow slope.*

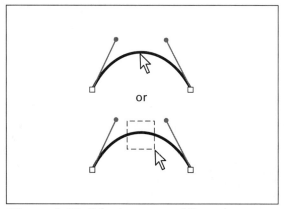

Figure 6.17 *Selecting a curved line segment without directly selecting its points.*

This type of selection will enable you to edit the structure of the curve but not its position in the document. Unlike a straight line segment, when a curve's points are hollow, moving the curve will not affect its points. Only the steepness of the curve will be affected by dragging the actual curved line segment. Using any of the transform tools, when a curve is selected this way, will affect only the shape of the curved line segment, not the position of its anchor points.

If anchor points appear hollow, other curved line segments attached to the selected curve will not be affected in most cases. Selecting a curve with only one of its anchor points being directly selected will display the direction handles for both curves connected by that anchor point. Choose the Direct Selection tool from the toolbox and click directly on the anchor point or drag a marque around it (see Figure 6.18). The point will be shown as a solid square, and the direction handles for that point will be displayed. If the selected anchor point is an end point, only the direction handles for one curve will be active. A selected anchor point that connects two curves may have one or two direction handles. Both curves must have a direction handle at the selected anchor point in order for that anchor point to display two handles. When an anchor point is directly selected, all the direction handles of the curves attached to that anchor point will be displayed (see Figure 6.19). This type of selection allows you to manipulate the direction handles and adjust the position of the directly selected anchor point.

When both anchor points of a curved line segment are directly selected, the direction handles for that curve will not be displayed. Choose a Direct Selection tool from the toolbox and click on the first anchor point, then hold down the **Shift** key and click on the second anchor point. You can also use the marque selection to select both points simultaneously (see Figure 6.20). The anchor points will be shown as solid squares to indicate that they are directly selected. The direction handles for that curve will not be displayed, because this type of selection allows you to manipulate the curve while keeping the relationship between the direction handles constant. This means that the basic structure of the curve will be constrained relative to how it is being manipulated. For instance, dragging the curve will change its position, not its shape.

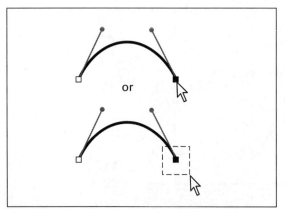

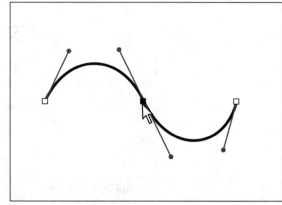

Figure 6.18 *Selecting one of curve's anchor points.*

Figure 6.19 *Selecting an anchor point that connects two curves.*

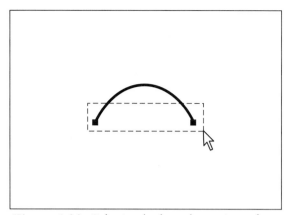

Figure 6.20 *Selecting both anchor points of a curve.*

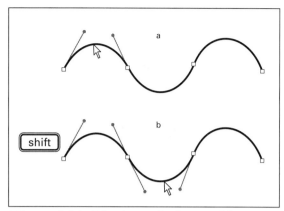

Figure 6.21 *Selecting multiple curved line segments within a path.*

Using the four Transform tools on a curve that has its anchor points directly select-ed will affect both direction handles and anchor points, but maintain the original rela-tionship between those elements. Line segments attached to that curve will also be affected when the curve is edited by moving or transforming.

Selecting Multiple Curved Line Segments

The Direct Selection tool is used to select curved line segments; simply choose it from the toolbox and click on the first curved line segment. After holding down the **Shift** key and clicking on the next curved line segment, the direction handles for both curved line segments will be displayed. The anchor points of the whole path will now appear hollow (see Figure 6.21 a, b). Both curves can be edited by dragging one of them directly or changing the length and angle of their direction handles one at a time. You can continue to select multiple curves while holding down the **Shift** key. All of the selected curves will have both of their handles displayed. Curves that are not selected will display only one handle if they are next to a selected curve, or no handles if not adjacent to a selected curve.

The Shift key may be used as a toggle between selecting and deselecting multiple curves. Clicking on a selected curve while holding down the **Shift** key will deselect it and will hide its handles without affecting other selected curves.

Two curves can be selected by clicking on—or dragging a marque around—the anchor point that connects them, while using the Direct Selection tool. The anchor point will be shown as a solid square, and the direction handles for both curves will be displayed (see Figure 6.22). Directly selecting more than one anchor point on a path of curved line segments will not display the direction handles at the directly selected anchor points. The direction handles will be displayed at indirectly selected anchor points immediately before or after the directly selected anchor points (see Figure 6.23).

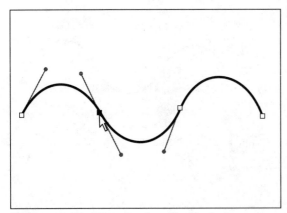

Figure 6.22 Direction handles for both curves are displayed.

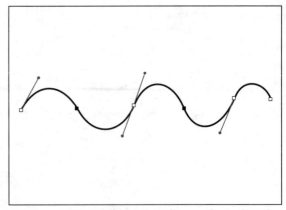

Figure 6.23 Direction handles at the indirectly selected anchor points are displayed.

Manipulating Curves

As we have seen, curved line segments can be manipulated in much the same way as straight line segments. The effects of those manipulations, however, differ, depending on the way in which a curved line segment is selected. A curved line segment may also be manipulated by changing the length and angle of its direction handles, which a straight line segment does not have.

Editing a curve by altering its direction handles will affect the original structure of the curve. This may be done by either dragging the direction handles themselves, or by manipulating the curve in any way without directly selecting its points. In this section we will discuss both situations. For a more detailed explanation of how the direction handles affect the structure of the curve, read Chapters 7 and 8.

Move

To move a curved line segment without affecting its shape, both anchor points must be directly selected. If a curve exits by itself, any of the selection tools can be used; but a curve that is a part of a path must be moved using the Direct Selection tool.

Choose the appropriate selection tool from the toolbox and click and drag the selected curved line segment in the direction you want to move it (see Figure 6.24). To move a curved line segment a specific distance on a specific angle, click on the Selection tool in the toolbox while holding down the **Option** key, or select Move from the Edit menu. This will bring up the Move dialog box, where you can input the desired information. If a curved line segment is part of a path, the basic structure of the line segments attached to that curve will be altered (see Figure 6.25).

While dragging, you will see both the original curved line segment and the one you are moving. When you have finished the move, release the mouse button and the original curved line segment will disappear, leaving only the newly moved one. Dragging a curved line segment without directly selecting its anchor points will not move the curve. Instead, the length of the direction handles will be affected, thereby altering the slope of the curve (see Figure 6.26 a, b). Manipulating a curve by dragging its outline, without selecting its anchor points, is a technique that can be used to alter the curve's shape without affecting other curves attached to it by smooth points.

However, I do not recommend utilizing this technique, because the shape of the curve is very difficult to control in this manner. Chapter 8 will examine this subject in greater detail.

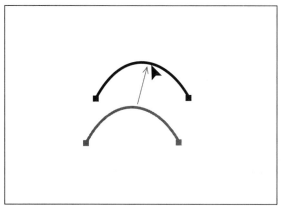

Figure 6.24 *Moving a curved line segment.*

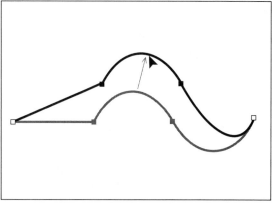

Figure 6.25 *Moving a curved line segment that is part of a path.*

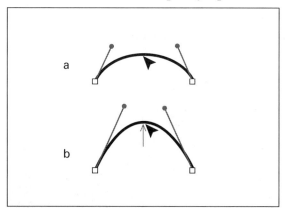

Figure 6.26 *Moving a curved line segment without directly selecting its points.*

Cut, Copy, Paste, and Delete

The cut, copy, paste, and delete functions affect a curved line segment the same regardless of whether its anchor points are directly selected. The only distinction is whether other line segments will be affected. For the most part, selecting an anchor point and performing any of these operations will affect all line segments attached to that anchor point.

To delete a curved line segment, select it (as usual) with the Direct Selection tool and choose Clear from the Edit menu—or press the **Delete** key. Deleting a curved line segment will erase it from your document, or you can choose to keep it temporarily in the clipboard by cutting it. To cut a curved line segment, select it with a Direct Selection tool and choose Cut from the Edit menu, or simply press **Command + X**. Copying a curved line segment will leave a temporary duplicate in the clipboard as well, but it will leave the originally selected curve unaffected.

To copy, select the curved line segment and press **Command + C**, or choose Copy from the Edit menu. A curved line segment that is currently being stored in the clipboard may be pasted back into your document. To do so, choose Paste from the Edit menu or press **Command + V**. The object currently stored in the clipboard will now appear in the center of your screen.

The Four Transform Tools

A curved line segment may be manipulated using any of the four Transform tools. The effects of these tools will differ based on how anchor points are selected.

Rotate

To rotate a curved line segment without affecting its shape, both anchor points must be directly selected. Choose the Rotate tool from the toolbox and click to establish a focal point (see Figure 6.27); the cursor will become an arrowhead to indicate that the selected object is ready to be rotated. Move the cursor away from the axis of rotation and drag the mouse in a circular motion around the axis of rotation. While dragging, you will see both the originally selected segment and the one you are rotating (see Figure 6.28). Release the mouse button, and the original curved line segment will disappear, leaving the rotated curve.

To rotate a curved line segment by a specific angle, hold down the **Option** key—while clicking—to establish the axis of rotation. The Rotate dialog box will appear and request the desired angle. If the selected segment is part of a path, line segments attached to it will be affected by the rotation (see Figure 6.29).

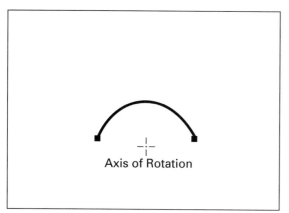

Figure 6.27 *Establishing the axis of rotation.*

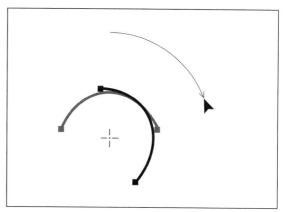

Figure 6.28 *Rotating a curved line segment.*

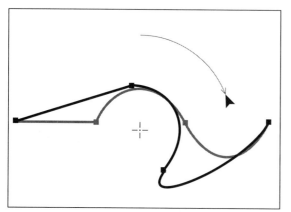

Figure 6.29 *Rotating a curved line segment that is part of a path.*

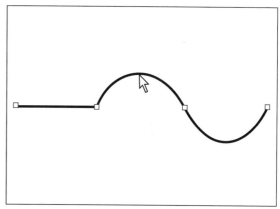

Figure 6.30 *If a curved line segment is selected, as shown, the effects of the Rotate tool will be similar to dragging the curve's outline.*

To rotate a curved line segment without affecting the segments attached to it, select the segment with the Direct Selection tool, but do not select its anchor points (see Figure 6.30). This action, however, will not produce the same results as rotating with the anchor points selected. As you drag around the axis of rotation, the direction handles change their length but not their angle, and the anchor points remain stationary. This produces effects similar to dragging the curved line segment without directly selecting its anchor points with the Direct Selection tool. Almost all control over the shape of the curve will be lost and the resulting segment will often be undesirable. To understand what exactly is happening to the curved line segment and its direction handles during this operation, read Chapter 8, the "How the Direction Handles Work" section.

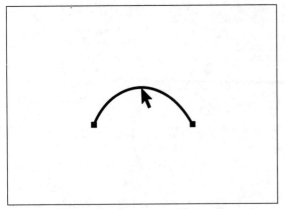

Figure 6.31 *Selecting a curve for scaling.*

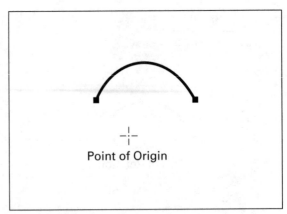

Figure 6.32 *Establishing the point of origin.*

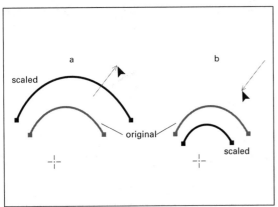

Figure 6.33 *Scaling a curve.*

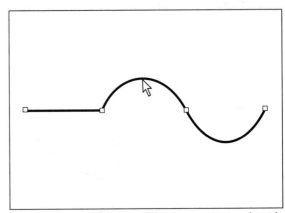

Figure 6.34 *If a curved line segment is selected, as shown, the effects of the Scale tool will be similar to dragging the curve's outline.*

Scale

When scaling a curved line segment, both the selected anchor and direction points will move closer to or further away from the focal point and each other. As the anchor points change their position relative to the focal point and each other, the distance between them will increase or decrease. This alone is not enough to scale a curved line segment. The direction points will also change their position while scaling, making the direction handles longer or shorter. This will change the shape of the curve relative to the horizontal and vertical percentages of scaling. To scale a curved line segment, select both anchor points of that line segment—even though the direction points and handles are not visible, they are assumed to be selected (see Figure 6.31). Choose the Scale tool from the toolbox and click in the document window to establish the focal point or point of origin (see Figure 6.32). The cursor will turn into an arrowhead to indicate that the selected curved line segment is ready to be scaled. Move the cursor away from the point of origin and drag toward or away from the point of origin to scale the object (see Figure 6.33 a, b). While dragging, both the original segment and an image of the one being scaled will be visible. When you release the mouse button, only the newly scaled curve will remain.

You may enter precise vertical, horizontal, and uniform percentages for scaling in the Scale dialog box. To access this dialog box, hold down the **Option** key while clicking to establish the point of origin. After entering the desired percentages, click **OK** for the scaling to take place, or **Copy** to create a duplicate of the scaled object. If the selected curved line segment is part of a path, the line segments attached to it will be affected by the scaling.

To scale a curved line segment without affecting the segments attached to it, select the segment with the Direct Selection tool, but do not select its anchor points (see Figure 6.34). This, again, will not produce the same results as scaling with the anchor points selected. As you drag to and from the point of origin, the direction handles will change their lengths, although the anchor points retain their position. This produces effects similar to those that occur when the curved line segment is dragged without selecting its anchor points with the Direct Selection tool. Almost all control over the shape of the curve will be lost and the resulting segment will often be undesirable. To understand what exactly is happening to the curved line segment and its direction handles during this operation, read Chapter 8, the "How the Direction Handles Work" section.

Reflect

To reflect a curved line segment, select both of its anchor points (see Figure 6.35). Choose the Reflect tool from the toolbox and click in the document window to establish the focal point (see Figure 6.36). The pointer will change into an arrowhead to indicate that the object is ready to be reflected. To establish the angle for the axis of reflection, click for the second time while positioning the cursor at the desired angle to the first click. The axis of reflection will be established by the angle of an imaginary

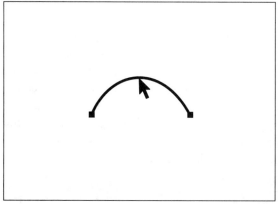

Figure 6.35 *Selecting a curve for reflecting.*

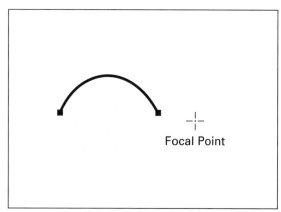

Figure 6.36 *Establishing the focal point.*

line between the two clicks. The object will be reflected as you perform the second click (see Figure 6.37).

To vary the axis of reflection while the curved line segment is being reflected, click and drag the mouse in a circular motion around the focal point (first click); this will rotate the axis of reflection as you drag. The further away from the focal point you start dragging, the more control over the angle of the axis of reflection you will have. While dragging, both the original segment and the reflected counterpart will be visible on the screen. When you release the mouse button, the original selection is deleted, leaving the reflected curved line segment.

You may enter a precise angle for the axis of reflection in the Reflect dialog box that appears if you hold down the **Option** key as you click to establish a focal point. Select either the vertical, horizontal, or angled axis of reflection. Click **OK** for the reflection to occur, or **Copy** to reflect a duplicate.

If the selected curve is part of a path, segments attached to it will be affected by the reflection (see Figure 6.38). To reflect a curved line segment without doing so, select the curved line segment with the Direct Selection tool, but not its anchor points. This, however, will not produce the same results as reflecting with the anchor points selected. The consequences of this were mentioned earlier and will be discussed in more detail in Chapter 8.

Shear

To shear a curved line segment, select both of its anchor points (see Figure 6.39), choose the Shear tool from the toolbox, and click in the document window to establish a focal point (see Figure 6.40). The cursor will turn into an arrowhead to indicate that the object is ready to be sheared. Move the cursor away from the focal point and start dragging (see Figure 6.41).

While dragging, you will see both the originally selected curved line segment and the one being sheared. When the mouse button is released, only the newly sheared curve will remain.

To use the Shear dialog box, hold down the **Option** key while clicking to establish a focal point. Select either the horizontal or the vertical axis and the angle of shearing. You may also input a specific angle for the axis as well as the shear angle. Click **OK** to complete the action, or **Copy** to create a duplicate of the sheared object.

If the selected curve is a part of a path, segments attached to it will be affected by the shear function (see Figure 6.42). To shear a curved line segment without affecting the segments attached to it, select the curve with the Direct Selection tool, but do not select its anchor points. As we have seen previously, this will not produce the same results as shearing an object with selected anchor points. The results of this have been mentioned earlier and will be expanded upon in Chapter 8.

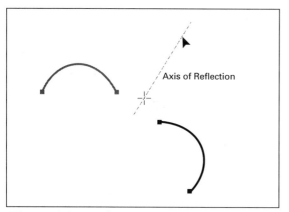

Figure 6.37 *Reflecting a curve.*

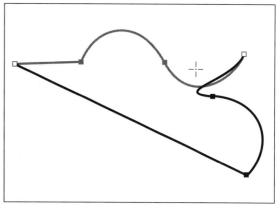

Figure 6.38 *Reflecting a curve that is part of a path.*

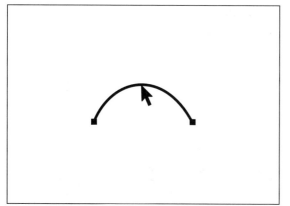

Figure 6.39 *Selecting a curve for shearing.*

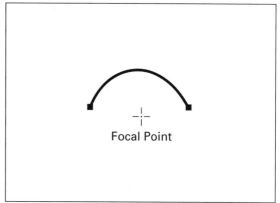

Figure 6.40 *Establishing the focal point.*

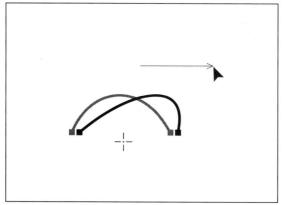

Figure 6.41 *Shearing a curve.*

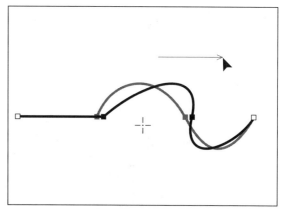

Figure 6.42 *Shearing a curve that is part of a path.*

Manipulating Curves with Direction Handles

The most precise way to manipulate a curve's shape is by changing the length and angle of its direction handles. The length of these handles will determine the slope of the curve, while the angle of the handles determines in which direction the curve will travel. So far, we have been manipulating the direction handles indirectly by using the Transform tools.

To manipulate the direction handle directly, select the curved line segment—or one of its anchor points—with the Direct Selection tool. The direction handles and direction points will now be displayed. Click and drag a direction point to change the length and angle of that direction handle. While dragging, you will see both the original curve and the one being altered (see Figure 6.43). Once the curve is the desired shape, release the mouse button and the original curve will disappear, leaving the newly altered curved line segment.

Holding down the **Shift** key while dragging will constrain the angle of the direction handle to 45-degree increments, relative to the X and Y axes. The length of the

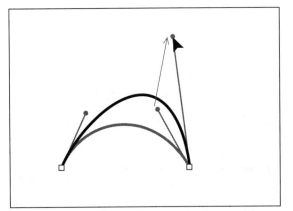

Figure 6.43 *Changing a curve's shape with direction handles.*

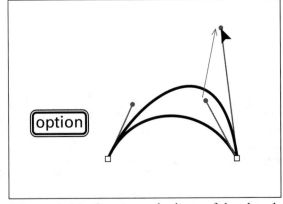

Figure 6.44 *Creating a duplicate of the altered curve.*

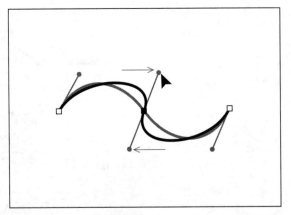

Figure 6.45 *Manipulating a direction handle at a smooth anchor point.*

direction handle itself will not be constrained. Holding down the **Option** key while performing the drag will, of course, result in the creation of an altered duplicate while the original remains unaffected (see Figure 6.44). The two curved line segments will not be attached, but their anchor points will be directly on top of each other.

Altering the angle of a direction handle that stems from a smooth point—connecting two curved line segments—will affect the angle of the direction handles of both segments. The shape of both curves will be altered (see Figure 6.45).

To alter the shape of any curve with two direction handles, each handle must be adjusted individually. Sometimes, you'll need to adjust both handles a few times to get the curve to look *just right.*

There is an infinite number of variations on the shapes a curve can take. Therefore, there is an infinite number of positions the direction handles can be in. To narrow these possibilities to the types of curves that are best suited for a specific rendering, you must understand how the position of the direction handles affects the shape of a curve. This will be discussed in greater detail in the next few chapters.

7 *Single Ideal Curve*

The Basic Concept of an Ideal Curve

Most renderings are created using a combination of straight and curved lines. Straight lines are easy to recognize, as they have a definite beginning and end. A corner where two straight lines meet is where one segment ends and the other begins. The angle or the direction of that corner does not affect that relationship.

This is not so with curved lines. Dividing a continuous curved outline into curved line segments involves a thorough knowledge of the variety of curves that can be created, and how they can be combined to trace that outline in the most effective and precise manner.

A good way to start is by examining the most basic and efficient curve that can be created in Illustrator: the *ideal curve*. An ideal curve is a section of a circle not longer than a semicircle. Any type of swerving, bending, winding, or twisting outline can be divided into a number of ideal curves (see Figure 7.1).

Since Adobe Illustrator is capable of creating many types of curves, using only ideal curves to build a rendering may not always be the most efficient choice. Once you have learned how to construct and use an ideal curve, it will be easier to understand how and when to create other kinds of curves.

The Bump

A *bump* describes the convex side of a curve. Any curved path will have a number of bumps of different sizes and steepness (see Figure 7.2); curves can be created with one or two bumps. Curves with two bumps, however, are harder to control and therefore are not as efficient. The ability to divide a curved path into a number of bumps is the

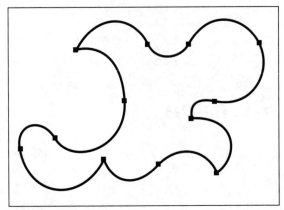

Figure 7.1 *Outline divided into ideal curves.*   ***Figure 7.2*** *Different size bumps.*

key to figuring out where is the ideal place for curved line segments and their anchor points to be. We will discuss in greater detail how to recognize bumps in a path in Chapter 11.

Technical Description of an Ideal Curve

An ideal curve is a single curved line segment not greater than a semicircle consisting of two anchor points and two direction handles (see Figure 7.3). If you have more than two anchor points, you have more than one line segment. An ideal curve should have only one bump, and it should be somewhat symmetrical.

To determine if a curve is symmetrical, draw a line perpendicular and centered, with an imaginary line between the two anchor points. If the two sides of the curve look like mirror images, then the bump is symmetrical (see Figure 7.4).

An ideal curve should be tangent to its direction handles and never intersect them. It should also fall in the area defined by two straight lines stretching across its anchor points, and perpendicular to the imaginary line between the anchor points, (see Figure 7.5).

Four Rules for Creating an Ideal Curve

The next four rules are designed to help you better understand how the direction handles should be constructed to create an ideal curve. These rules can also be applied to creating most types of curves in Illustrator.

Rule 1: The direction handles of any curve are always on the convex side of that curve (see Figure 7.6). Imagine that the direction point is like a magnet, and the peak

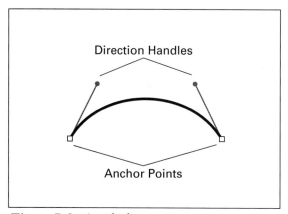

Figure 7.3 *An ideal curve.*

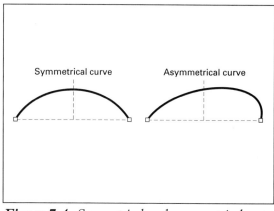

Figure 7.4 *Symmetrical and asymmetrical curves.*

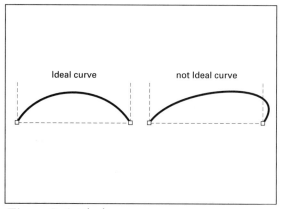

Figure 7.5 *Ideal curve area.*

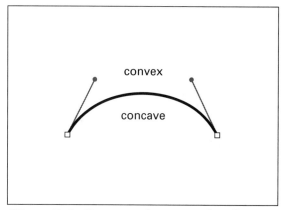

Figure 7.6 *Convex and concave sides of a curve.*

of the curve is attracted to it. The bump or the convex side of the curve will always be pulled toward the direction points.

Rule 2: The handles of an ideal curve should be on an acute angle to the imaginary line between its anchor points (see Figure 7.7). If a handle is on an obtuse angle to the imaginary line between the two anchor points, then the curve will be pulled out of the area defined by lines running through the anchor points and perpendicular to the imaginary line between the anchor points (see Figure 7.8). Making both handles on an obtuse angle will create two bumps in a curve (see Figure 7.9).

Rule 3: The length of the handles of an ideal curve should be about one-third the length of the curve if the curve were stretched into a straight line (see Figure 7.10). This means that you must know how long the curve will be before you begin drawing it. This is a very important idea in using Illustrator and it is applied in other situations that will be discussed later.

Rule 4: Both handles of an ideal curve should be similar in length and angle. This is to ensure that the bump of an ideal curve will by symmetrical (see Figure 7.11).

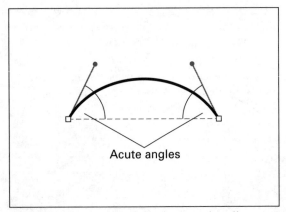

Figure 7.7 *Angles of the direction handles.*

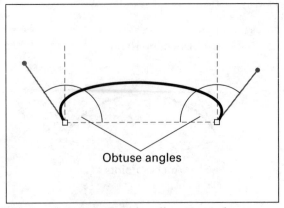

Figure 7.8 *Direction handles set on obtuse angles.*

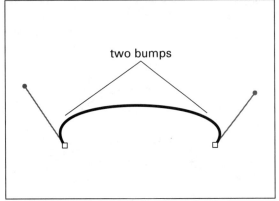

Figure 7.9 *A curve with two bumps.*

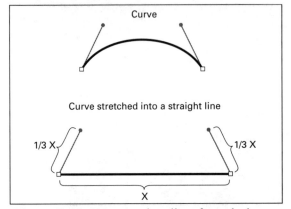

Figure 7.10 *Direction handles of an ideal curve should be a third of the length of a curve.*

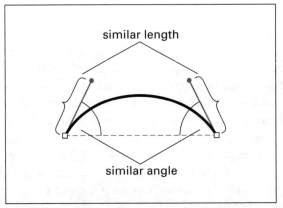

Figure 7.11 *Direction handles of an ideal curve should be of similar length and angle.*

Drawing an Ideal Curve

We are now ready to create an ideal curve. In order to concentrate on the physical steps of drawing a curve and not be distracted by the aesthetic aspects, we will create a curve that will require you to follow specific angles and measurements. You can estimate these measurements on your screen or choose Show Info from the Window menu to see precisely how far and on what angle the cursor is being moved.

We will start by creating the first anchor point and direction handle for the curve. Choose the Pen tool from the toolbox and press the mouse button in the document to establish the first anchor point. Without releasing the mouse button, drag for one inch on a 60-degree angle. Release the mouse button, and the first anchor point and a direction handle will have been created (see Figure 7.12). Now click the mouse button about two inches to the right of the first anchor point. Try to keep the two points horizontally aligned. Without releasing the mouse button, drag for an inch on a -60-degree angle (see Figure 7.13). Note that when you clicked to establish the second anchor point, the curve was created; and as you dragged a second direction handle, the curve changed shape. The second direction handle was dragged in the opposite direction, because the second direction handle of the curve you just drew—and the first direction handle for the next curve—are created simultaneously. The second direction handle of the curve always pulls out automatically while you are creating the first direction handle for the next consecutive curve.

It is normal for you to feel a bit clumsy at this point. Drawing curves with the Pen tool requires not only a thorough knowledge of how curves are created, but also many hours of practice. Keep repeating the steps for creating a curve until you feel more comfortable with your hand-eye coordination. You must be able to create a single ideal curve with ease in order to continue with the more advanced sections of this book.

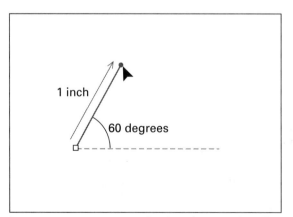

Figure 7.12 *Creating the first direction handle.*

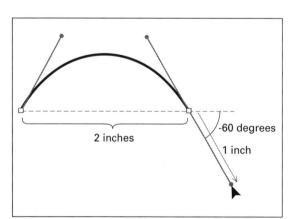

Figure 7.13 *Creating the second direction handle.*

Manipulating an Ideal Curve with Direction Handles

Next we will discuss a very limited movement of the direction handles to demonstrate a basic relationship between the angle and length of direction handles and the ideal curve. Once you have understood the logic behind this relationship, you will be able to predict how the position of the direction handles will affect any curve.

One of the factors that determines how a curve will look is the angle of its direction handles. To make the slope of a curve steeper, the direction handles should be on a greater angle to the imaginary line between the anchor points. To make a shallower curve, construct the direction handles on a lesser angle to the imaginary line between the anchor points (see Figure 7.14).

The other factor that determines how a curve will look is the length of the direction handles. If a slope is made steeper, it also becomes longer in length (see Chapter 6). In order to keep the relationship between the curved line segment and its direction handles at (1:3) (Rule 3), the direction handles have to be made longer for a steeper

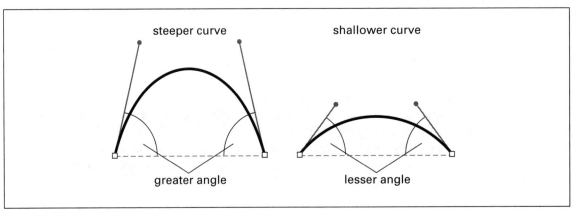

Figure 7.14 *Steep and shallow curves.*

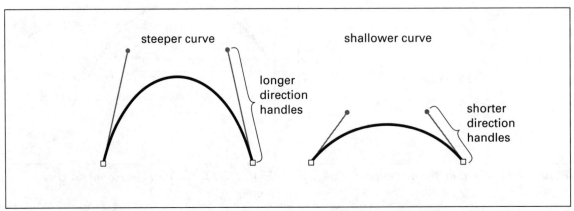

Figure 7.15 *Relationship of the length of the direction handles to the slope of the curve.*

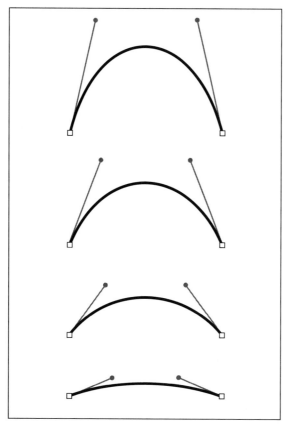

Figure 7.16 *Relationship of the length and angle of the direction handles to the slope of the curve.*

curve. The length of a curve with a shallow slope is shorter; therefore, the direction handles must also be made shorter to remain about one-third of the length of the curve (see Figure 7.15). To summarize, a steeper curve will have direction handles that are longer and at a greater angle to the imaginary line between the anchor points, while a shallower curve will have direction handles that are shorter and at a lesser angle to the imaginary line between the anchor points.

Figure 7.16 demonstrates the progression of an ideal curve from a steep to a shallow slope in four steps. Note the relationship of the direction handles to the ideal curve. Try to duplicate these steps on your computer using the ideal curve created earlier. Keep in mind that the direction handles are manipulated one at a time.

8 *More about Curves*

Adobe Illustrator allows you to create almost any shape of curve. The shape of the curve will directly relate to the position of its direction handles. In this chapter, we will discuss the logic behind how the construction and manipulation of direction handles affects the shape of a curve. The ideal curve, described in the previous chapter, is the most efficient curved line segment you would use to outline a path. There are some exceptions to this rule, but knowing why and when to apply those exceptions requires an expert understanding (which you will have upon the completion of this book) of how curved line segments are created and combined to form paths.

There is virtually no limit to the size and angle of direction handles. It is, however, difficult to understand how to manipulate the direction handle of an already created curve in order to change its shape. It is even more difficult to construct a direction handle before the curve has been drawn. As we have seen previously, one of the most important aspects of drawing a curve is visualizing how it should look before you begin to construct the first direction handle for that curve.

First Direction Handle

First, you must consider the direction in which the curve will travel; this direction hinges on two important questions: Where will the second anchor point be placed, and in what direction is the bump of the curve facing? The first direction handle should be dragged toward the direction of the second anchor point on the side where the bump of the curve will be. Figure 8.1 shows the angle of the first direction handle for various positions of the second anchor point and direction of the bump.

The next consideration you must take into account is how long and how steep the curve will be. The length of the curve will dictate the length of the direction handles.

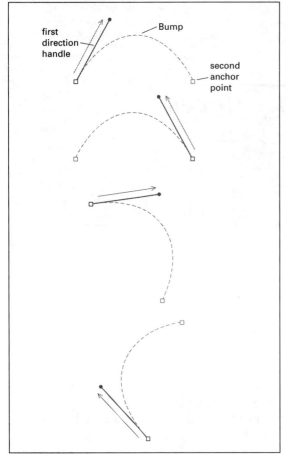

Figure 8.1 *Various positions of how the first direction handle should be constructed in order to create a curve shown with the dotted line.*

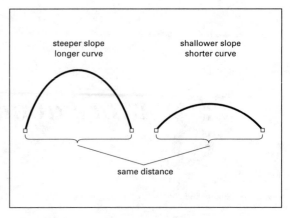

Figure 8.2 *Different slope curves.*

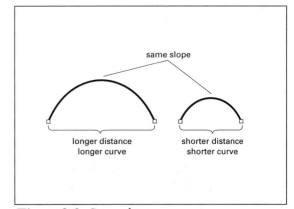

Figure 8.3 *Same slope curves.*

Once the length of the curve is established, the length of the direction handles is determined by dividing the length of the curve by three (see Rule 3, Chapter 7). The length of the curve is determined by two factors: the distance between its two anchor points and the slope of the curve. A curve with a steeper slope will be longer in length than a curve with a shallow slope, assuming that the distance between their anchor points is the same (see Figure 8.2). A curve with a greater distance between its anchor points will be longer in length than a curve with a shorter distance between its anchor points, assuming their slope is similar (see Figure 8.3).

The final decision you must make in constructing a direction handle is the angle on which it should be. You already have a clue to this angle from the position of the second anchor point and the direction of the bump. After the position of the second anchor point and the direction of the bump have been determined, the angle of the direction handle is narrowed down to 90 degrees. Figure 8.4 shows the area where the

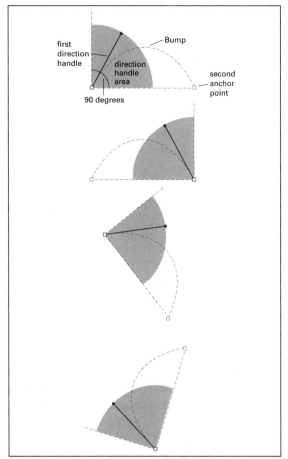

Figure 8.4 *The angle possibilities for the first direction handle of various curves are shown in gray.*

angle of the direction handle can still be varied after the position of the second anchor point and the direction of the bump have been established. This area is determined by drawing two perpendicular lines: The first line is an imaginary straight line between the two anchor points. The second line is drawn from the anchor point where the first direction handle is, and should also be perpendicular to the imaginary line between the anchor points and drawn on the convex side of the curve.

The angle of the direction handle within this area must be approximated by determining the slope of the curve. The greater the slope of the curve, the greater the angle of the direction handle to the imaginary line between the two anchor points. The lesser the slope, the lesser the angle.

You now have enough information to construct a direction handle perfect in length and angle for the curved line segment you are about to create. By visualizing the slope and length of the curve, the direction of its bump, and the location of the second anchor point before you begin to draw the curve, you will be able to construct a proper direction handle. This may seem like a lot to consider before you even click the mouse button, but after some practice it will become routine. Later in the book, we will discuss some of the ways to reduce the guesswork involved in determining all those factors.

Second Direction Handle

Once you have constructed the first direction handle, you should already know where the second anchor point will be placed. To construct the second direction handle, you must click and drag from the second anchor point. The most important thing to remember about making a second direction handle is that you must *drag in the opposite direction*. All the elements that determine the length and angle of the first direction handle apply to the second as well. The length of the second handle is still established by the distance you drag the mouse, but the angle of the second direction handle is at 180 degrees to the angle you drag (see Figure 8.5). This is because while you are constructing the second direction handle for the existing curve, the first direction handle for the next curve you will draw is being constructed simultaneously. As you drag, you will see both handles being created at that anchor point. This anchor point is the second anchor point of the curve that you just drew, and the first anchor point of the curve you are about to draw. The length of both handles will be identical and they will always be at 180 degrees to each other. These factors can be altered once both direction handles have been created.

When two direction handles stemming from the same anchor point are at 180 degree angles to each other, the transition between the two curves at that anchor point

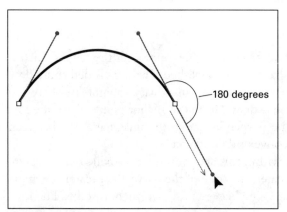

Figure 8.5 *The second direction handle is constructed while you drag at 180 degrees to its angle.*

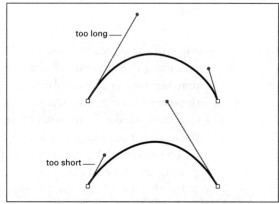

Figure 8.6 *The second direction handle has to compensate for the first direction handle being too long or too short.*

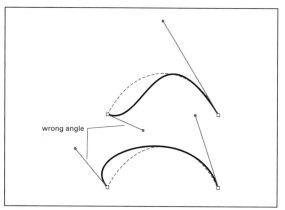

Figure 8.7 *The second direction handle cannot compensate for the first direction handle being at a wrong angle.*

will be smooth. Altering that 180-degree relationship will create a corner at the anchor point. Drawing more than one consecutive curve will be discussed in Chapter 9.

Determining the length and angle of the second direction handle is somewhat easier. While you are dragging to construct the second direction handle, the curve will be visible on your screen. The shape of the curve will change as you drag the second direction handle. This enables you to adjust the length and angle of the direction handle until the curve is of the desired shape. The only time you may run into a problem is if the first direction handle of that curve was not constructed properly. If it was made too short or too long, the second handle has to compensate (see Figure 8.6). This will make the curve less efficient and harder to control.

An even bigger problem will arise if the angle of the first direction handle is wrong. In most cases, compensating with the second direction handle will not help. Figure 8.7 shows the curves that must be created with a dotted line. The first direction handles were constructed incorrectly, and even with the help of the second handle, the curves (shown solid) could not be made a desired shape. This demonstrates that the construction of the first direction handle is very important and should be well thought out before proceeding.

Of course, the way Illustrator was designed, most mistakes are easily fixed. If either of the direction handles was improperly constructed, simply choose the Direct Selection tool from the toolbox and drag the direction point until the length and angle of the direction handle creates the desired curved shape.

How the Direction Handles Work

In Chapter 6 we discussed how to manipulate the direction handles: The most precise way is by dragging the direction point. How, exactly, the position of the direction handles affects the shape of a curved line segment will be discussed next.

The most important thing to remember about how the direction handles affect the shape of a curve is that the peak of a curved line segment is attracted to the direction points. This is why the bump of a curve will always be facing toward the direction points. If you are trying to achieve an even curve, the direction handles should be about the same length and at similar angles to the imaginary line between the two anchor points (see Figure 8.8). The portion of the curved line segment closest to one of the direction handles will be affected more by that direction handle when the length or angle of that direction handle is altered (see Figure 8.9). Positioning the direction handles so that they are drastically different in size and angle to the imaginary line between the anchor points will result in an uneven, asymmetrical curved line segment.

Since the peak of the curve is always attracted to the direction points, constructing the direction handle so that the direction points are farther away from the imaginary line between the anchor points will result in a steeper curve. If one of the direction points is further from the imaginary line between the anchor points than the other direction point, the slope of the curve will be steeper on that side.

The steepest slope is achieved when the direction handles are constructed perpendicular to the imaginary line between the anchor points (see Figure 8.10); the shallowest slope is a straight line. A curved line segment will become a straight line when both direction handles are positioned at a 0-degree angle to the imaginary line between the anchor points (see Figure 8.11). In this case, the length of the direction handles will not affect the shape of the segment if the length of the direction handle does not exceed the length of the distance between the two anchor points. Creating straight line segments with direction handles is not recommended, because the direction handles are designed to create only curved line segments. Creating straight line segments with anchor points that do not contain direction handles is much more efficient and easier to control.

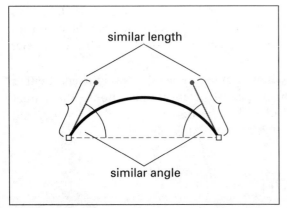

Figure 8.8 *Direction handles should be of similar length and angle.*

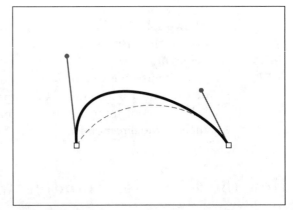

Figure 8.9 *Left side of the curve is affected more by the left direction handle.*

Another important relationship between the direction handles and the curved line segment is that the curve will always be tangent to the direction handles at anchor points. The definition of a *tangent* is as follows: two lines—one straight and one curved—or both curved, are said to be tangent to each other when they coincide for a very short distance on either side of the *point of contact*. The point of contact is the anchor point and is infinitesimal (that is, the distance where the two lines touch cannot be measured), because that distance is a point and has no dimension. The two lines are the direction handle and the curved line segment; the direction handle being a straight line, and the curved line segment being the curved line.

In some cases, it might seem like the direction handle and the curved line segment touch for a distance that is greater than a point. Figure 8.12 shows a curve and straight line that are tangent to each other. At first glance, it may seem like the distance where they touch is greater than a point. When that figure is enlarged (see Figure 8.13), it

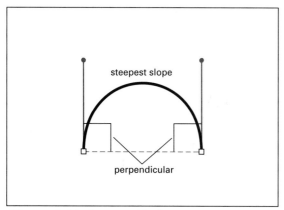

Figure 8.10 *Steepest ideal curve.*

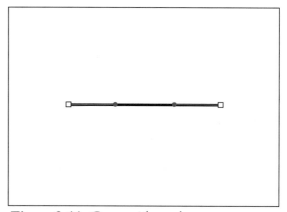

Figure 8.11 *Curve with no slope.*

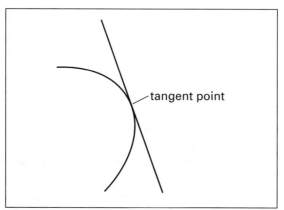

Figure 8.12 *Curve tangent to a straight line.*

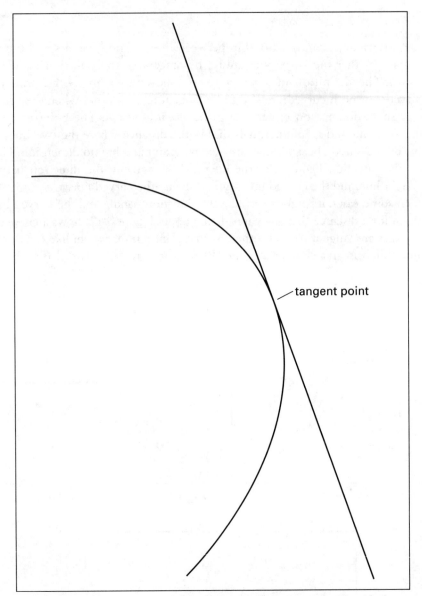

tangent point

Figure 8.13 *The exact tangent point cannot be precisely identified.*

can be observed that the distance between the two lines is decreasing to a point where it can no longer be measured with the naked eye. In fact, the exact spot where the two lines touch cannot be established on a two-dimensional level, because they touch for a distance of only a point, which we know has no dimension or area.

The direction handle and the curved line segment are tangent to each other in the same way. When we look at the direction handle and the curve, we are seeing only half of the tangent formation. If the anchor point is an end point, the direction handle

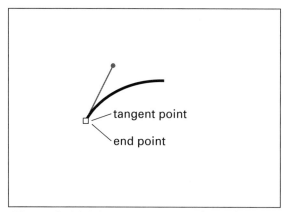

Figure 8.14 *Tangent point is at the end point.*

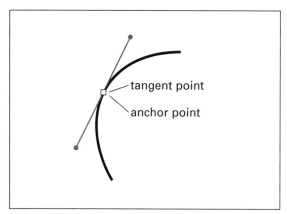

Figure 8.15 *Tangent point is at the anchor point.*

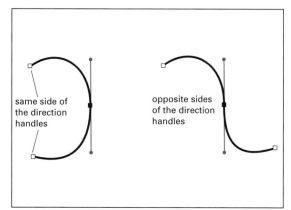

Figure 8.16 *Two different tangent formations.*

and the curved line segment stop at the tangent point, which is the end point (see Figure 8.14).

If the anchor point is a smooth point, then you can see the whole tangent formation. The curved line and the direction handle will continue on the other side of the anchor point (see Figure 8.15). In this case, you also see two tangent formations: one with the curve continuing in the same direction, and the other with the curve changing its direction at the anchor point. This will depend on where the second anchor point is placed. Let's assume that we have two curved line segments connected by a smooth anchor point. If both end points are placed on the same side of the direction handles stemming from the smooth anchor point, then the curve will keep going in the same direction. If, however, the end points are placed on the opposite sides of the direction handles stemming from the smooth anchor point, then the curve will change its direction at the tangent point (see Figure 8.16).

Understanding how the curved line segment is tangent to the direction handles is very important, because it is a constant throughout all the curved line segments created in Adobe Illustrator. Having the ability to predict how a curve will look relative to its direction handle is crucial to being able to create the curves you want.

Curves to Avoid

In the great variety of curved line segments that can be created with Illustrator, there are some that should be avoided because they are inefficient and hard to control.

In general, the length of the direction handles should be kept at about one-third of the length of the curved line segment. The angle of the direction handles should be no greater than 90 degrees to the imaginary line between anchor points. In some cases, diverging from those specifications is not detrimental to the shape of the curve. However, extremely altering those guidelines will create ineffective curves that will be hard to control.

Having control over a curve means that you can fine tune it to the desired shape with minimum manipulation. If the curve is drawn properly and the anchor points are placed correctly, you should be able to adjust that curve without drastically altering the shape of the curves adjacent to it. If a curve must be drastically adjusted, the shape of the curves connected to it with smooth points must be altered in a chain reaction. By learning how these mistakes are made, and how inefficient curves occur, it will be easier for you to avoid creating them. Avoiding the types of curves discussed next will help you to create smooth, efficient, trouble-free paths.

There are two types of curves that result from improper use of the Pen tool. The Pen tool is initially used to create the direction handle. Afterward, the only way to manipulate the handle is with a selection tool. A mistake is often made by trying to adjust a direction handle with the Pen tool. The mouse button is clicked at the direction point. This, of course, will not affect the direction handle when you drag. Instead, another anchor point and a direction handle will be created. A curved line segment will be drawn between the first anchor point and the spot where you clicked with the Pen tool. This creates a curved line segment where one was not desired (see Figure 8.17).

Another mistake often made with the Pen tool is when you attempt to drag an alternate direction handle from the first anchor point of a path. Alternate direction handles can be created with the Pen tool at an end point that is not the first point of a path (this will be discussed later). When you begin a path, click to establish the first anchor point, and drag to pull out a direction handle from that point. If the first attempt at creating the direction handle at the desired length and angle fails, the only way to adjust that handle will be with a selection tool. If you try to create an alternate direction handle from that anchor point with the Pen tool, a curved line segment will be created with both of its anchor points located in the same spot (see Figure 8.18 a, b).

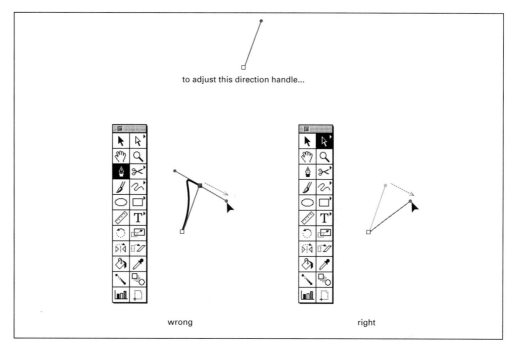

Figure 8.17 *Adjusting a direction handle after it has been constructed.*

The next few curves to avoid are created as a result of improper direction-handle positioning. One of the most common inefficient curves is the double-bump curve or the S curve. This curve is often created because of an incorrect breakdown of the outline to be traced. If an outline includes a smooth S shape (see Figure 8.19), there is a tendency to trace it using only one curved line segment (see Figure 8.20). This will eliminate one anchor point from the total path; minimizing the number of anchor points is desirable. However, a great amount of control over the shape of the curved line segment is lost. A double-bump curve is created when the direction handles are placed on the opposite sides of the imaginary line between the anchor points. As you know, the bump of the curve is controlled by the two direction handles. The S curve has two bumps, but you still have only two direction handles (see Figure 8.21). The control over the shape of the curve is diminished by at least 50 percent. For maximum control, an S shape should be created using two curved line segments.

Another improper placement of the direction handles results when they are made too long. The direction handles are considered too long when their length is greater than half the length of the curve. To achieve an even looking curve, both direction handles should be about the same length and angle. If one of the direction handles is too long or too short, the other handle has to compensate by being either too short or too long (see Figure 8.22 a, b, c). The shape of the curve in those cases can still be kept even and symmetrical. The control over the shape of the curve, however, is no longer

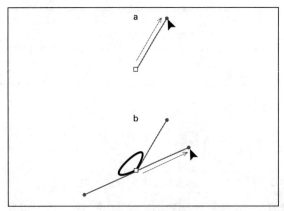

Figure 8.18 *An alternate direction handle cannot be created from the first point of a path.*

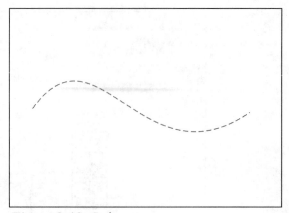

Figure 8.19 *S shape.*

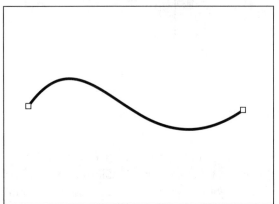

Figure 8.20 *S shape created with one curved line segment.*

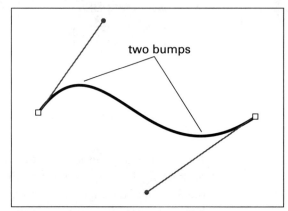

Figure 8.21 *S shape has two bumps.*

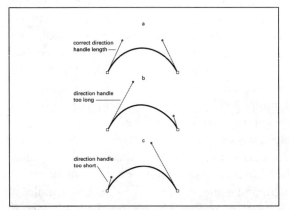

Figure 8.22 *Curves created with direction handle length being too short or too long.*

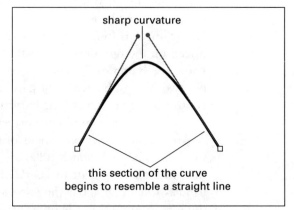

Figure 8.23 *Both direction handles are too long.*

evenly distributed between the two direction handles. The longer direction handle will have a greater influence over the shape of the curve than the shorter one.

If both handles are made too long, the integrity of the curve starts to diminish. The section of the curve closer to the anchor points will start to resemble a straight line, and the actual curvature of the curved line segment will be very small and sharp (see Figure 8.23). If that is the shape you are trying to achieve, it is best done with two straight line segments and one curved line segment (see Figure 8.24).

Taking this a step further, the direction handles are made so long that they start to overlap. This will exaggerate the sharp curve until it starts to look like a corner (see Figure 8.25). If the direction handles are made even longer, the curve will start to loop over itself (see Figure 8.26). This may look like a neat effect, but in fact it is a highly inefficient curve over which you will have almost no control.

The direction handles may be made as long as you want without intersecting them, as long as they are constructed at a right or obtuse angle to the imaginary line between the anchor points. This, however, brings up a whole new set of problems.

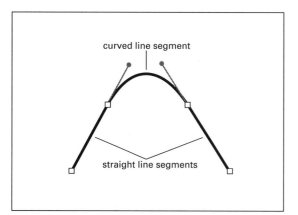

Figure 8.24 *Path created with two straight line segments and an ideal curved line segment.*

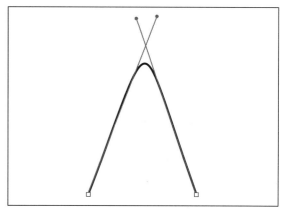

Figure 8.25 *Direction handles are too long and are intersecting.*

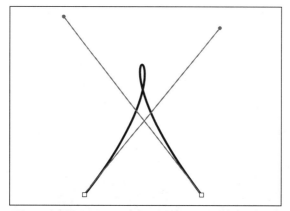

Figure 8.26 *Curved line segment starts to loop.*

When the direction handles are at a 90-degree (right) angle to the imaginary line between the anchor points and are made too long, the curve starts to become a straight line as it nears the anchor points (see Figure 8.27). This shape should be created using only two straight lines segments and one curved line segment (see Figure 8.28). When the direction handles are at an obtuse angle to the imaginary line between anchor points, that curve is already inefficient. As mentioned earlier, and as will be discussed in greater detail in Chapter 11, the best way to break up a continuous curved outline in Adobe Illustrator is by using curved line segments that are less than a semicircle. Constructing direction handles that are on an obtuse angle to the imaginary line between the anchor points results in a curved line segment that is larger than a semicircle (see Figure 8.29). Making those direction handles longer will exaggerate this condition even more (see Figure 8.30).

Another type of curved line segment that does not give you full control is the curve with only one direction handle. This kind of curve obviously gives you only half the amount of control over its shape than a curve with two direction handles. This

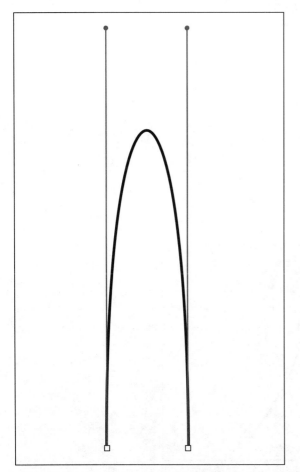

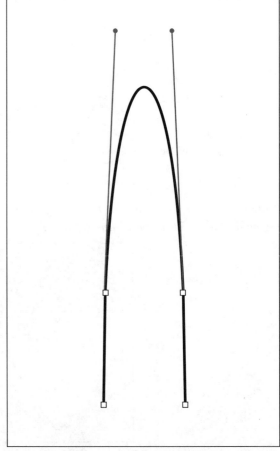

Figure 8.27 *Direction handles are too long.*

Figure 8.28 *Path created with two straight line segments and one curved line segment.*

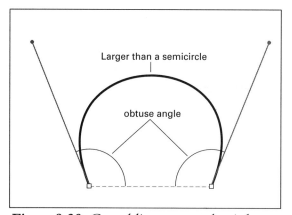

Figure 8.29 *Curved line segment that is larger than a semicircle is harder to control.*

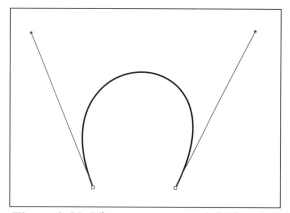

Figure 8.30 *The more exaggerated the length and angle of the direction handles, the more difficult it is to control the shape of the curve.*

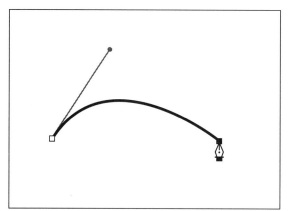

Figure 8.31 *Curve with a first direction handle and no second direction handle.*

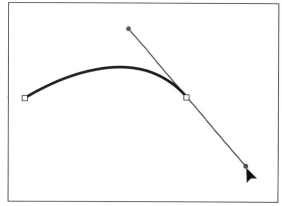

Figure 8.32 *Curve with a second direction handle and no first direction handle.*

happens in one of two ways: If you have dragged out a direction handle from the first anchor point and then clicked to establish the second anchor point without dragging, there will be no direction handle at the second anchor point (see Figure 8.31). If you clicked to establish the first anchor point and—without dragging a direction handle from it—clicked and dragged a direction handle from the second anchor point, there will be no direction handle at the first anchor point (see Figure 8.32). Either way, you will have a curved line segment with only one direction handle.

The preceding discussion had two major purposes: to show you some of the extreme cases of curved shapes that can be created in Illustrator, and to reinforce your knowledge of how direction handles affect the curves' shapes. There are no rules in the Adobe Illustrator manual telling you to never create these curves. As a matter of fact, since you have been given the capability to create these curves, you are expected to utilize them.

Knowing how all types of curves, efficient or not, are created is an important part of understanding how Adobe Illustrator works. The only way to avoid creating an undesirable curve is to know how to create it in the first place. Once you have learned how to create all kinds of curves, you will be able to make your own decisions about what types of curves to make and when to make them.

9 Drawing Consecutive Straight and Curved Line Segments

Straight Line Segments

Perhaps the simplest application of the Pen tool is creating a path that consists solely of straight line segments. The only information the computer needs from you is where the line segment should begin and end.

After choosing the Pen tool from the toolbox, the cursor will display a Pen tool icon with an (X) next to it, indicating that a path is ready to be constructed. Click (do not drag) where you want the path to begin (see Figure 9.1). An anchor point will be created and the Pen tool cursor will no longer display an X, indicating that a path is under construction. This anchor point is the beginning end point of the path.

Next, move the cursor to a spot where the straight line should change direction. When a straight line changes direction, there is a visible corner; this corner could be of any angle. Click (do not drag) at that corner. A straight line segment will be created between the two anchor points (see Figure 9.2). The last anchor point created will be displayed as a solid square, while all other anchor points on that path will be displayed as hollow squares. Continue to click at every corner of your outline; straight line segments will be automatically created and connected to each other at the anchor points (see Figure 9.3).

If the shape of the path does not exactly match the outline you are tracing, you can adjust it by moving the anchor points in two ways: The first technique allows you to continue creating the path once you have adjusted it, without any extra steps. This technique, however, works only if the Direct Selection tool was the last selection tool used. As the path is being constructed with the Pen tool, hold down the **Command** key. The Pen tool cursor will become a Direct Selection tool cursor. Continue holding the **Command** key as you drag the anchor point, or points, to a new location until you have achieved the desired shape. Once you release the **Command** key, the cursor

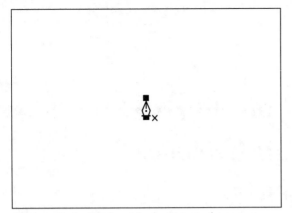

Figure 9.1 *Click with the Pen tool to create the first point.*

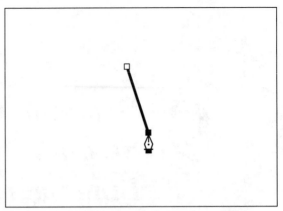

Figure 9.2 *Click a second time in a different location to create a line segment.*

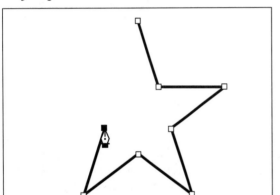

Figure 9.3 *Consecutive clicks with the Pen tool create a path.*

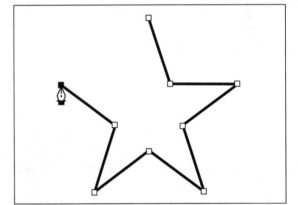

Figure 9.4 *Continue constructing the path after editing.*

will again become the Pen tool. Click to establish the next anchor point on your path, and the line segment created will be automatically attached to the previous anchor point on the path (see Figure 9.4).

The second technique requires going to the toolbox to choose the Direct Selection tool; the cursor will become the Direct Selection tool. Click and drag the anchor point or points until the desired shape is achieved (see Figure 9.5). To continue constructing the path after the adjustment, choose the Pen tool from the toolbox. Position the cursor at the last anchor point. The Pen tool icon will now display an (/hr) next to it, indicating that it is directly on top of an end point. Click the mouse button and the (/hr) symbol will disappear, indicating that a path is ready to be continued. Click to establish the next anchor point and to create a straight line segment connecting to the existing path (see Figure 9.6 a, b).

When you have traced the desired outline, you have a choice of whether to close the path or leave it open. If you choose not to close the path, do not click on the

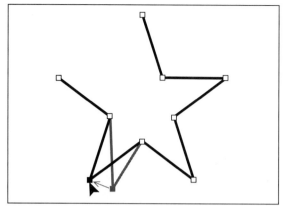

Figure 9.5 *Drag an anchor point to a new location to adjust the shape of the path.*

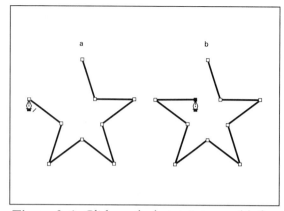

Figure 9.6 *Click on the last point created before continuing constructing the path after editing.*

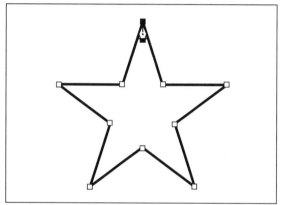

Figure 9.7 *Click on the first point of the path to close that path.*

beginning end point of the path. Once you have created the ending end point of the path, go directly to the toolbox and choose one of the selection tools. Click anywhere on the document page to deselect the path, or choose Select None under the Edit menu. The path will remain open, containing two end points.

If you choose to close the path, position the Pen tool cursor on the beginning end point of the path. The Pen tool cursor will display an o next to it, indicating that it is ready to close a path. When you click with the mouse button, a line segment will be drawn between the last anchor point created and the beginning end point (see Figure 9.7). The path will now be closed and consist solely of regular anchor points. The Pen tool cursor will display an (X) next to it, indicating that a path was completed and it is ready to begin a new path.

If the path was deselected before it was closed, it is still possible to close that path. To do so, choose the Pen tool from the toolbox and position it at one of the end points. The Pen tool cursor will display an (/hr) next to it, indicating that it is positioned directly on top of an end point. Click with the mouse button and move the cursor to the other end point. The Pen tool cursor will now display a o next to it, indicating that it is ready to close a path. Click with the mouse button to close the path. Other techniques on closing paths will be discussed in Chapter 11.

Curved Line Segments

Drawing consecutive curved line segments requires a thorough knowledge of curve construction and manipulation. Assuming you have read the previous sections of this book, you will now have enough information to continue with this section.

If you are tracing a specific outline that includes curved line segments, you must analyze how that outline can be broken down into segments and where the anchor points should be placed. A detailed explanation of how this is done will be discussed in Chapter 11, but for now we will concentrate only on the technical aspects of drawing consecutive curved line segments. (The figures in this section will be broken down into segments for you.)

First, we will look at how an outline consisting of similarly shaped curved line segments with smooth transitions is created. Figure 9.8 is a wave outline broken down so that you may see where the anchor points should be positioned.

To create a path consisting of curved line segments, you will need to construct direction handles. As you choose the Pen tool from the toolbox, the cursor will turn into a Pen tool icon with an (X) next to it, indicating that a new path is ready to be constructed. Press the mouse button to establish the first end point and drag in the direction you want the handle to be (see Figure 9.9). Once you release the mouse button, an anchor point with a direction handle will be created. The Pen tool cursor will no longer display an (X) to indicate that the path is under construction.

The next step involves clicking at the spot where the second anchor point should be, and dragging to create the first direction handle for the second curved line segment (see Figure 9.10). The first segment and its second direction handle will automatically be created. If you have constructed the first direction handle correctly,(see Chapters 7 and 8), the second direction handle for the first segment and the first direction handle for the second segment should be of the same length and not require any angle adjustment. Continue to click and drag at the suggested anchor point spots until the outline is traced (see Figure 9.11). Note that the last anchor point created will always be displayed as a solid square, while all other anchor points on that path will appear as hollow squares.

The preceding example involved outlining a path where the shape of all the curves was similar. In a situation like that, no adjustment of the direction handles from one segment to the next was required. The second example, however, will deal with an outline consisting of different shaped curved line segments. Tracing this type of outline will require adjusting the direction handles as you create the path.

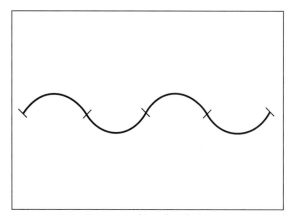

Figure 9.8 *Wave outline divided into curved line segments.*

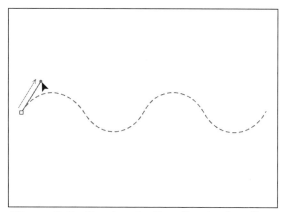

Figure 9.9 *Creating the first direction handle.*

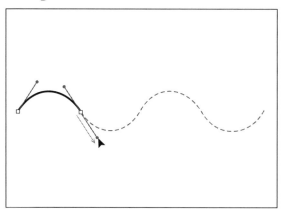

Figure 9.10 *Creating the second direction handle.*

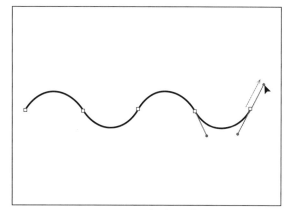

Figure 9.11 *Creating the last direction handle.*

If you are tracing the outline shown in Figure 9.12, after creating the first segment you will see that the first direction handle for the second segment is the wrong length (see Figure 9.13). There are two ways to adjust the direction handle while a path is in process: The first is to pull out an alternate direction handle. To do this, while still in the Pen tool, click and drag on the last anchor point. A new direction handle will be created. You will be able to drag the desired length for that direction handle without affecting the length of the second direction handle of the previous segment (see Figure 9.14)

The second way to adjust a direction handle while a path is being created, is to edit the length of the existing direction handle. Immediately after the second direction handle for the previous segment and the first direction handle for the segment you are about to draw are created, hold down the **Command** key. The cursor will turn into a selection tool, and you can drag the direction point of the first handle for the segment about to be drawn until it is the desired length (see Figure 9.15). When you release the

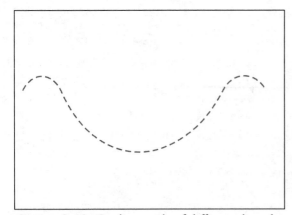

Figure 9.12 *Outline made of different shaped curves.*

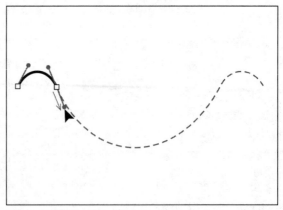

Figure 9.13 *The direction handle is too short for the second curve.*

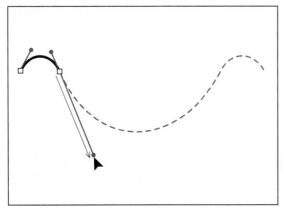

Figure 9.14 *Constructing an alternate direction handle.*

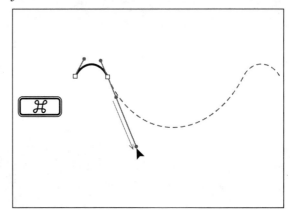

Figure 9.15 *Adjusting the existing direction handle.*

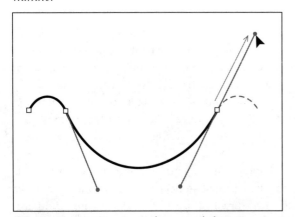

Figure 9.16 *Construct the second direction handle for the second curve.*

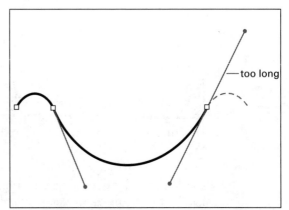

Figure 9.17 *The direction handle is too long for the third curve.*

Command key, the cursor will turn back into a Pen tool. Click and drag at the next anchor point to complete the curved line segment and create a direction handle for the next curve (see Figure 9.16).

After creating the second segment, a similar problem will occur. The direction handle for the next segment is now too long (see Figure 9.17). Use the same procedure—just described—to adjust the length of this direction handle.

If you wish to adjust a direction handle that is not currently displayed (only the direction handles of the most recently created curved line segment are displayed), or change the position of any anchor points, you may use one of the these two techniques.

If the last selection tool used was the Direct Selection tool, hold down the **Command** key while constructing the path with the Pen tool. The cursor will turn into the Direct Selection tool. To change the position of an anchor point, continue holding down the **Command** key and click and drag that point to a desired location (see Figure 9.18). To adjust the shape of a curved line segment, click on that line segment while still holding down the **Command** key. The direction handles will appear (see Figure 9.19). Continue holding down the **Command** key and drag the direction point to change the shape of the curved line segment (see Figure 9.20). Keep in mind that editing the shape of a curved line segment will affect the shape of the curve attached to it with a smooth anchor point. Once all the editing has been completed, release the **Command** key and the cursor will resume as the Pen tool. Click and drag to establish the next anchor point of the path, complete the current line segment, and create a direction handle for the next curved line segment (see Figure 9.21).

If the Direct Selection tool was not the last selection tool used, you will need to choose it from the toolbox. Adjust the anchor points or direction handles as just described and, once you have finished the editing, return to the toolbox to choose the Pen tool. Position the cursor at the last anchor point on the path; the Pen tool cursor

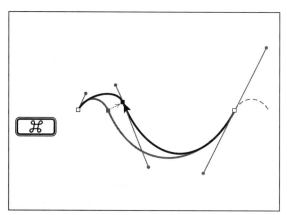

Figure 9.18 *Adjusting the position of an anchor point while the path is under construction.*

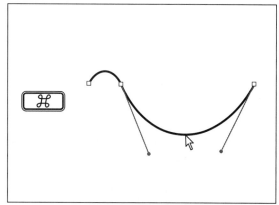

Figure 9.19 *Selecting a curve while the path is under construction.*

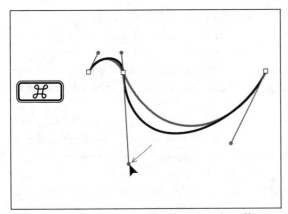

Figure 9.20 *Adjusting the direction handle while the path is under construction.*

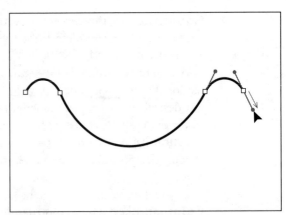

Figure 9.21 *Create the next line segment.*

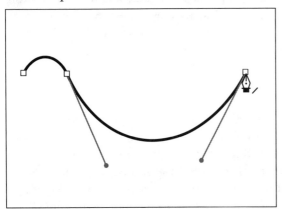

Figure 9.22 *Continuing the path construction after the edit.*

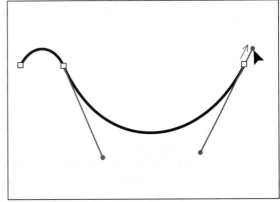

Figure 9.23 *Constructing a direction handle after the edit.*

will display an (/hr) next to it, indicating that it is directly on top of an end point (see Figure 9.22). Click and drag the mouse to construct a direction handle for the next curved line segment (see Figure 9.23). Continue constructing the path as you were before.

If you wish to leave the path open, choose a selection tool from the toolbox and click anywhere on the document to deselect the path, or choose Select None from the Edit menu.

If, however, you do choose to close a path with a smooth point, do not deselect the path. Instead, position the Pen tool cursor directly on the beginning anchor point of the path and the Pen tool cursor will display a o next to it, indicating that it is ready to close the path. Click and drag to close the path and create a direction handle for the last segment. You will be dragging in the opposite direction from the second direction handle of the last segment in the same way all other second direction handles are created. The only difference in this case is that no other direction handle will be created in the direction you drag (see Figure 9.24), because a direction handle already exists on that side. Although the length of the existing direction handle will not be affected, the angle of the existing direction handle will alter to keep the 180-degree relationship between the two direction handles, as it would at any smooth point.

Drawing consecutive curved line segments where the transition from one segment to the other is a corner requires creating corner anchor points. Figure 9.25 shows an outline where the curved line segments do not flow smoothly into each other.

To trace such an outline, start by creating the first anchor point and a direction handle in the same way as you would for any curved line segment. As you choose the Pen tool from the toolbox, the cursor will become a Pen tool icon with an (X) next to it, indicating that a new path is ready to be constructed. Click to establish the first anchor point, and drag in the direction of the bump of the curve to construct the first direction handle (see Figure 9.26). Next, click and drag to create the second anchor point and the second direction handle. The first curved line segment will be created (see Figure 9.27).

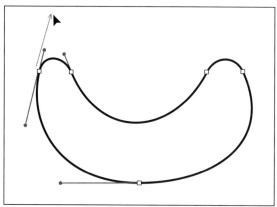

Figure 9.24 *Closing a path with a smooth anchor point.*

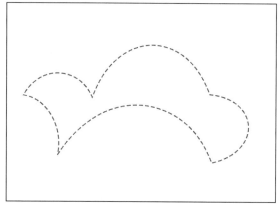

Figure 9.25 *Outline made of curves and corners.*

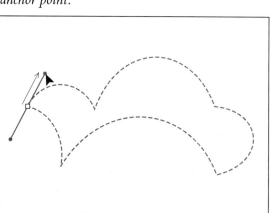

Figure 9.26 *Constructing the first direction handle.*

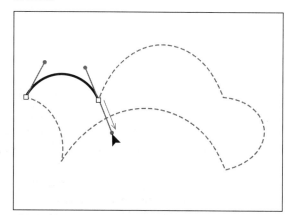

Figure 9.27 *Constructing the first curved line segment.*

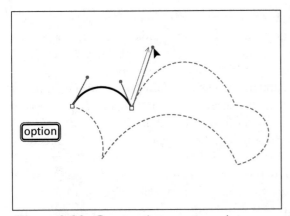

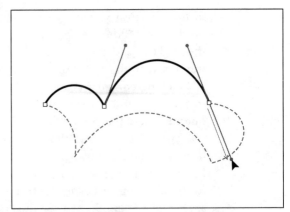

Figure 9.28 *Constructing a corner point.*

Figure 9.29 *Creating two curved line segments connected with a corner point.*

The second anchor point must be a corner point. To make an anchor point into a corner point, hold down the **Option** key and click and drag again on the last anchor point. When you are dragging for the second time—with the **Option** key held down—a new direction handle for the second curved line segment will be created (see Figure 9.28). You can drag that handle in whatever direction necessary to describe the second curve without affecting the shape of the previously drawn curved line segment. Once you have constructed the first direction handle at an appropriate angle and length, click and drag at the next anchor point to create the second direction handle. A curved line segment will be created attached to the first by a corner anchor point (see Figure 9.29).

Note that before the next curved line segment can be created, the last anchor point needs to be converted into a corner point as well: Use the procedure just described. Continue creating curved line segments with corner anchor points until the entire outline has been traced. If you need to adjust the shape of the previously drawn curved line segments, hold down the **Command** key. If the Direct Selection tool was the last selection tool used, the cursor will resume as that tool. Adjust the anchor point—or the direction handle—as needed while continuing to hold down the **Command** key (see Figure 9.30). After all the editing has been completed, release the **Command** key and the cursor will turn back into the Pen tool. Continue with the construction of the path as you had been previously (see Figure 9.31).

If the Direct Selection tool was not the last selection tool used, you must choose it from the toolbox. Adjust the anchor point or the direction handles, as needed. To continue constructing the path after the adjustments have been made, go to the toolbox and choose the Pen tool. When you position the cursor at the last anchor point on the path, the Pen tool cursor will display an (/hr) next to it, indicating that it is directly on top of an end point (see Figure 9.32). Hold down the **Option** key and click and drag the mouse to construct a direction handle for the next curved line segment (see Figure 9.33). Continue with the construction of the path (see Figure 9.34).

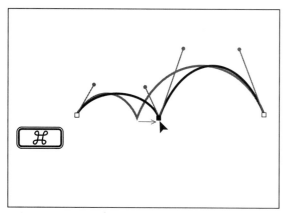

Figure 9.30 *Adjusting the position of an anchor point while the path is under construction.*

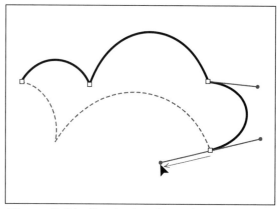

Figure 9.31 *Continuing the path construction after the edit.*

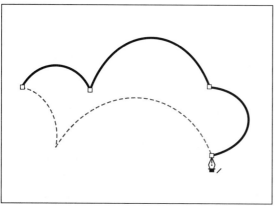

Figure 9.32 *Continuing the path construction after using the toolbox.*

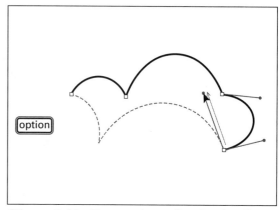

Figure 9.33 *Constructing a direction handle at a corner point.*

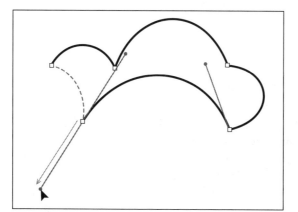

Figure 9.34 *Creating the next curved line segment.*

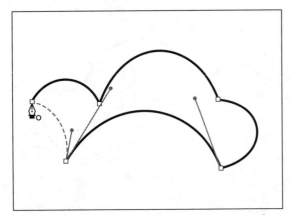

Figure 9.35 *A small circle appears next to the Pen tool when it is positioned on the first point of an existing open path.*

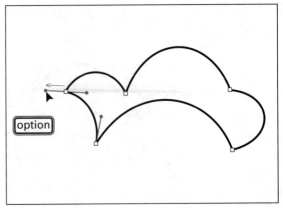

Figure 9.36 *Closing a path of curved line segments with a corner point.*

If you wish to leave the path open, choose a selection tool from the toolbox and click anywhere on the document to deselect the path, or choose Select None from the Edit menu. To close the path with a corner point, do not deselect the path, but position the Pen tool cursor directly on the beginning anchor point of the path. The Pen tool cursor will display a o next to it, indicating that it is ready to close the path (see Figure 9.35). Hold down the **Option** key, click and drag to close the path, and create a direction handle for the last curved line segment (see Figure 9.36).

Knowing the difference between smooth and corner anchor points—and when to use one or the other—is crucial in constructing paths. Corner points should be used only when there is an obvious corner on the outline. If an outline is flowing smoothly from one curve to the next, a smooth anchor point should be used. In many cases, the annoying tendency of the smooth anchor point to change the shape of a curve you do not want to affect makes many people shy away from using smooth anchor points. This is not advisable, because smooth anchor points do serve an important purpose: They keep smooth transitions between curved line segments.

Even though you can imitate a smooth transition at a corner anchor point by manually aligning the direction handles to be 180 degrees to each other, a small discrepancy will be greatly visible once that artwork is printed at a high resolution. If you are having trouble shaping your path to the desired outline by adjusting direction handles at a smooth point, try moving that anchor point to a better location or creating more anchor points. The most effective way to break down an outline into segments, and how to choose the optimal place for the anchor points, will be discussed in Chapter 11.

Combining Straight and Curved Line Segments

A path that consists of a combination of straight and curved line segments can be created by making corner anchor points where the straight and curved line segments meet. These corner points are constructed similarly to the corner points where two curves meet. The main difference between the two types of corner points is that a corner point that connects a curved and a straight line segment will have only one direction handle. Straight line segments have no direction handles; therefore, a corner anchor point that connects a curved and a straight line segment will have only one direction handle for the curved line segment (see Figure 9.37).

To draw a curved line segment that follows a straight line segment, choose the Pen tool from the toolbox. The Pen tool cursor will display an (X) next to it, indicating that a path is ready to be constructed. Click (do not drag) with the cursor where you want the straight line segment to begin. An anchor point will be created and the Pen tool cursor will no longer display an (X), indicating that the path is under construction (see Figure 9.38). Next, move the cursor to wherever you want the straight line segment to end and the next segment to begin. Again, click (do not drag) with the cursor, and the second anchor point will be created along with a straight line segment connecting the two anchor points (see Figure 9.39). Neither of the two anchor points just created will have direction handles. Since the Pen tool cursor was clicked, not dragged, anchor points were constructed without direction handles and a straight line segment was created.

To continue the path with a curved line segment, the last anchor point needs to have a direction handle for the curved line segment you are about to draw. To construct a direction handle at an end anchor point of a straight line segment, position the Pen tool cursor directly on top of that anchor point. Click and drag with the cursor to construct a direction handle. Note that the length and the angle of the direction handle should be relative to the shape of the curved line segment you are about to draw

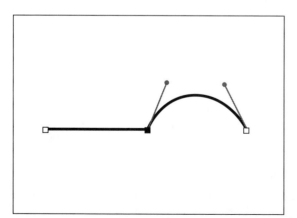

Figure 9.37 *Corner point connecting a curved and a straight line segment.*

Figure 9.38 *Creating the first point.*

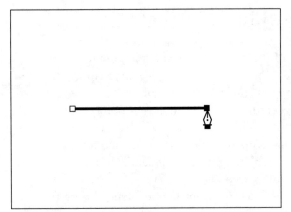

Figure 9.39 *Creating a straight line segment.*

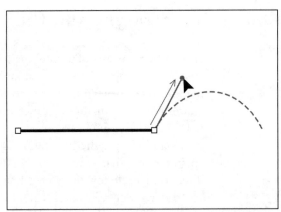

Figure 9.40 *Constructing a direction handle for a curved line segment connected to a straight line segment.*

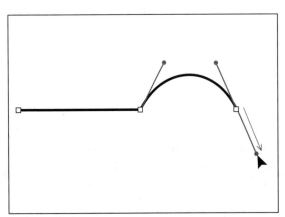

Figure 9.41 *Creating a curved line segment connected to a straight line segment.*

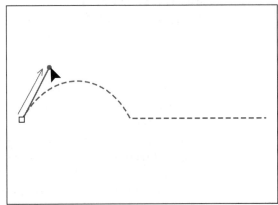

Figure 9.42 *Constructing a direction handle for a curved line segment.*

(see Figure 9.40). When the direction handle is of desired length and angle, release the mouse button and move the Pen tool cursor to the spot where you want the curved line segment to end. Click and drag to construct an anchor point with a direction handle, and a curved line segment will be created (see Figure 9.41).

An important thing to note about drawing a curved line segment following a straight line segment is that the direction handle for the curved line segment cannot be created at the same time you are constructing an anchor point for the straight line segment. The straight line segment and its anchor points must be created first. To create a direction handle, you must go back to the last anchor point again and click and drag for a direction handle. Dragging the cursor as you are constructing an anchor point for a straight line segment will create a curved line segment instead.

To draw a straight line segment following a curved line segment, choose the Pen tool from the toolbox. The Pen tool cursor will display an (X) next to it indicating that a new path is ready to be constructed and that you may click and drag to create

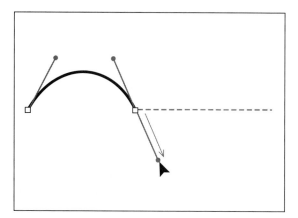

Figure 9.43 *Creating a curved line segment.*

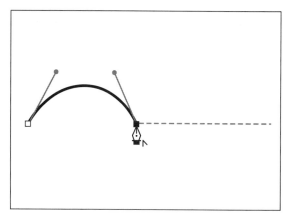

Figure 9.44 *Eliminating one of the direction handles at an end point.*

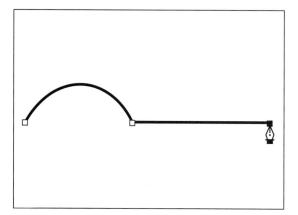

Figure 9.45 *Creating a straight line segment connected to a curved line segment.*

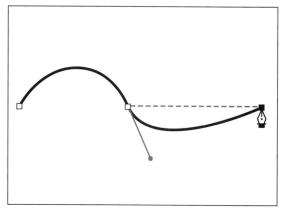

Figure 9.46 *If a direction handle is not eliminated, a second curved line segment will be created.*

the first anchor point and a direction handle for a curved line segment (see Figure 9.42). Release the mouse button and move the cursor to the spot where you want the curved line segment to end; click and drag to create a second anchor point, and a direction handle and a curved line segment will be drawn (see Figure 9.43). Keep in mind that when you are dragging to construct the second direction handle, you must drag in the opposite direction, thereby creating another direction handle for the next curved line segment. If the next line segment is straight, that direction handle has to be eliminated. Position the Pen tool cursor directly on top of the last anchor point. Click (do not drag) the cursor, and the second direction handle at that anchor point will disappear (see Figure 9.44). Next, move the cursor to where you want the straight line segment to end, and click the mouse button. A straight line segment will be created connected to the curved lined segment (see Figure 9.45). If you do not go back to the last anchor point and click to eliminate the unwanted direction handle, the second line segment will be a curve (see Figure 9.46).

Smooth Transitions between Curved and Straight Line Segments

The anchor points that connect straight and curved line segments to each other should be corner points. Corner points will, generally, create a visible corner on the path. Sometimes, however, there is a need to have a smooth transition between curved and straight line segments. One example where this could be the case is a rounded corner rectangle. Adobe Illustrator creates automatic rounded corner rectangles (see Chapter 5) by connecting four straight and four curved line segments with corner points. There are, however, no visible sharp corners on a rounded corner rectangle. This effect can be duplicated when you use the Pen tool.

The transition between a curved and a straight line segment is kept smooth by aligning the curve's direction handle to the angle of the straight line segment. The best results are achieved when the Shift key is used to constrain the angle of the straight line segment and the curved direction handle. First, you must find out at what angle your straight line segment will be drawn; if the straight line segment has already been drawn, choose the *Measure tool* from the toolbox (see Figure 9.47). You will see the cursor become a (+) when moved into an active window; position it directly on top of the first anchor point of the straight line segment and click the mouse button; the *Info Palette* will appear (see Figure 9.48). Move the cursor to the second anchor point of the straight line segment and click the mouse button. The Info Palette will display the distance and the angle at which the cursor was moved. The angle displayed is the angle of the straight line segment.

To construct a direction handle at the same angle as the straight line segment, go to the File menu and select Preferences > General. Enter the angle of the straight line segment in the Constrain Angle option and press the **OK** button. Holding down the **Shift** key will now constrain the movement of the cursor to 45-degree increments, starting at that angle. Choose the Pen tool from the toolbox and position the cursor at an end point of the straight line segment. Hold down the **Shift** key and click and drag to create a direction handle; the direction handle will be constructed at the same angle as the straight line segment (see Figure 9.49). When the direction handle is of the desired length, release the mouse button and then the **Shift** key, and click and drag to create an anchor point and a direction handle where you want the curved line segment to end. A curved line segment will be created attached to the straight line segment with a smooth transition (see Figure 9.50).

If a straight line segment has not yet been drawn, you may set the Constrain Angle option before you start constructing the path. If you are using a template, you can measure the angle of the straight line to be drawn by clicking directly on the template with the Measure tool. Enter the constrain angle in the General Preferences dialog box, choose the Pen tool from the toolbox, and click where you want the straight line segment to begin. Hold down the **Shift** key and click in the general area where you want the straight line segment to end. A straight line segment will be created at the

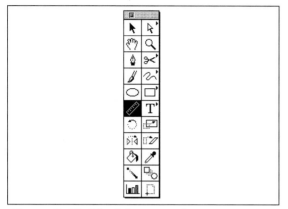

Figure 9.47 *The Measure tool.*

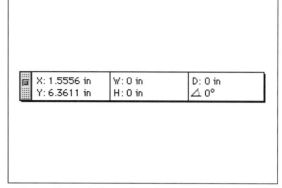

Figure 9.48 *The Info palette.*

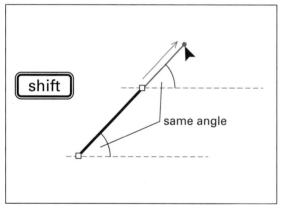

Figure 9.49 *Constructing a direction handle at the same angle as the straight line segment.*

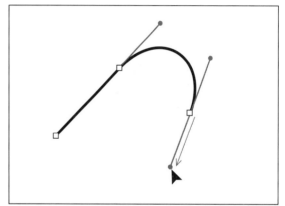

Figure 9.50 *Creating a curved line segment that flows smoothly into a straight line segment.*

angle you have specified in the Constrain Angle option. While still holding down the **Shift** key, click and drag at the last anchor point to construct a direction handle at the same angle. Release the **Shift** key and click and drag to complete the curved line segment.

To continue a path with a straight line segment connected by a smooth transition to an existing curved line segment, you must measure the angle of a direction handle at the end point of the curved line segment. Choose the Direct Selection tool from the toolbox and click on the curved line segment—the direction handles of that line segment will be displayed (see Figure 9.51). Choose the Measure tool from the toolbox and click at the end point of the curved line segment, and the Info Palette will appear (see Figure 9.52). Move the cursor to the direction point of the curve's direction handle at that end point, and click the mouse button (see Figure 9.53). The Info Palette will show the angle measurement. Set the Constrain Angle option to that angle

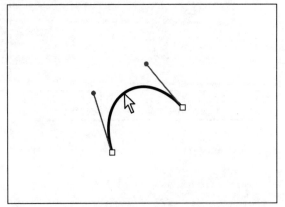

Figure 9.51 *Displaying the direction handles.*

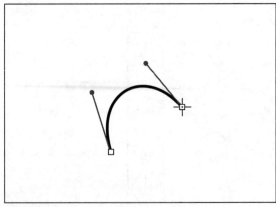

Figure 9.52 *Click on the anchor point with the Measure tool.*

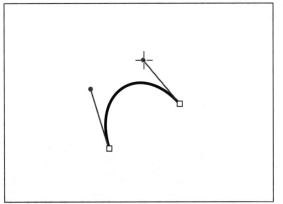

Figure 9.53 *Click on the direction point after clicking on the anchor point to find out the angle of the direction handle.*

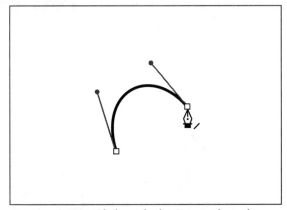

Figure 9.54 *Click with the Pen tool on the end point.*

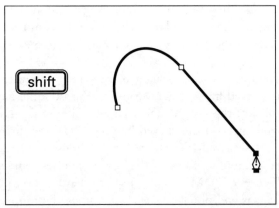

Figure 9.55 *Hold down the Shift key to create a straight line segment on the same angle as the direction handle.*

and press the **OK** button. Choose the Pen tool from the toolbox and position it directly on the end point of the curved line segment (see Figure 9.54). The Pen tool cursor will display an (/) next to it indicating that it is directly on top of an end point. Click the mouse button and the Pen tool cursor will no longer display an (/) next to it, indicating that a path is under construction. Move the cursor to a general area where you want the straight line segment to end, hold down the **Shift** key, and click the mouse button. A straight line segment will be created connected to the curved line segment with a smooth transition (see Figure 9.55).

If the curved line segment has not yet been drawn, you can set the constrain angle before you start constructing the path. If you are using a template, you can measure the angle of the straight line to be drawn after the curve by clicking directly on the template with the Measure tool. Enter the constrain angle in the General Preferences dialog box. Choose the Pen tool from the toolbox, and click and drag to create the first anchor point and the direction handle for a curved line segment (see Figure 9.56). Move the cursor to where the curved line segment ends and the straight line segment begins. Click and drag to create the second anchor point and construct the second direction handle. While dragging, press and hold the **Shift** key; the direction handle that you are constructing will snap to the constrain angle. (Note: Make sure you press the **Shift** key after you have clicked at the second anchor point. If the Shift key is pressed before the second anchor point is established, the relationship between the first and second anchor points will be constrained.)

Release the mouse button and then the **Shift** key once the direction handle is of the desired length (see Figure 9.57). The second direction handle for the curved line segment will be constructed at the specified constrain angle. Position the Pen tool cursor directly on top of the last anchor point, click the mouse button, and the unwanted direction handle will disappear (see Figure 9.58). Move the cursor to the general area where you want the straight line segment to end, hold down the **Shift** key, and click the mouse button. A straight line segment will be created connected to the curved line segment with a smooth transition (see Figure 9.59).

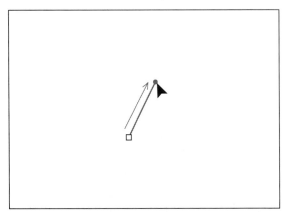

Figure 9.56 *Construct a direction handle.*

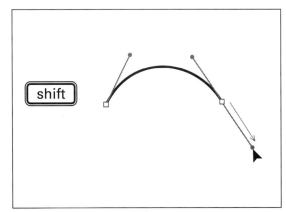

Figure 9.57 *Hold down the Shift key to construct a direction handle at the set constrain angle.*

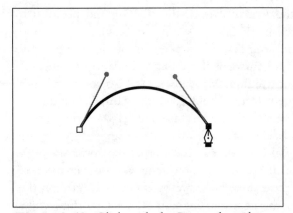

Figure 9.58 *Click with the Pen tool on the last point to eliminate one of the handles.*

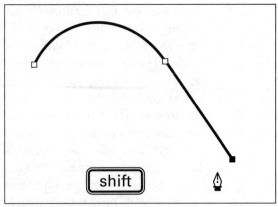

Figure 9.59 *Hold down the Shift key to construct a straight line segment at the set constrain angle.*

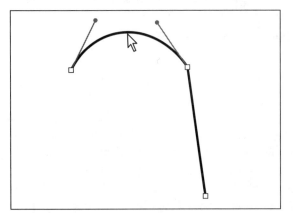

Figure 9.60 *Displaying the direction handles.*

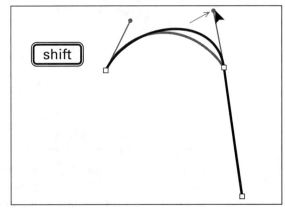

Figure 9.61 *Hold down the Shift key to adjust the direction handle to the set constrain angle.*

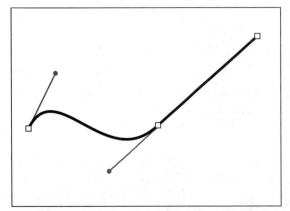

Figure 9.62 *An inefficient curve is created.*

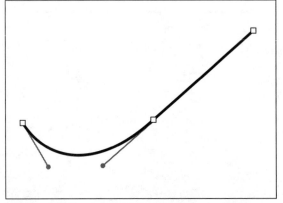

Figure 9.63 *Adjust to create a more efficient path.*

If you wish to create a smooth transition between a curved and straight line segment on an existing path, measure the angle of the straight line segment as described previously. Input that angle in the Constrain Angle option in the General Preferences dialog box, and hit the **OK** button. Next, choose the Direct Selection tool from the toolbox and click on the curve to be adjusted (see Figure 9.60). The direction handle for that curve will now be displayed. Hold down the **Shift** key and click on the direction point of the direction handle at the anchor point that connects the curve and the straight line. The direction handle will snap to the constrain angle. Adjust the length of the direction handle to achieve the desired curve shape. The transition between the curved and the straight line segments at that anchor point will now be smooth (see Figure 9.61). Once you have developed good hand-eye coordination in Illustrator, you will be able to align the angle of the direction handle to the angle of a straight line without measuring and constraining.

In some cases, aligning the angle of a direction handle to the angle of a straight line segment drastically changes the shape of the curved line segment until it is no longer efficient (see Figure 9.62). When this happens, you may need to adjust the other direction handle of that curve, or reposition the anchor points, to achieve a more efficient path outline (see Figure 9.63). The ideal placement of anchor points in a path will be discussed in Chapter 11.

10 *Working with Templates*

Creating a Template

Creating and using templates is an essential part of working with Adobe Illustrator. When you are rendering an illustration, a template could be a sketch or a reference that you use as a guide for building the final image. Just as in traditional illustration, before producing the final art, you would need to compile some reference material and create sketches. For instance, if you were creating a painting, the reference material would be placed under a piece of tracing paper to obtain a sketch. The sketch would then be transferred to the surface (e.g., canvas) on which the actual painting will be done. This creates a general guideline for you to follow as you fill the shapes in with color until the whole sketch is covered and the painting is done. Templates in Illustrator are used in exactly the same way.

Since Adobe Illustrator is an object-oriented program—and the images are created by compiling various shaped paths—your template should be made in a way that outlines those paths in the clearest way. The ideal template has clean, even outlines without any shading. It is best not to use photographs or images with shading as templates, because Adobe Illustrator displays templates with only two levels of gray (black and white), and much of the detail will be lost (see Figure 10.1). If your reference material is, however, a photograph or shaded drawing, there is one extra step you can take now—in the creation of the template—to save yourself time and frustration later.

Lay a piece of tracing paper over the reference image and trace it using clean and even outlines. While you are doing that, think of how this image will be created in Illustrator. Imagine that you are working in Illustrator, and each shape must be a continuous closed path combined and overlaid as if it were a cut-paper collage. By doing this, you have already begun the thought process necessary to create an image in Illustrator. Once you have an outlined drawing or sketch, you are ready to make it

Original photo

Adobe Illustrator template

Figure 10.1 *Original photo and a template created from it.*

into a template. You may use a black-and-white or a color scanner to scan in your sketch. If the sketch is very clean and evenly outlined, you can scan it as line art; although, in most cases, you will get better results by scanning in gray scale. Once a gray-scale image has been scanned, you can adjust the contrast and brightness of that image to make it cleaner and clearer looking. This can be done in Adobe Photoshop or another scanning program. Once you are satisfied with the way the scan looks, save it as a *PICT* file.

Any PICT file can be used as a template in Illustrator. To open a template in Illustrator, the application must be launched first. You cannot open a template from the desktop. Once in Illustrator, go to the File menu and choose Open to open the template file. A document window will appear on your screen with a grayed-out template on the page. The template image cannot be manipulated in any way and will not print. Use the template as a guide while you create paths outlining all the shapes. When you save, you will be asked to name the file and specify the format. An Adobe Illustrator document will be created separate from the PICT template file, and this will be your live Adobe Illustrator artwork file. If you still need the template to be a part of the Adobe Illustrator document, make sure that the PICT template file is always in the same folder as the Adobe Illustrator file. The template will then be automatically opened when you open the Illustrator artwork file. If, however, you no longer need the template, trash the PICT file and the next time you open the Illustrator file you will be asked to find the template or choose None. Click on None, and the Illustrator file will be opened without the template.

While working with a template in Illustrator, you may need to select different views and previews of the document to clearly see what you are doing. For instance, if you are working in Preview mode, paths that are filled with color will obstruct your view of the template. In this case, it may be necessary to choose Artwork under the View menu, or press **Command + E**. This will not display any paint style attributes of the objects, making them transparent and enabling you to see the template underneath. To return to Preview mode, choose Preview from the View menu, or press **Command + Y**. If you are working on a fairly complex image, the template itself may sometimes interfere with the clear picture of what you are doing. Hiding the template will give you a better view for detailed work. This is done by going, again, to the View menu and selecting Hide Template, or by holding down both the **Command** and **Shift** keys and pressing W. To show the template again, you may press the same keys (**Command + Shift + W**) or select Show Template from the View menu.

Placed EPS Images

Templates are not the only things you can use as guides for drawing in Illustrator. Files saved in *EPS* (Encapsulated PostScript) format can be placed into the Adobe Illustrator document. While in an active document in Adobe Illustrator, go to the File menu, choose Place Art, and choose the EPS file you wish to place. This can be any image: color or black-and-white, scanned, or created on the computer. A box representing the EPS image will be placed in your document, and the placed image will be displayed in full color or gray scale when the document is in Preview mode. You may choose whether to show the placed image by using the Document Setup dialog box found in the File menu. In Artwork mode, the placed image will not be displayed but will be represented by a picture box describing its boundaries. The placed EPS artwork may be manipulated in Illustrator with any of the transform tools. You cannot, however, adjust any paths or segments, or apply paint style attributes to the EPS image.

To use a placed EPS file as a guide for constructing paths, it is best to lock it. You can do this by selecting the EPS image and choosing Lock from the Arrange menu, or by pressing **Command + 1**. The image will now be unselectable and unaffected by any tools. You may start creating your paths right on top of the EPS artwork. When you are done, select Unlock All from the Arrange menu, or press **Command + 2** and delete the EPS image from your document.

Using a placed EPS image instead of a template will give you a clearer guide to follow for creating paths. It does have its drawbacks, however. Placed EPS images usually take up a large amount of the computer's operating memory. This will slow down your operations noticeably and will increase your chance of running out of memory. In addition, in order to see the actual EPS image, you must work in Preview mode, which will further slow down your computer and impair the viewing options. For instance, if you create a path filled with color on top of the placed EPS image, you will no longer be able to see the image under the colored path. Going to Artwork view will not display the EPS image at all. Using templates is a much better option, as it gives you greater flexibility over viewing your artwork and does not affect the memory or speed of your computer.

Tracing Templates

Doing the preparation work before starting a rendering can be a valuable step, as it will save you a lot of time and frustration during the actual construction of an image in Illustrator. Accruing reference materials, and setting up a template, is a main part of that preparation. When you create an outline drawing—to be used as a template—either from a reference picture or your imagination, you will be separating that image into shapes that will then be translated into Illustrator paths. This practice will help you better understand and visualize how to build those shapes in Illustrator. You will also gain a better idea of which tool is the best to use to create different shapes.

For instance, if the outline is very irregular and organic looking, an Auto Trace or Freehand tool may be the best tools to use (see Figure 10.2).

On the other hand, if the outline is smooth and sharp-edged, the Pen tool would work best (see Figure 10.3). If there are rectangles and ovals in your outline, then, obviously, the Rectangle and Oval tools should be used. When an Auto Trace tool is

Figure 10.2 *Image with an irregular, rough outline.*

Figure 10.3 *Image with a smooth outline.*

used, the characteristics of a template become even more important. Since you can control only the beginning and end of an autotraced outline, the path will directly reflect the property of the template. If a template is clean and precise, the autotraced path will be easier to control and will have fewer nicks and unusual shapes. However, if a template is cluttered and dirty—for example, if you are using a scanned photograph—the direction and length of the autotrace path will be harder to control. Since the autotrace path allows a continuous outline on a template, any stray markings on the template may diverge the path shape away from the desired outline. Figure 10.4 shows how the Auto Trace tool, set to the same tolerance level, outlines two different templates.

There are two methods that you can use to gain more control over what the Auto Trace tool outlines on your template: one is by specifying the beginning and the end of the autotrace path by clicking and dragging from the spot where you want the path to begin or where you want it to end. Choose the Auto Trace tool from the toolbox, make sure that the template is visible on the document page, move the Auto Trace tool cursor to the spot where you want the path to begin, and click and drag to the spot where you want the path to end. Once you release the mouse button, the autotrace path will follow the template outline between those two points.

Dirty template

Clean template

Resulting autotraced image

Resulting autotraced image

Figure 10.4 *Templates and the resulting autotraced images.*

If you do not wish to specify the beginning and the end of the autotrace path, you may simply click with the Auto Trace tool in the area you want outlined. This will create a path tracing the continuous outline of the template until that outline returns to the beginning point. This can occasionally create a path that may be too complex to print or preview. Depending on your template, you should choose how to trace its outline carefully.

Another method of controlling the autotrace outline is by setting the *Auto Trace Gap Level* in the General Preferences dialog box. While the Auto Trace tool is follow-ing a template, it may run into small gaps or bumps in the outline. The Auto Trace Gap option allows you to set the tolerance level to 0, 1, or 2 pixels. This means that if the Auto Trace Gap option is set to 0, the path will trace every tiny gap and bump in the outline. This will also produce a very complex path with many line segments and anchor points. With the Auto Trace Gap option set to 2, the path will ignore gaps or bumps that are 2 pixels large. The path created will have fewer segments and anchor points. The Auto Trace tool will almost never follow the template outline exactly, and in most cases you will need to fine-tune the path shape by moving the anchor points and editing the direction handles.

Using the Freehand tool to trace a template will give you somewhat greater control over selecting specific areas of the template you wish to trace. Since you can guide the Freehand tool by moving the mouse, the direction and the duration of the path outline is easier to control. The tracing of the template will still not be exact, however, because the Freehand tool responds to deviations in movement of the mouse. This can be somewhat controlled by setting the Freehand Tolerance level in the General Preferences dialog box. The tolerance can be set from 0 to 10 in increments of 1/100 of a point. Setting the Freehand Tolerance level to 0 will detect any small variation in the mouse movement and will create bumps and gaps in your outline. A setting of 10 will reflect only the general movement of the mouse, creating smooth outlines but with no detail. A setting of about 3 to 5 is a good general setting that will create outlines that are true to the form you are tracing, and with minimal bumps and nicks.

If your outline needs to have perfectly straight lines and smooth flowing curves, using the Pen tool is the best solution. The path outline will no longer rely on how the computer interprets the template or movements of the mouse. The only variant in the path shape will be the placement of the anchor points and the construction of the direction handles, both completely controlled by you.

11 *Constructing Complex Paths*

Before You Begin

You now have all the basic technical knowledge necessary to construct and manipulate paths in Illustrator. The following discussions will concentrate on the procedures that will take you from a blank document page to full-fledged illustration. You may already have in mind an image that you would like to do. How you get from that idea to the final product will vary based on your style, working routine, and, of course, what you exactly need to get done.

The techniques discussed next are what I have found to be the most efficient and time-saving. You will undoubtedly discover your own as you acquire more expert knowledge of Adobe Illustrator. If you are designing a page that is mostly text with some simple graphic elements, such as rules and boxes, then you may not need to know any advanced path techniques, and Adobe Illustrator might not even be the best program to use. If, on the other hand, you need to create anything from a graphic logo to a complex illustration, Adobe Illustrator can be the ideal tool.

Even if you are the kind of person who never draws a sketch before doing the final art, having a template in Illustrator as a guide will save you a lot of time and frustration while you are constructing the image. If the graphic you are creating consists only of shapes automatically provided in Illustrator, such as ovals, rectangles, stars, and polygons, then having a template guide is not that crucial. However, if your image calls for complex shapes that can be created only with the Pen tool, a template is an essential element.

To draw any given shape, a path must be constructed outlining that shape. While constructing a path, you must decide whether it will consist of straight or curved line segments or both, where those line segments will begin and end, what length and angle the direction handles for the curved line segments will be, and whether the anchor points are smooth or corner. These are only some of the factors you would have to consider when creating a shape. Having a template will help eliminate having to make some of those decisions while constructing paths. The next section will deal with how to analyze and outline a shape with the most efficient path.

Breaking Down an Outline into Segments

If you have a specific shape to draw, you may choose to outline it using the Freehand tool. However, in most cases this will produce a path that has too many segments and anchor points. The memory that Adobe Illustrator files require relates, in part, to the number of anchor points in your document. If you are doing a complex illustration, using the Freehand tool to construct the paths will produce an overwhelming number of anchor points; this may cause PostScript errors and printing problems. You may set the Freehand Tolerance Level to a high number to reduce the number of anchor points; this, however, will not allow you to trace an outline exactly. Using the Pen tool for precise outlines with a minimum number of anchor points is the best solution, although it does require the user to provide a great deal of information. The first and most important step is analyzing the shape you will need to outline and breaking it down into line segments. Once a shape has been broken down into straight and curved line segments, you will already have the information about where the anchor points should be placed.

The simplest shape to divide into segments is one that consists of only straight lines. The beginning and the end of each segment are clearly visible. Figure 11.1 shows an abstract shape composed of straight lines; anywhere there is a corner, an anchor point should be placed. This will describe the beginning of one segment and the end of another. If you are creating a closed path, it does not matter where you begin constructing it, because closed paths have no beginning or end; although an open path must be started at one of its end points. To create a path consisting solely of straight lines, click with the Pen tool at every corner to establish anchor points and create straight line segments between them. Do not drag the Pen tool, because that will create a direction handle for a curved line segment. The angles and lengths of the straight line segment will be determined by where you place the anchor points.

If a particular segment needs to be on a specific angle, the Shift key can be used to constrain a segment to that angle. The default constrain angle is set to 0 degrees. Holding down the **Shift** key while clicking to establish the anchor points will constrain the resulting line segment to increments of 45 degrees, starting at 0 degrees. Therefore, if you need to draw a line that is vertical, horizontal, or on 45-degree angle, leave the Constrain Angle option at 0 degrees. However, if the angle of the line you need to draw must be on another specific degree, input that angle into the Constrain Angle option. The Constrain Angle option can be found in the File menu after selecting Preferences > General.

To constrain a line segment to the specific angle, click to establish its first anchor point, hold down the **Shift** key, and click in the general area where you want the line

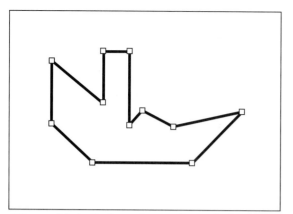

Figure 11.1 *Path made up of straight line segments.*

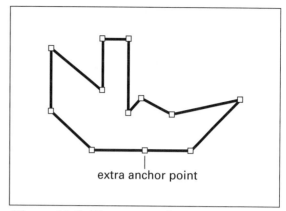

Figure 11.2 *Too many anchor points.*

segment to end. An anchor point will be created at the specified angle to the first anchor point, thereby creating a line segment on that angle. The position of the Pen tool cursor will not be the exact position of the anchor point if the Shift key is held down. The computer estimates the closest position to the Pen tool cursor for the placement of the anchor point at the set constrain angle. For instance, if the Constrain Angle option is set to 0 degrees, clicking with the Pen tool—while holding down the **Shift** key at 20 degrees to the first anchor point—will place the second anchor point at 0 degrees to the first one. Clicking with the Pen tool while holding down the **Shift** key at 25 degrees to the first anchor point will place the second anchor point at 45 degrees to the first one.

Remember to always release the mouse button before releasing the **Shift** key, or the anchor point will be placed at the exact location of the cursor regardless of the constrain angle. The construction of a path to outline the shape in Figure 11.1 requires some lines that will be constrained to vertical and horizontal angles, and other lines that do not need to be on a specific angle. The lines that do not need to be on a specified angle should be estimated by placing the Pen tool cursor in the exact spot where the anchor point will be established. Having a template as a guide will be very helpful in making these estimations.

The shape in Figure 11.1 can be easily separated into line segments. It consists of 11 line segments connected by 11 anchor points. Creating more segments than that will contribute to the path's inefficiency in two ways: First, the path will have more anchor points than required, which—multiplied by hundreds of points in a complex illustration—will create numerous unnecessary anchor points in your document. Second, the integrity of the straight lines may be compromised. If an extra anchor point is placed in the path (see Figure 11.2), the desired straight line will no longer be continuously even. The location where an anchor point exists will always stand a chance of becoming a corner. Even a slight degree difference between the two segments attached at that anchor point may create a visible bump on a high-resolution printout.

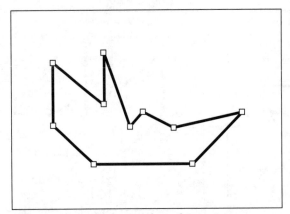

Figure 11.3 *Not enough anchor points.*

On the other hand, if not enough anchor points are used, it will be impossible to create a path to outline the shape. Figure 11.3 shows what would happen if even one anchor point were omitted.

This brings us to the conclusion that there is an optimal number of anchor points that should be used to construct a path outlining any given shape. Too many anchor points will cause your path to not be as efficient as it could be. Too few anchor points, and the path will not be the shape you need. Breaking down a shape that consists of curves into segments is not as obvious.

As mentioned in Chapter 2, how the shapes divide will depend on your interpretation. For instance, if you wanted to draw an outline of a map of the United States, one of the decisions you would have to make is how detailed you want that outline to be. This interpretation will, in part, influence how many segments and anchor points you will need to draw. How much detail your outline requires will be dictated by how large the final image will be, what you are trying to express with that image, and the style in which you choose to express it. An outline that graphically represents the map of the United States may have very few segments and anchor points, just enough to be able to recognize it (see Figure 11.4). If, however, you are trying to achieve a more realistic rendering of the map, more segments and anchor points are required (see Figure 11.5). As your rendering becomes more realistic, the level of detail will increase, necessitating the construction of more segments and anchor points.

One of the most typical misinterpretations made while rendering in Illustrator is the final scale of the image. Since in Illustrator you can work on an image at great magnification—1,600 percent of the actual size—there is a tendency to put too much detail into the artwork. This should be considered when working in Illustrator, as some of the details you spend a lot of time on at 1,600 percent magnification may not even be visible when you output the image at its actual size. Your time will be wasted and the path will have more segments and anchor points than are needed, making it inefficient. It is always a good idea to decide what size your final image will be, and print out samples of it to gain a better idea of how much detail you actually need.

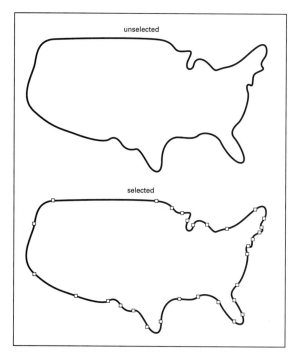

Figure 11.4 *Less detail uses less anchor points.*

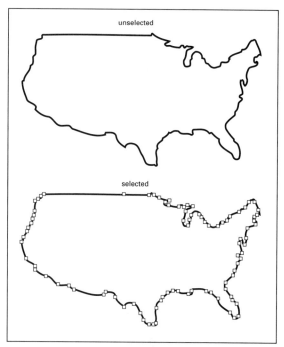

Figure 11.5 *More detail uses more anchor points.*

Realize, though, that viewing your artwork in Illustrator at actual size may not always give you the proper representation of how the image will look when it is printed. Because your computer screen is generally 72 dots per inch (dpi) and the laser output is 300 dpi, the detail seen on the printout may not always be as clearly visible on your computer screen.

I've found that there is a way to view your artwork on the screen in close approximation to the amount of detail you will see printed. Since a laser writer's resolution is 300 dpi and the screen is 72 dpi, zooming in on your image at 300 to 400 percent will give you a fairly accurate representation of the printed image. To zoom in or out on your artwork, choose the Zoom In tool from the toolbox (see Figure 11.6). If you wish to zoom in on a specific area in your artwork, position the Zoom In tool icon at the center of that area and click the mouse button. The image will be displayed at the next magnification level, with the specified area in the center of the screen (see Figure 11.7).

To zoom out of your artwork, hold down the **Option** key and you will see the plus (+) sign in the magnifying glass icon change to a minus (–) sign. Click on the mouse button while holding down the **Option** key, and the image will zoom out to the next reduction level (see Figure 11.8). You can also zoom in on a specific area by dragging the Zoom In tool icon diagonally across that area. A marque will be created, outlining the area you want to magnify. Release the mouse button, and the marqued area will fit to the size of your screen. This will skip through a few magnification levels, depending on the area you have marqued (see Figure 11.9 a, b).

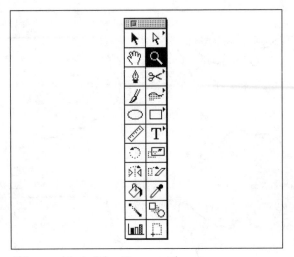

Figure 11.6 *The Zoom tool.*

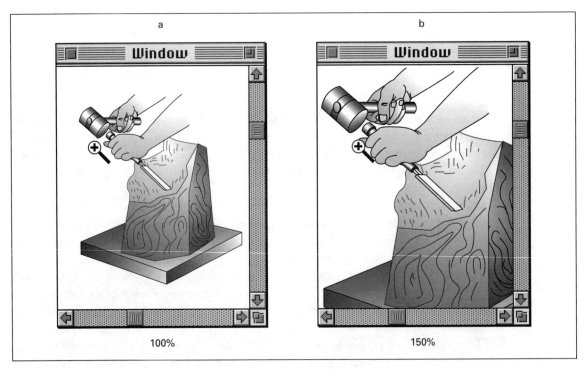

a

b

100%

150%

Figure 11.7 *First zoom level is 150 percent of the actual size.*

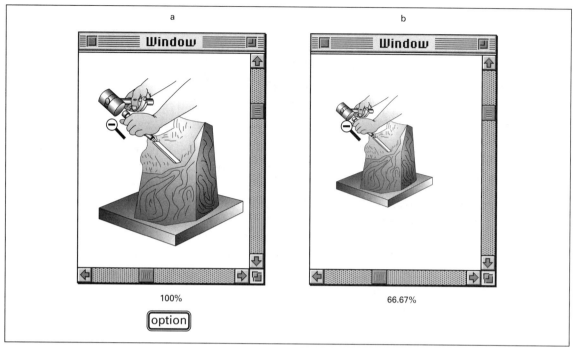

Figure 11.8 *First zoom out level is 66.67 percent of the actual size.*

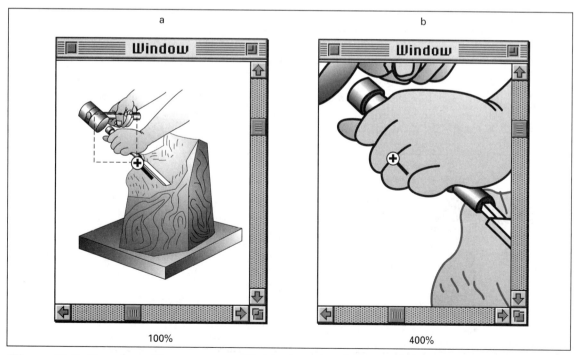

Figure 11.9 *Dragging a Zoom marque will skip through a few magnification levels.*

Zooming in or out of your artwork does not affect the actual size of the image, only your view of it. All of the elements in the document are proportionally magnified or reduced: the artwork, the art board, the page, and all the units of measurement. To view the artwork in actual size (100 percent), double-click on the Zoom tool in the toolbox or choose Actual Size from the View menu; you may also press **Command + H**. You can choose from 17 different magnification levels ranging from 6.25 percent to 1,600 percent of the actual size of the artwork.

Until you have become more accustomed to translating how your image will look from the screen to hard copy, it is a good idea to make printouts as you go along to get a better idea of the amount of detail you need to apply. Also, to help determine how much detail your rendering will have, it is a good idea to create a tight outline pencil drawing of your image to be used as a template. Most of the interpretation work will be done by executing this step. Whether you are drawing from your imagination or using reference material, translating those images into an outline sketch will enable you to establish the amount of detail your final art will have. The appearance of your finished rendering will also dictate which tool is best to use to create it in Illustrator. If the outline of your image is so detailed that there is no visual distinction between line segments, and the shape consists of many tiny lines and curves, a Freehand or Auto Trace tool may be your best choice.

Freehand and Auto Trace tools set at low tolerance levels produce outlines that are very irregular, with many bumps and glitches. This could be a desired effect when the outline of your image calls for a lot of random detail—that is, that the general shape represents a specific image—but when the shape is magnified, the detail does not depict any particular image. Figure 11.10 shows an outline of a tree that was created with a Freehand tool. The general shape represents a tree, but a magnification shows no particular image. Since using the Freehand tool does not give you much control over the detail, the outline takes on a random appearance.

In cases like this, no breakdown of the outline into segments is required, because the specific placement of line segments and anchor points cannot be controlled with the Freehand or Auto Trace tools.

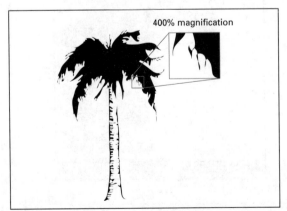

Figure 11.10 *Detail is abstract.*

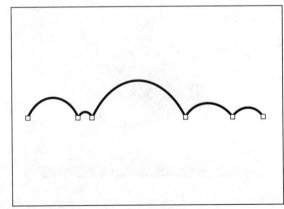

Figure 11.11 *Curved outline with visible corners.*

On the other hand, your artwork may call for just as much detail that is not random. For example, if you are drawing a crowd of people, where people's faces must be rendered realistically, the detail is great but not random. In a case like this, a Pen tool can be used to outline the faces at a high magnification level.

After you have decided the amount and type of detail your artwork will have, and created the appropriate template, you should be able to make the decision about which tool will be best to use. If your artwork calls for the Freehand or Auto Trace tools—or can be constructed with shapes automatically provided in Illustrator (ovals, rectangles, polygons)—you can proceed with the construction of the image. If, on the other hand, the Pen tool is best suited for creating your artwork, further analysis of the outline is required.

As discussed earlier in this chapter, if your outline consists solely of straight lines, breaking it down into line segments is an easy task. The anchor points are simply placed at all the corners where lines change direction. Most shapes do consist of both straight and curved lines, and a shape consisting of curved lines can still have defined corners. The shape in Figure 11.11 is comprised of curves, but the corners are still clearly visible. In a case like this, breaking down the outline into line segments can be achieved by identifying the corners, as in the straight lines outline.

The anchor points are constructed as corner points, and the curved line segments are created as discussed in Chapter 9. The shape in Figure 11.11 can be traced with five curved line segments and six anchor points, two of which are end points. All five curved line segments are less than a semicircle and can be easily designed with two anchor points and two direction handles apiece. If, however, a shape includes a curve that is larger than a semicircle, the most efficient way to trace it will require more than two anchor points and two direction handles; Figure 11.12 shows such a curve. Even though it is possible to outline this shape with a single curved line segment with two anchor points and two direction handles, it might not always be the most efficient path.

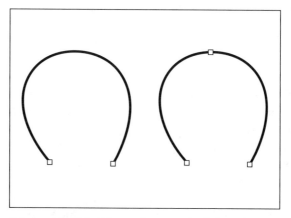

Figure 11.12 *The outline on the left is drawn with one curve and is more difficult to control than the outline on the right, which is drawn with two curves.*

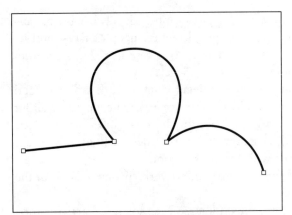

Figure 11.13 *The lack of control over a curve that is connected to other line segments with corner points is not a factor.*

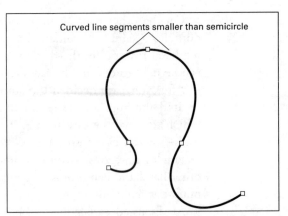

Curved line segments smaller than semicircle

Figure 11.14 *The lack of control over a curve that is connected to other line segments with smooth points can be a factor.*

To refresh your memory, the most efficient path is one that consists of the minimum number of anchor points without compromising control. In the case of the shape in Figure 11.12, tracing it with one line segment will give you the minimum number of anchor points, but the control over the shape of the path will be somewhat diminished. If this particular shape exists by itself, or it is not connected to any other segments with smooth anchor points, the lack of control over it may not be a factor (see Figure 11.13). As long as you can achieve the exact shape desired, it is not always necessary to conform to the ideal-curve rules (see Chapter 7). If, however, you are having trouble constructing the curved line segment to the desired shape, or if it is connected to other segments with smooth anchor points (see Figure 11.14), breaking it down into more segments may be required.

By constructing an additional smooth anchor point to divide the segment in half, two curved line segments smaller than semicircles will be created, allowing you to have more control (see Figure 11.14). Separating this particular shape into two segments will result in two ideal curves with two anchor points and two direction handles, respectively.

The greatest control over a shape is achieved when its direction handles are at an acute angle to the imaginary straight line between its two anchor points. If the shape in Figure 11.12 is traced using only one curved line segment, its direction handles will be at an obtuse angle to that imaginary line (see Figure 11.15). Fine-tuning the shape of such a curved line segment can be more difficult. If there are other curved line segments attached to it with smooth anchor points, control over fine-tuning the shape may be further diminished.

Since adjusting the direction handles of one curve will affect the shape of an adjacent curve, the variety of positions at which the direction handles can be placed is somewhat restricted. In addition, if one of those curved line segments is not an ideal curve and you do not have optimal control over its shape, fine-tuning that curve can be frustrating. By dividing a shape into ideal curves, more control is gained.

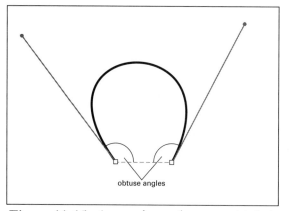

Figure 11.15 *A curve larger than a semicircle is created when its direction handles are at an obtuse angle to the imaginary straight line between the anchor points.*

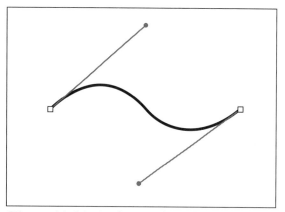

Figure 11.16 *Outline made with one curved line segment.*

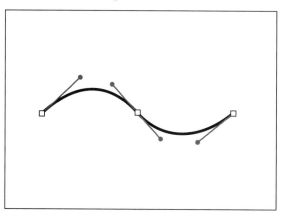

Figure 11.17 *Outline made with two ideal curves.*

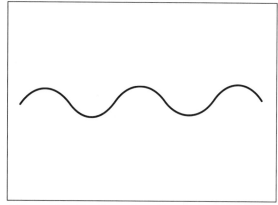

Figure 11.18 *Curved outline with no visible corners.*

Our discussion continues with Figure 11.16. The shape shown here can also be outlined by using only one curved line segment with two anchor points and two direction handles. However, you may have problems similar to those experienced with the previous shape. The two direction handles exhibit the most control over a single bump, and the curve in Figure 11.16 has two bumps. If you are able to construct the direction handles in such a way as to achieve this exact shape, no further breakdown will be needed. In this case, however, the shape of each bump will be dictated by only one direction handle; as a result, all the fine-tuning possibilities will not be available.

Having adjacent curved line segments connected with smooth anchor points will decrease those possibilities even more. Constructing a path of this shape with two curved line segments will give you more control over the shape of each bump (see Figure 11.17). This brings us to the conclusion that the optimal placement of anchor points is at the beginning and end of each bump—provided that the bump is not larger than a semicircle.

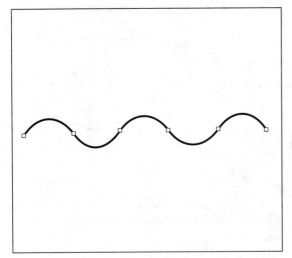

Figure 11.19 *Outline divided into ideal curves.*

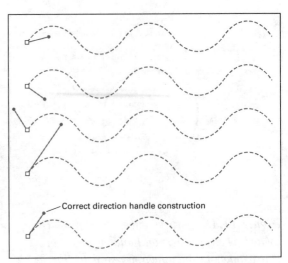

Correct direction handle construction

Figure 11.20 *The first four direction handles are constructed at either the wrong angle or the wrong length.*

Let us look at a few more shapes consisting of curves, and analyze how they should be broken down into segments to achieve the most efficient path. Figure 11.18 shows a simple wave shape; all the curves run smoothly into each other, creating no visible corners. Your first assumption should be that all the anchor points will be smooth. This shape also has a definite beginning and an end, which means that it will be an open path with two end points.

The best place to start constructing this path is at one of the end points, and then continue until the other end point is reached. Next, count the number of bumps on this shape; you should count five bumps, three facing up and two facing down. Each one of those bumps will be a curved line segment, and the smooth anchor point will be placed at the beginning and end of each curved line segment (see Figure 11.19). You have now divided the shape into line segments, which will create a path with the least amount of anchor points and the most control over the shape of each segment.

Further analysis of this shape reveals that all the curved line segments are approximately the same size and shape, which means that all the direction handles will be relatively the same length and angle. If you construct the direction handles in accordance with the rules given to you in Chapters 7 and 8, no adjustment of those handles from one curve to the next will be required. Simply click and drag with the Pen tool to create the first direction handle at about a third of the length of the curve, in the direction of the curve, and on an angle between 0 and 90 degrees to the imaginary straight line between the curve's anchor points. Make sure that the angle of the direction handle puts it on the convex side of the bump.

Figure 11.20 shows all the wrong possibilities of how a direction handle should be constructed, and one correct way. Once the first direction handle has been properly created, follow the same procedure for all the other direction handles until you reach the other end point and the shape is traced. Keep in mind that while constructing the

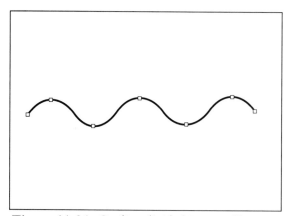

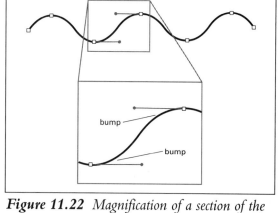

Figure 11.21 *Outline divided into inefficient curves.*

Figure 11.22 *Magnification of a section of the outline shows a curved line segment with two bumps.*

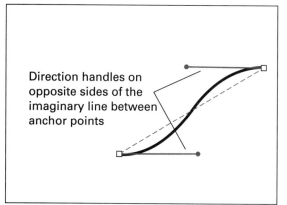

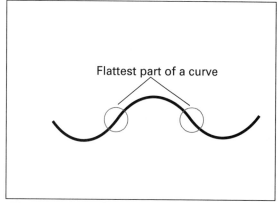

Figure 11.23 *A curved line segment with two bumps.*

Figure 11.24 *Flattest part of a curve is where the bump changes direction.*

second direction handle for a curve with a bump facing up, you are also constructing the first direction handle for the curve with a bump facing down. The same rules apply to bumps facing down as to bumps facing up.

Let's now discuss why this type of breakdown is ideal for this particular shape. Figure 11.21 shows a different placement of the anchor points that will still achieve the same shape. The number of anchor points in this configuration is increased by one. This result breaks the first rule of path construction. Using more anchor points, however, is not the main concern in this case, as the location of those anchor points is more detrimental to the path shape. Even though the first and last segments are still considered ideal curves, the segments in between are not. Looking closely at those segments, we can see that they consist of two bumps (see Figure 11.22). The bumps are very subtle, but they nonetheless require the direction handles to be placed on the opposite sides of the imaginary straight line between the anchor points of that segment (see Figure 11.23). As discussed in Chapters 7 and 8, this does not give you the

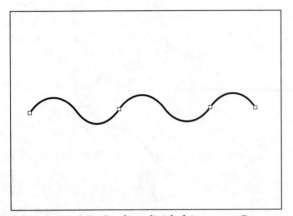

Figure 11.25 *Outline divided into two S-shaped curves and one ideal curve.*

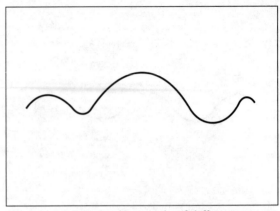

Figure 11.26 *Outline made of different size bumps with no visible corners.*

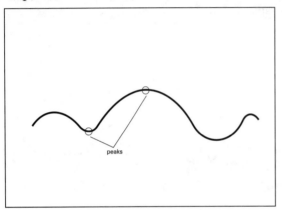

Figure 11.27 *Identifying peaks of two consecutive bumps.*

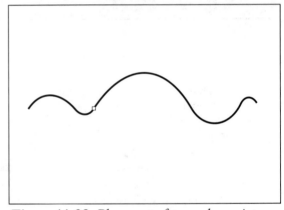

Figure 11.28 *Placement of an anchor point.*

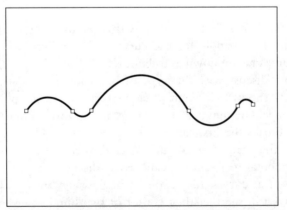

Figure 11.29 *Ideal placement of anchor points for this outline.*

optimal control over the shape of that segment. Furthermore, the shape of a curve immediately preceding and following an anchor point, tends to be the flattest part of that curve. Placing the anchor points at the peaks of the bumps may flatten that area and hinder that curve's integrity. The spot where one bump is flowing into the next and begins to change direction is a better place for an anchor point, as that area tends to be flatter, anyway (see Figure 11.24).

A path of this shape can also be achieved by using only four anchor points. This conforms to the first path construction rule, but not the second. The number of anchor points used is fewer, but their placement will create some curved line segments with two bumps. Once again, the control over the shape of the segments is diminished (see Figure 11.25).

The next shape we will look at is similar to the previous one, except that the bumps are different sizes (see Figure 11.26). In this case, the breakdown is the same because the anchor points are placed at the beginning and end of each bump. The exact spot where one bump ends and the next one begins, however, is a bit more elusive, because the bumps are of different sizes. Nonetheless, if you carefully observe each bump, you should be able to identify the best spot for an anchor point. Start by identifying the peaks of two consecutive bumps (see Figure 11.27); the anchor point will be somewhere between those two peaks. In a case where both bumps are similar in size, the anchor point will be located close to the center between the two peaks. In this situation, however, the two bumps are drastically different in size. Since the larger bump will also be longer in length, the anchor point positions should reflect that fact. Placing the anchor points closer to the peak of the smaller bump will create a curved line segment that is longer for the large bump and shorter for the small bump (see Figure 11.28). Using this theory, you should be able to determine all the other anchor point locations (see Figure 11.29).

The actual construction of this shape will be a bit trickier than the previous one. Since all the bumps are of different sizes, the direction handles will also vary in length, and some adjustment of the direction handles will be required as you construct the path. This procedure was discussed in Chapter 9.

So far, we have looked at shapes whose bumps are easily recognizable, although this will not always be the case once you begin creating a greater variety of shapes with Illustrator. Figure 11.30 shows a shape where the bumps are not as clearly defined. You should, nevertheless, be able to pinpoint some of the more obvious bumps (see Figure 11.31). In light of that, you may decide to place the anchor points midway between those bumps (see Figure 11.32). You will soon find out that more anchor points are needed to create a path of this shape. This particular shape actually consists of seven bumps. Three of them you have already identified—these are the short, steep curves that are facing up and down. In other words, the convex side of the bump is pointing up or down. The other four bumps are long, shallow, and facing to the left (see Figure 11.33).

One reason why it may be more difficult to identify all the bumps in this shape is because some of the consecutive bumps are curving in the same direction. The wave

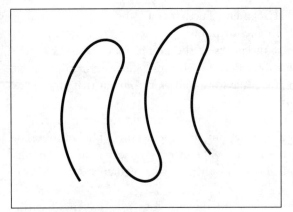

Figure 11.30 *Outline where bumps are not clearly defined.*

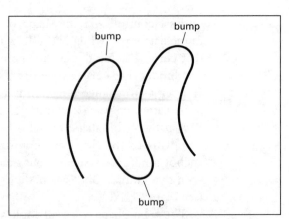

Figure 11.31 *Identifying the obvious bumps.*

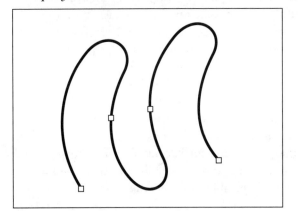

Figure 11.32 *This anchor point placement is not sufficient to trace this outline.*

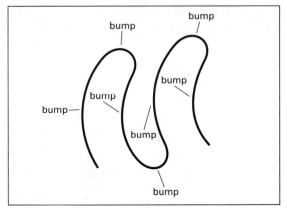

Figure 11.33 *Identifying other bumps.*

shape discussed earlier had the line change direction with each consecutive bump. If you could pinpoint the spot where the curve changed direction, you could find the anchor point location. In this instance, all the bumps do not change direction from one to the next, so it is important to look for a drastic change in the curvature of the line. If you follow the outline of the shape from left to right, you will be able to see such an occurrence. At first, the curve bends slightly as it goes up (see Figure 11.34); as it starts to reach the top, the bend becomes more drastic and continues that way until it gets to the other side (see Figure 11.35). The outline then travels downward, bending slightly again (see Figure 11.36).

Such a drastic change in curvature is what you should look for when the change in direction is not present. The anchor points are then located at the spots where the change in curvature begins. The optimal placement of anchor points for this shape will divide it into four long, shallow curved line segments and three short, steep ones (see Figure 11.37).

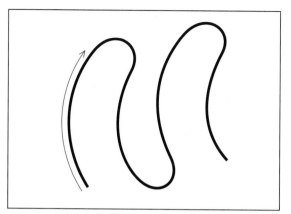

Figure 11.34 *Following the outline to identify the first bump.*

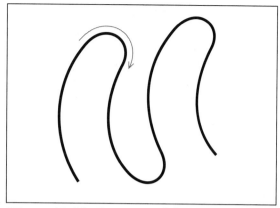

Figure 11.35 *Continuing following the outline to identify the second bump.*

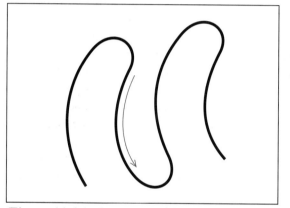

Figure 11.36 *Continuing following the outline to identify the third bump.*

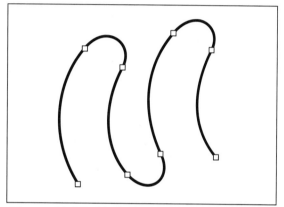

Figure 11.37 *Ideal placement of anchor points.*

Figure 11.38 *Spiral outline.*

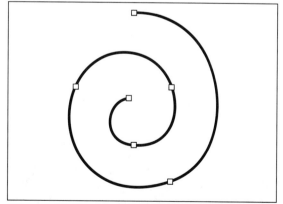

Figure 11.39 *Ideal placement of anchor points.*

What if a shape has no drastic change in curvature or direction? The best example of such a shape is a spiral (see Figure 11.38). The outline keeps traveling in the same direction, while the radius of the curve gets slightly smaller. Separating a shape like this is easier than you may think: Simply follow along the outline and place an anchor point before it reaches a semicircle. Continue placing anchor points to create curved line segments as large as possible without being larger than a semicircle (see Figure 11.39). To compensate for the decreasing radius of the curve, some adjustment of the length of the direction handle must be made to the path as you are constructing.

Using Anchor Point Guides

With the information just presented, you should be able to divide any outline into line segments to construct the most efficient path. Figure 11.40 shows a shape that consists of all the combinations shown earlier. In order to draw a shape like this in Illustrator, you must first break it down into straight and curved line segments and establish where the anchor points will be placed. In addition, you must determine—at each anchor point—whether it will be a smooth or a corner point and how the direction handles will be constructed for each curved line segment. This is a great deal of information to process before you even begin to construct your first anchor point. Until you have become more proficient in constructing paths, it is best to separate that information as much as possible.

Of course, the very first thing you must do is create a template; you can scan the shape in Figure 11.40 right from the book. Afterward, you must carefully examine the

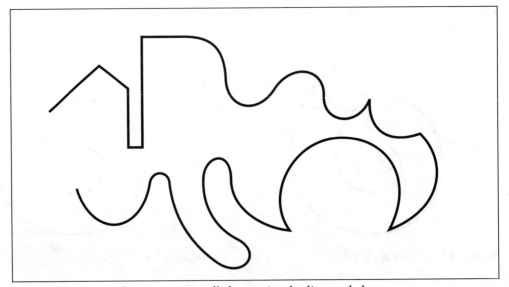

Figure 11.40 *Outline containing all the previously discussed shapes.*

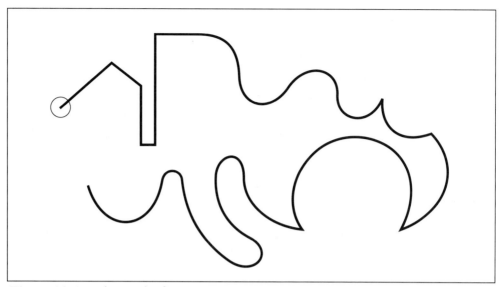

Figure 11.41 *Placing the first point guide circle.*

shape and decide where the anchor points will be placed. Next, create a small circle just large enough so that the center point is clearly visible, and position that circle with its center point at the exact spot where the first anchor point will be placed (see Figure 11.41). This is best done in the Artwork mode. This circle and its duplicates will be used as guides for the placement of all the anchor points. Hold down the **Option** key and move the circle to the next anchor point location. A duplicate of the circle will be made, while leaving the first one in its original position. Continue making duplicates of the circle and placing them at optimal anchor point locations. If necessary, refer to the previous section for hints on where to place anchor points on the path.

Once all the anchor point locations have been established for that shape, select all the circles by dragging a marque around them, pressing **Command** + **A**, or by choosing Select All from the Edit menu. Group them together by choosing Group from the Arrange menu, or by pressing **Command** + **G** and going to the Objects menu and choosing Guides and then Make, or pressing **Command** + **5**. The circle outlines will now become dashed lines so as to not obstruct your view of the artwork. Now that all the anchor point locations have been identified, you can concentrate on other aspects of constructing the path.

Please note that it will not be necessary to go through this procedure for every path you need to construct in every rendering you create in Illustrator. This is simply an exercise to help you think about the anchor point locations before proceeding with the path construction. After practicing this technique on a few different shapes, you will be able to visualize the anchor point locations while the path is under construction without the anchor point guides. Once you have reached that point, you are well on your way to becoming an Adobe Illustrator expert.

Converting Anchor Points

In some cases, there may be a need to convert a smooth anchor point to a corner anchor point, or vice versa. For example, if you constructed the wrong type of anchor point by mistake, or decided to change the shape of a path by changing the anchor points.

The Convert Direction Point tool is chosen by dragging to the right of the Scissor tool (see Figure 11.42). Add Anchor Point and Delete Anchor Point tools are also located to the right of the Scissor tool and will be discussed in the next section.

A smooth anchor point can be converted into a corner anchor point in two ways: with the direction handles remaining at that anchor point, and with the elimination of the direction handles. If you wish for the direction handles to remain, they must be made visible before proceeding with the conversion. With the Direct Selection tool, select either the anchor point to be converted or a curved line segment attached to it, and the direction handle (or handles) will appear. After you have chosen the Convert Direction Point tool from the toolbox, the cursor will turn into a plus (+) sign when moved into the active window. Position the cursor directly on top of a direction point and click and drag to change the angle of that direction handle. You will notice that the other direction handle at that anchor point will not be affected, indicating that the anchor point is now a corner point (see Figure 11.43). Once the anchor point has been converted, further adjustments to either of the direction handles at that anchor point can be made using the selection tools.

If you do not wish for the direction handles to remain, they need not be visible. However, selecting the path or that anchor point may still be necessary in order to see where the actual anchor point is located. In this case, simply click with the Convert Direction Point tool directly on the anchor point and both direction handles will disappear, turning the anchor point into a corner point (see Figure 11.44).

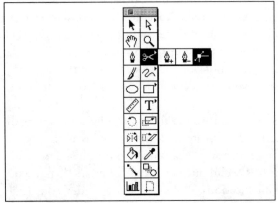

Figure 11.42 *Convert Anchor Point tool.*

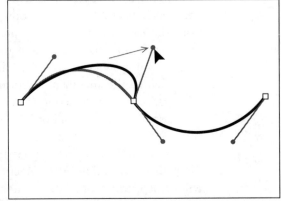

Figure 11.43 *Converting a smooth anchor point to a corner anchor point.*

Both corner points with direction handles and those without may be converted to smooth anchor points with the Convert Direction Point tool. You will need to select the path so that the anchor point to be converted is visible, and choose the Convert Direction Point tool from the toolbox. Position the cursor directly on the anchor point and click and drag in the direction in which the path was originally created, which can be determined by the order in which the line segments were constructed. If you are not sure in which direction to drag, it should become apparent as soon as you begin dragging. While you drag, two direction handles will be created at that anchor point. If the anchor point already had direction handles, new ones will be constructed—one in the direction of the drag, and the other at 180 degrees to the drag, creating a smooth transition between the two curved line segments connected at that anchor point (see Figure 11.45). If you drag in the wrong direction, the two curved line segments will create a loop at the anchor point (see Figure 11.46). To remedy this, simply change the direction of the drag, and after the two direction handles have been created, they can be further adjusted with the selection tools. Keep in mind that adjusting a direction handle at a smooth point will affect the other direction handle at that point, thereby changing the shape of the other curved line segment.

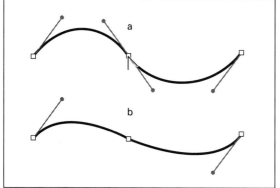

Figure 11.44 *Eliminating both direction handles at an anchor point.*

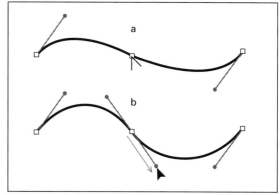

Figure 11.45 *Converting a corner anchor point to a smooth anchor point.*

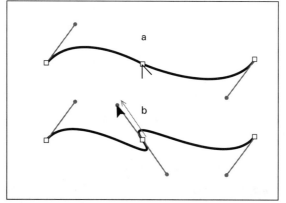

Figure 11.46 *Dragging in the wrong direction.*

Adding and Removing Anchor Points

The other two tools found next to the Scissor tool are the Add Anchor Point tool and the Delete Anchor Point tool. The Add Anchor Point tool will create an anchor point on an existing path. To do so, choose the Add Anchor Point tool from the toolbox by dragging to the right of the Scissor tool (see Figure 11.47) and the cursor will turn into a plus (+) sign when moved into the active window. The path to which you wish to add an anchor point does not need to be selected. However, to ensure that you do not try to add an anchor point where one already exists, you would be wise to select the path. If you do attempt to add an anchor point where one exists, a dialog box will appear telling you that the program cannot perform this operation.

With the Add Anchor Point tool selected, click directly on the outline of a path. An anchor point will be created in that spot and will be directly selected while the rest of the path is being indirectly selected. Adding an anchor point to a straight line segment

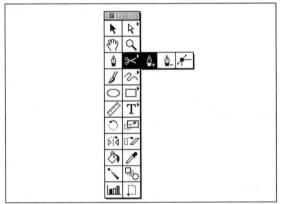

Figure 11.47 Add Anchor Point tool.

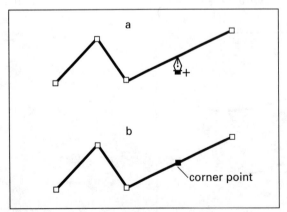

Figure 11.48 Adding a corner anchor point.

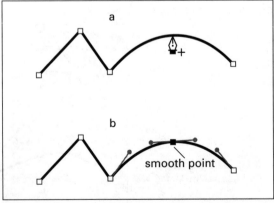

Figure 11.49 Adding a smooth anchor point.

will create a corner point with no direction handles (see Figure 11.48). Adding an anchor point to a curved line segment will create a smooth point with two direction handles (see Figure 11.49). The shape of the path will remain the same, regardless of how many anchor points you add. Adding anchor points does, however, give you the ability to manipulate the path into shapes unachievable with fewer anchor points.

A second way to add anchor points to a path is with the Add Anchor Points filter. To do so, select the path and go to Add Anchor Points in the Objects submenu of the Filters menu. An anchor point will be added at the center of each line segment of that path (see Figure 11.50). Each time you repeat the filter command, more anchor points will be added to the path. In a closed path, the number of anchor points is doubled, and in an open path it is doubled minus one. The anchor points, once again, will be smooth on curved line segments and corner on straight line segments.

To delete an anchor point from a path, select the path and choose the Delete Anchor Point tool from the toolbox by dragging to the right of the Scissor tool. The cursor will turn to a plus (+) sign when moved into the active window, and you may position the cursor directly on top of the anchor point you wish to delete. Click the mouse button and the anchor point will be deleted. If the anchor point that you removed was an end point, the effect will be the same as selecting that point and pressing the Delete key or choosing Clear from the Edit menu. Both the end point and the line segment attached to it will be deleted (see Figure 11.51). If the anchor point was not an end point, the effect of the Delete Anchor Point tool will differ from simply using the Delete key or Clear command.

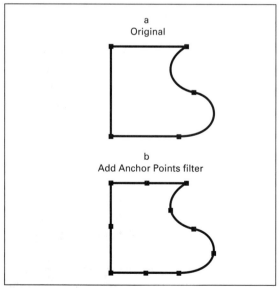

Figure 11.50 *Add Anchor Points filter.*

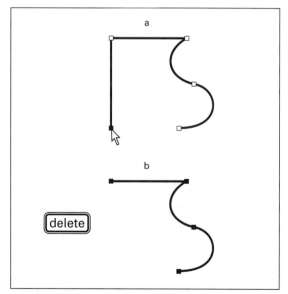

Figure 11.51 *Deleting an end point.*

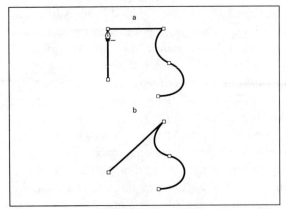

Figure 11.52 *Removing a corner anchor point.*

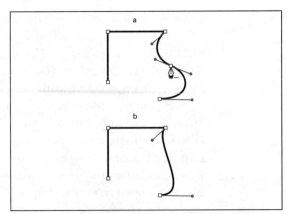

Figure 11.53 *Removing a smooth anchor point.*

When the Delete Anchor Point tool is used on a regular anchor point, the anchor point and the line segments attached to it are still deleted. In their place, however, a line segment is created between the two anchor points adjacent to the one you have deleted. If the two line segments connected at the anchor point that you deleted with the Delete Anchor Point tool were straight line segments, the line segment created between the two adjacent anchor points will also be straight (see Figure 11.52 a, b). If, however, one or both of the line segments connected at the deleted anchor point were curved, the line segment created between the two adjacent anchor points will be curved.

The direction handles for the newly created curved line segment will be the same direction handles used for the curved line segments that were deleted. This will, in most cases, create a curved line segment that will have direction handles that are too short (see Figure 11.53 a, b). This is because one line segment now exists in the space where two line segments used to be, while the length of the direction handles remained the same. In addition, if one of the deleted line segments was a straight line segment and the other curved, the resulting curved line segment will have only one direction handle. Some adjustment to the resulting curved line segment will be necessary in order to create the desired shape and make it an efficient line segment.

Cutting Paths

The Scissor tool may be used to make a closed path open or to split an open path into two. The Scissor tool can be used on a line segment or an anchor point that is not an end point.

To cut a path, choose the Scissor tool from the toolbox; the cursor will turn into a plus (+) sign when moved into the active window. Click directly on the outline of the path anywhere you wish to make a cut, and two end points will be created at that location. If you clicked on an existing anchor point, no visual difference will be apparent. The two end points created are positioned right on top of the other, creating the illusion of one anchor point (see Figure 11.54 a, b). Both end points will also be selected, so going immediately to the Direction Selection tool and dragging those points will not give you any indication that the path was cut (see Figure 11.55). Both end points will be moved simultaneously as you drag. To move these end points individually, choose the Direct Selection tool from the toolbox and click in an empty space on the document page to completely deselect the whole path. Then, click and drag at the spot that was cut. The top end point will be moved, while the other end point remains in its place; the cut in the path will become clearly visible (see Figure 11.56).

The order in which the line segments of the path were created will determine which end point will be placed on top. For instance, if you cut the path at an anchor point, the resulting two end points will each belong to one line segment connected at

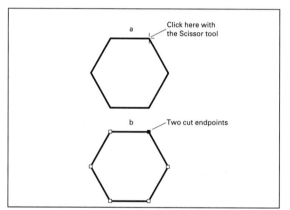

Figure 11.54 *Cutting a path results in two end points in the same location.*

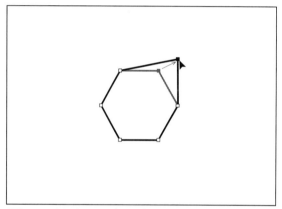

Figure 11.55 *Both end points will move if they are selected.*

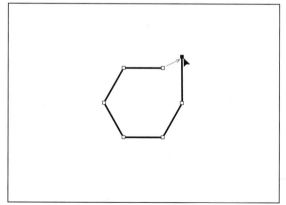

Figure 11.56 *Only the top point moves when it is selected.*

the anchor point that was there before you made the cut. The line segment that was created last will have its end point on top. To move the end point that is underneath, while allowing the top end point to remain in its place, choose the Direct Selection tool immediately after making the cut. Hold down the **Shift** key and click where the two selected end points are located. The top end point will be deselected, while the end point underneath will remain directly selected. Press any of the arrow keys on the keyboard, and the directly selected bottom anchor point will be moved a distance specified in the Cursor key text field under the keyboard increments in the General Preferences dialog box. (see Figure 11.57). If by pressing once does not move the anchor point far enough, you can press the arrow key a few times or set the Cursor key distance to a larger number.

If you have cut an open path, that path will now be two open paths. While the procedure is the same for separating the end points, it is easier to see which end point is on top and which one is underneath. After you have made the cut, deselect the entire path and click again on the spot that was cut. The top end point will be directly selected and the rest of the anchor points on that path will be shown as hollow squares. No anchor points on the other path will be displayed (see Figure 11.58), which will enable you to determine which end point is on top and which one is underneath.

If the cut was made on a line segment and not an anchor point, the resulting effect is visually similar to adding an anchor point. The physical difference is that instead of creating one anchor point that connects two line segments, two end points are created that are not connected. All the end-point separating procedures are the same as for cutting at an anchor point.

If you wish to cut out and delete a section of a path, it can be done in one of two ways: If the section you want to delete begins and ends at anchor points, the use of the Scissor tool is not required. Simply select, with the Direct Selection tool, the anchor points belonging to the section you want to delete—not including the first and last

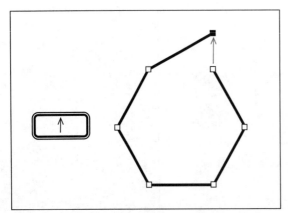

Figure 11.57 Moving with an arrow key.

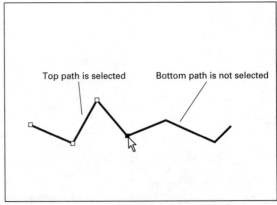

Figure 11.58 Identifying the top path.

anchor points of that section (see Figure 11.59); the anchor points where the undesired section begins and ends must remain unselected. Choose Clear from the Edit menu, or press the **Delete** key and that section will be deleted (see Figure 11.60). If the section you wish to remove does not begin and end at anchor points, some cuts will need to be made.

Choose the Scissor tool from the toolbox and click at the spot where the undesired section begins (see Figure 11.61). Move the cursor to the spot where the section ends and click the mouse button again (see Figure 11.62). You have now made two cuts in the path, one at each end of the section to be removed. Next, go to the toolbox, choose the Regular Selection tool (solid arrow), and click anywhere along that section. All the anchor points of that section will be shown as solid squares. No anchor points of the remaining path will be displayed (see Figure 11.63). Choose Clear from the Edit menu, or hit the **Delete** key and the selected section will be deleted, leaving behind the rest of the path (see Figure 11.64).

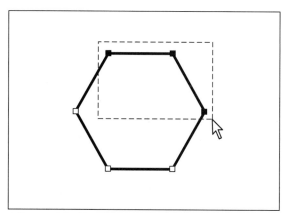

Figure 11.59 *Selecting multiple anchor points.*

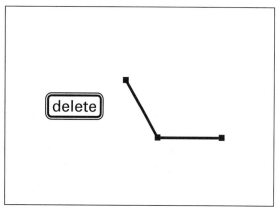

Figure 11.60 *Deleting multiple anchor points.*

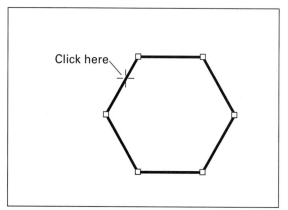

Figure 11.61 *Cutting a path's outline.*

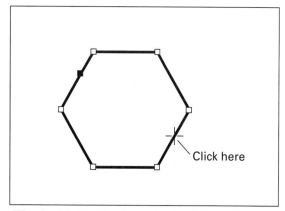

Figure 11.62 *Cutting a section of a path.*

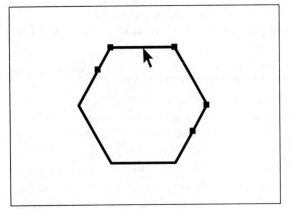

Figure 11.63 *Selecting the cut section.*

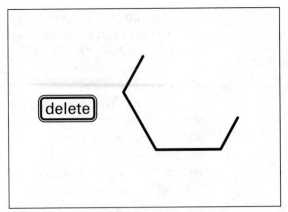

Figure 11.64 *Deleting the cut section.*

Averaging Anchor Points

In Illustrator, more often than not, sections of a particular shape are created as separate paths that are later combined to form that shape. End points of an open path can also be joined together to create a closed path. In these cases, the Join command should be used. The Average command is often used in combination with joining, although it has some significant applications of its own. This command's function is to align anchor points on a vertical or horizontal axis, or both.

To average anchor points, you will need to directly select them (see Figure 11.65) by choosing Average from the Object menu, or by pressing **Command + L**, which will cause the Average Dialog box to appear. Choosing the Horizontal option will move all of the selected anchor points up or down on the page until they are horizontally aligned (see Figure 11.66), and the Vertical option will align the points on a vertical axis by moving them left and right (see Figure 11.67).

If you clicked on Both, the selected anchor points would be moved to a location that is an average distance between the two, and placed on top of each other (see Figure 11.68). Averaging two or more anchor points, which are not end points, on both axes should be done with caution. This is because when anchor points are averaged in this way, all of the selected and averaged anchor points will be in the same location and appear as only one anchor point.

Used in certain situations, this can produce some interesting effects. For example, create a circle with the Oval tool and, while all the anchor points are still selected, choose Average from the Object menu or press **Command + L**. The resulting shape will be a four-leaf clover (see Figure 11.69 a, b). The Average command can be applied to any combination of anchor points: The anchor points can belong to the same path or different paths, they can be regular anchor points or end points, and the number of points that can be averaged is unlimited. This will allow you to align sections of various paths without affecting the rest of those paths.

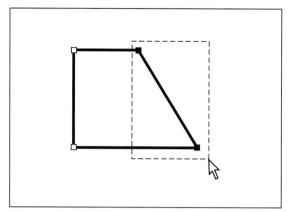

Figure 11.65 *Selecting points to be averaged.*

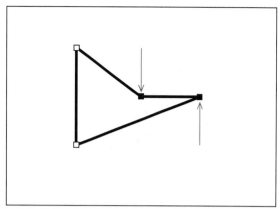

Figure 11.66 *Average horizontally.*

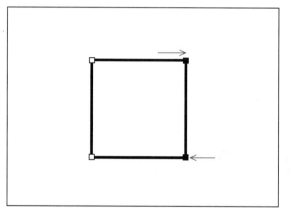

Figure 11.67 *Average vertically.*

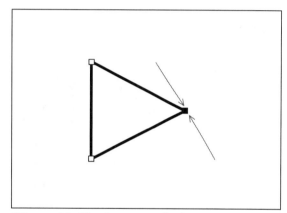

Figure 11.68 *Average on both axes.*

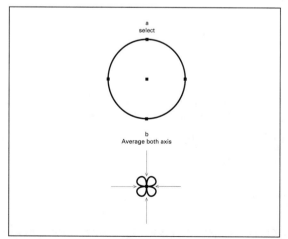

Figure 11.69 *Averaging all points of a circle on both axes.*

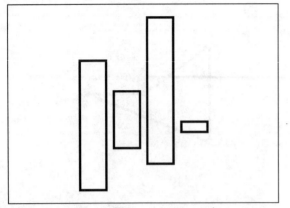

Figure 11.70 *Different size rectangles.*

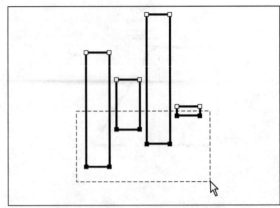

Figure 11.71 *Select the two bottom points of each rectangle.*

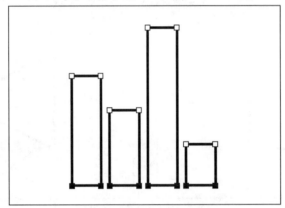

Figure 11.72 *Average the bottom points of each rectangle on horizontal axis.*

For instance, if you had constructed a number of rectangles in different positions (see Figure 11.70) and then wished to align all of their bases, the Average command can be used. Select the two bottom anchor points of each rectangle (see Figure 11.71), choose Average from the Object menu or press **Command + L**, and select Horizontal Axis. All the bases of the rectangles will be aligned, while the tops will remain in their original position (see Figure 11.72). The Average command also plays an essential part when used in combination with the Join command—discussed next.

Joining End Points

Two end points can be joined together to form one smooth or corner anchor point, or joined with a straight line segment between them. However, the Join command can be applied only to two selected end points. The end points can be a part of the same

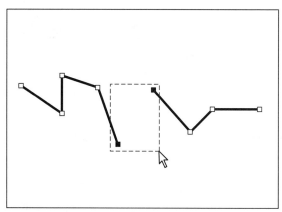

Figure 11.73 *Select two end points.*

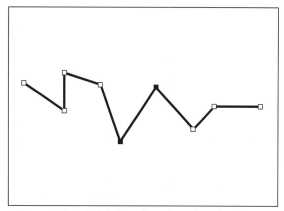

Figure 11.74 *Joining the selected end points.*

path or of two different paths. When two end points of an open path are joined, the path will become a closed path, while joining two end points from two separate open paths will combine those two paths into one open path.

To join two end points with a straight line segment, directly select any two end points (see Figure 11.73) and choose Join from the Object menu, or press **Command + J**. A straight line segment will be drawn between the two end points, connecting them (see Figure 11.74). If you wish for the joining line segment to be perfectly vertical or horizontal, average the two end points on an appropriate axis before joining them.

A second way to join two end points is to combine them into a single anchor point. The most important step in this procedure is making sure that the two end points are placed in the same location, on top of each other. The easiest way to do this is by averaging them on both axes, as described earlier. This, however, will move both end points to a new location (the average distance between the two selected end points), which may not always be desirable (e.g., one of the end points is already in an optimal location).

To position both end points in the same place without changing the location of both points, one of the end points must be moved manually. Since a point does not have any physical dimension, identifying its exact location may be difficult. The *Snap to Point* option in the General Preferences dialog box can be used to increase the precision placement of the end point. To utilize this, make sure the Snap to Point option in the General Preferences dialog box is checked (see Figure 11.75) and choose the Direct Selection tool from the toolbox. Drag one of the end points until it is directly on top of the other point (see Figure 11.76). With the Snap to Point option selected, when you are within a close distance to the second end point, the point you are dragging will *snap* into the second point's position. This is a very subtle action that you may not detect your first time, but you will—after a few tries—get a feel for how one point snaps into another. Although, visually, it will seem like the points are already joined (see Figure 11.77), this is not the case; the points will still need to be selected

General Preferences

┌─ Tool behavior ──────────────────┐
Constrain angle: `0` °
Corner radius: `0.5 in`
Freehand tolerance: `2` pixels
Auto Trace gap: `0` pixels

☒ Snap to point
☐ Transform pattern tiles
☐ Scale line weight
☐ Area select
☐ Use precise cursors

Ruler units: [**Inches** ▼]
Type units: [**Points/Picas** ▼]

┌─ Keyboard increments ─┐
Cursor key: `0.01 in`
Size/leading: `2 pt`
Baseline shift: `2 pt`
Tracking: `20` /1000 em

┌─ Edit behavior ─┐
Undo levels: `50`
☐ Paste remembers layers

Greek type limit: `6 pt`

[Cancel]   [OK]

Snap to point option

Figure 11.75 *General Preferences dialog box.*

and joined. Note that at this time, only one of those end points has been selected. To join the two end points, you will need to select them by dragging a marque around the points with the Direct Selection tool (see Figure 11.78). (Simply clicking at that location will select only the top end point, not both.) Once both end points have been selected, go to the Objects menu and choose Join, which will cause the Join dialog box to appear, allowing you to specify a corner or a smooth point (see Figure 11.79). In an instance where one or both line segments attached to the end points are straight,

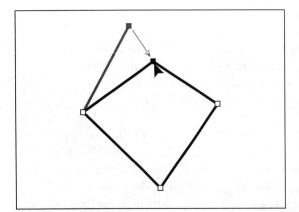

Figure 11.76 *Positioning one end point on top of another.*

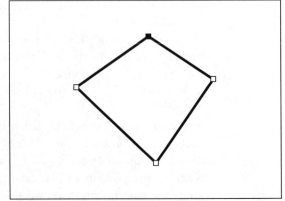

Figure 11.77 *Only one end point is selected.*

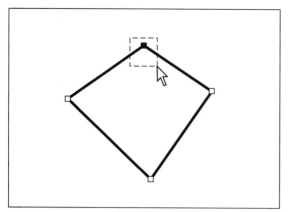

Figure 11.78 *Selecting both end points.*

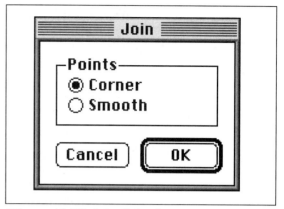

Figure 11.79 *Join dialog box.*

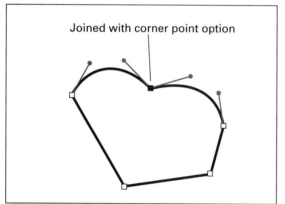

Figure 11.80 *Joining with a corner point.*

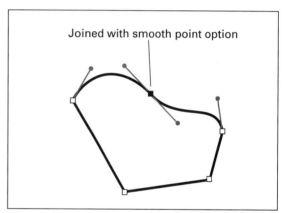

Figure 11.81 Joining with a smooth point.

choosing either option will not make a difference, as a corner point will be created regardless. If, on the other hand, both line segments attached to the end points are curved, each option will produce a different result.

Choosing the Corner Point option will create a corner anchor point that connects the two curved line segments without altering their shape (see Figure 11.80). If Smooth Point is chosen, the shape of one of the curved line segments may be altered. This will occur when the two curved line segments do not already flow smoothly into each other. The program will have to adjust the angle of one of the direction handles in order to create a smooth transition between the two segments (see Figure 11.81).

The sharper a corner is between the two curved line segments, the more drastic the change in shape of one line segment will be. This could be an unpleasant surprise if you are not prepared. One way to predict which of the curved line segments will change shape is to decipher their layering. The curved line segment that is on top will dictate the shape of the one underneath. If the two end points you are joining belong to separate paths, determining which one is on top will be fairly simple. Make sure that both paths are unselected and click at the joining spot with the Direct Selection tool. The path that is on top will be selected (see Figure 11.82).

If the end points belong to the same open path, determining which one is on top will require one extra step. Deselect the path, and click and drag one of the end points; the end point that is on top will move (see Figure 11.83). Go immediately to the Edit menu and choose Undo or press **Command + Z**, and the moved end point will return to its position.

If you are joining two separate paths with different paint styles, the resulting path will take on the paint style of the top path. This tip will be useful to help you achieve the desired paint style after the two paths are joined.

As mentioned earlier, only two end points can be joined at a time, but you should not worry about joining while other anchor points are selected. As long as they are not end points, any anchor points that are selected additionally will have no effect on the Join command. This may be helpful in a situation where you were joining two end points of the same path, but were not exactly sure where the two end points were (this is a very likely occurrence in a case where a path may have a very large number of points). You could simply select the whole path with the Regular Selection tool and perform the Join command; the program will automatically know which two points you want to join, because a single path has only two end points.

The same technique, however, cannot be used when joining two end points of two separate open paths, because the number of end points in this case is four (two for each open path). You must be sure to directly select only the end points you wish to join.

If anchor points of other paths are in close proximity to, and are interfering with, the points you need to select, the *Hide* or *Look* commands should be used. The Hide command will make the selected path or paths invisible on your screen so that they do not interfere with the paths on which you wish to work. The Look command will

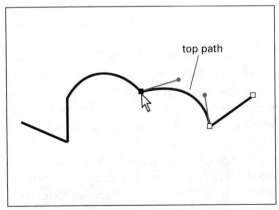

Figure 11.82 Identifying the top path.

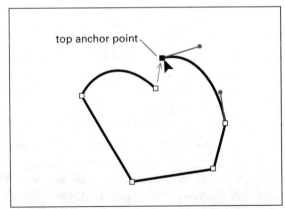

Figure 11.83 Only the top end point will move.

make the selected paths unselectable and uneditable, but still leave their image on the screen. To Hide a path, select it and either choose Hide from the Arrange menu or press **Command + 3**. To Hide all unselected paths, select the paths you do not wish to hide and press **Option + Command + 3**. To lock a path, select it and choose Lock, found in the Arrange menu, or press **Command + 1**. To lock all unselected paths, select the path you do not wish to lock and press **Option + Command + 1**.

An unlimited number of paths can be added to the already hidden or locked paths by selecting the paths and performing the commands. When you unlock or choose to show the hidden paths, however, all the locked or hidden paths will be unlocked and visible. To show all the hidden paths, go to the Arrange menu and choose Show All, or press **Command + 4**. To unlock all the locked paths, choose Unlock from the Arrange menu or press **Command + 2**. Selecting and manipulating obstructed paths and using the Hide and Lock commands will be further discussed in Chapter 13.

Once all interfering paths have been locked or hidden, selecting the desired end points will be easier. Do not forget to Show All and/or Unlock the paths once you have finished joining the end points.

Cutting and joining paths is an essential part of working in Illustrator, as certain images that would otherwise take a great deal of effort to construct may be easily created by cutting and joining shapes automatically created in Illustrator. These commands will prove especially helpful if the image you wish to create consists primarily of geometric shapes. The following example demonstrates how an image can be constructed by cutting and joining a few circles and rectangles.

Figure 11.84 shows the outline of a wrench, which can be created using any of the drawing tools available in Illustrator. The fastest and most precise way of constructing it, however, is by using the Oval and Rectangle tools. First, be sure that the Snap to Point option has been selected in the General Preferences dialog box, and that the Oval and Rectangle tools are set to draw from center (see Chapter 5). Choose the Rectangle tool from the toolbox and click inside the active window; enter **.5 inches** for width and **2 inches** for height, and press **OK** (see Figure 11.85). Next, choose the

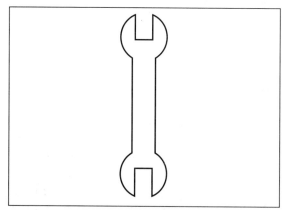

Figure 11.84 *A wrench shape.*

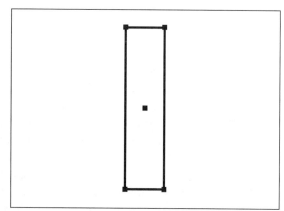

Figure 11.85 *Create a .5" × 2" rectangle.*

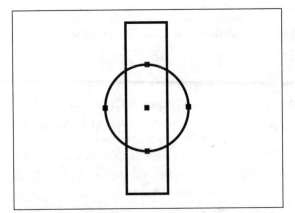

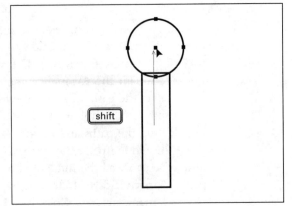

Figure 11.86 *Create a 1" × 1" circle centered with the rectangle.*

Figure 11.87 *Move the circle vertically.*

Oval tool and click on the center of the rectangle in your document; enter **1** in diameter and press **OK** (see Figure 11.86). From the toolbox, choose the Regular Selection tool (solid arrow) and—while holding down the **Shift** key—drag the circle upwards until the top two corners of the rectangle align exactly with the lower half of the circle's outline (see Figure 11.87).

Next, release the mouse button, then the **Shift** key. Hold down the **Shift** and **Option** keys, dragging the circle downward until the two bottom corners of the rectangle align with the top half of the circle's outline. The original circle will be duplicated while you drag it (see Figure 11.88). Choose the Rectangle Tool again and click on the center of the top circle; entering **3/8 inches** for width and **3/4 inches** for height. Choose the Regular Selection tool, and hold down the **Shift** key, dragging the resulting rectangle upward until the top edge of the rectangle is outside the circle outline (see Figure 11.89). Again, release the mouse button, then the **Shift** key, and hold down the **Option** and **Shift** keys while dragging the same rectangle downward so that the its bottom edge is outside the bottom circle's outline (see Figure 11.90). You have now created all the elements necessary to construct a wrench outline and have positioned them in the proper locations.

To complete the wrench image, cutting, joining, and deleting unwanted sections of paths are required. If you followed the steps exactly to construct your shapes, the layering should be as follows: The large rectangle should be on the bottom layer, the two circles on top of it, and the two smaller rectangles on top of the circles. (The layering of paths and its effects will be discussed in greater detail in Chapter 13.)

Choose the Scissor tool from the toolbox, clicking at each place where the five shapes intersect. You should make a total of eight cuts: four where the top circle intersects the two rectangles, and four where the bottom circle intersects the two rectangles (see Figure 11.91). Where the small rectangles intersect the circles, the cuts were made in the rectangle's paths, because the Scissor tool affects only the topmost shape. For the same reason, only the circle's paths were cut at the spots where the circles intersect the large rectangle.

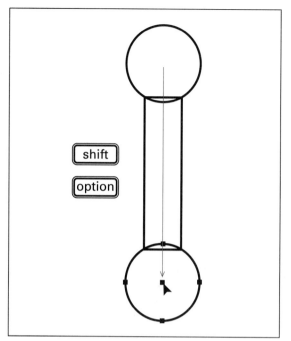

Figure 11.88 *Move and duplicate the circle vertically.*

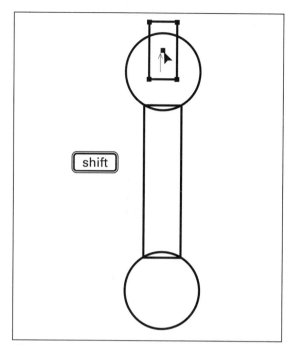

Figure 11.89 *Move the small rectangle vertically.*

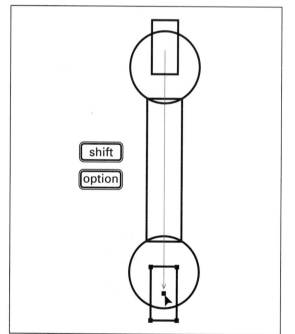

Figure 11.90 *Move and duplicate the small rectangle vertically.*

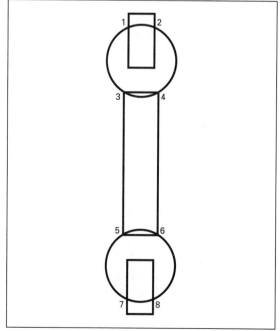

Figure 11.91 *Click with the Scissors tool in the eight spots, as shown.*

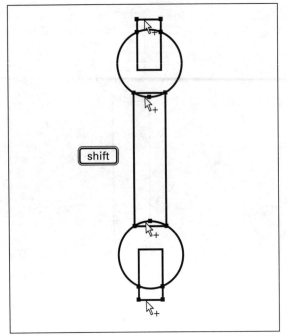

Figure 11.92 *Select the cut sections while holding down the Shift key.*

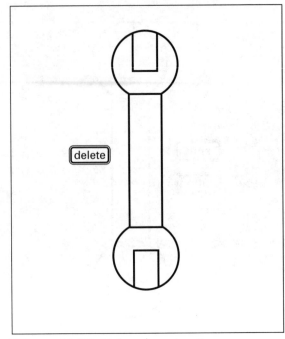

Figure 11.93 *Delete the cut sections.*

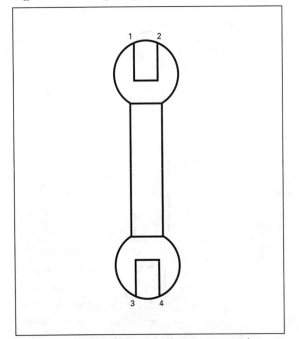

Figure 11.94 *Click with the Scissors tool in the four spots, as shown.*

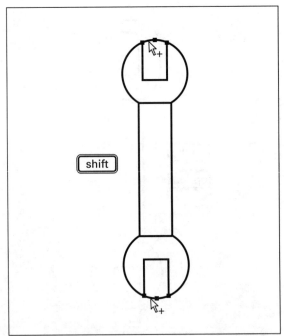

Figure 11.95 *Select the cut sections while holding down the Shift key.*

You may now delete these unwanted path sections. First choose Select None from the Edit menu, or press **Command + Shift + A**, and then choose the Group Selection tool from the toolbox (arrow with a +). Holding down the **Shift** key, click on the top edge of the top, small rectangle; the bottom edge of the bottom, small rectangle; and the sections of the two circles that are inside the large rectangle (see Figure 11.92). Once you have made these selections, press the **Delete** key, or go to the Edit menu and choose Clear. The resulting image should look like Figure 11.93.

Next, select the remaining sections of what used to be the two small rectangles and lock them. This will enable you to access the two circles underneath them in order to cut and delete the other unwanted sections of the circle's paths. Choose the Scissor tool and click precisely on the four spots where the small rectangles touch the circles (see Figure 11.94). Choose the Group Selection tool and click on the unwanted circle path section while holding down the **Shift** key (see Figure 11.95), then press the **Delete** key or choose Clear from the Edit menu. Again, choose the Direct Selection tool and click on the top and bottom edges of the rectangle outline while holding down the **Shift** key (see Figure 11.96). Press the **Delete** key again. The shape should now look like a wrench (see Figure 11.97).

The image, however, is not a whole continuous path, but a number of line segments and open paths. This is fine if you wish to only paint it with a stroke, but if you attempt to fill the shapes, the resulting image will look like Figure 11.98. In order to make the wrench image one closed path, the end points of all the line segments and open paths must be joined. To do so, choose the Direct Selection tool and drag a marque across one of the spots where a cut was made (see Figure 11.99). Both end points at that spot will be directly selected, and you should choose Join from the Object menu, or press **Command + J**. After repeating these steps for all the previously cut locations (see Figure 11.100), the resulting wrench shape will be one closed path and can be manipulated and painted as such.

Cutting and joining simple geometric shapes to construct more complex paths is one of the precision time-saving techniques used by expert Adobe Illustrator users. When creating an image consisting of geometric shapes, it is faster and more precise to use the automatically created geometric shapes and cut and join them together than to try to recreate those shapes with any of the other drawing tools. Illustrator is designed to give users several options for achieving the same results. The advantage to this is the ability to choose the technique that best suits a particular situation.

The wrench image could have also been rendered without cutting and joining, as some of the filters provided with Adobe Illustrator could be used to do some of the cutting and joining for you. For instance, if we return to Figure 11.90, where all of our geometric shapes were created and laid out in the right positions, we could use the filters to do the rest of the work. First, select the large rectangle and two circles with the Regular Selection tool (see Figure 11.101), and from the Filter menu choose *Pathfinder* and then *Unite*. The program will automatically combine those shapes into a single closed path, resulting in the shape shown in figure 11.102. Next, select the resulting shape and the two small rectangles, and in the Filter menu select Pathfinder

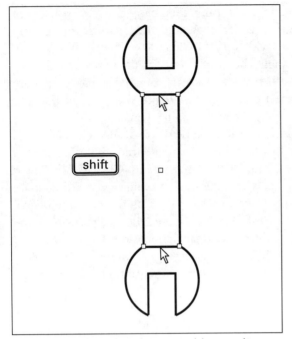

Figure 11.96 *Select the top and bottom line segments of the large rectangle.*

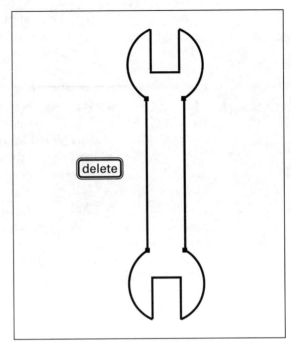

Figure 11.97 *Delete the top and bottom line segments of the large rectangle.*

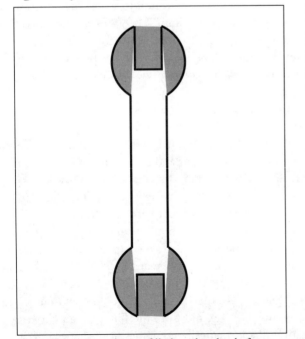

Figure 11.98 *Shapes filled with color before they are joined to be one closed path.*

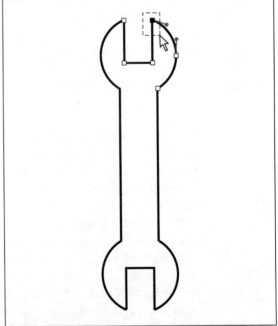

Figure 11.99 *Select both end points with a marque before joining.*

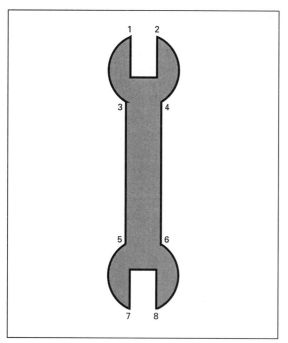

Figure 11.100 *Select both end points and join at the eight shown locations.*

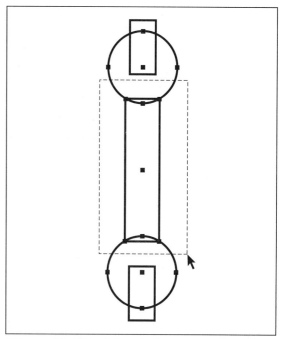

Figure 11.101 *Select the large rectangle and the two circles.*

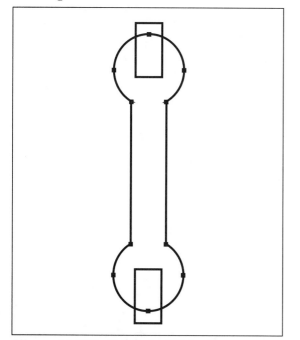

Figure 11.102 *Pathfinder/Unite filter.*

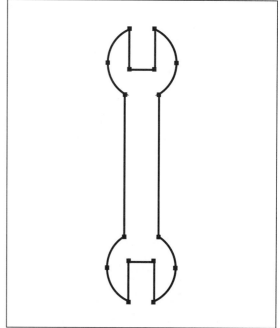

Figure 11.103 *Pathfinder/Minus Front filter.*

and then *Minus Front*. The two small rectangles will be used as cookie cutters to cut the dumbbell shape where they intersect (see Figure 11.103).

Using the Adobe Illustrator filters is a great way to shortcut some of the operations, but in no way replace them. Being aware of all the options available to achieve the same goal is very important when working in Illustrator. Every project presents its own unique set of challenges. Knowing a variety of ways to achieve a task will help you to apply the best combination of commands to a specific situation and allow you to discover faster, easier, and more efficient techniques on your own.

12 *Advanced Path Manipulation*

By now, you should have a thorough understanding of how to construct and transform paths in Adobe Illustrator. The next two chapters will deal with how to utilize and manipulate those paths to create the best-looking images in the most efficient manner. The features discussed in the following will not affect a path's shape so much as its attributes. Illustrator provides you with many options that may be applied to paths, such as paint style properties that can drastically change the way a path looks. Using a combination of these different path attributes will give you a limitless range of special effects.

Advanced Painting

As previously mentioned (Chapter 5), paths may be painted with fills, strokes, gradients, and/or patterns. This section will further explore path painting, and some advanced techniques will be revealed.

First, and most importantly, you must understand how the paint style affects a path. In Illustrator, all applied paint attributes are opaque; adding even 1 percent of a color to a path will completely cover all painted paths underneath. The only way to see through a path on the screen is to paint it with *None*.

A second important paint style characteristic to be aware of is that the *stroke* is always applied from the center outward, on the path outline. In other words, if you apply a 4-point stroke to a path, there will be 2 points on either side of the path's outline. The path outline will be perfectly centered on a stroke of any thickness (see Figure 12.1). *Fill* is always applied up to the inside of the path outline (see Figure 12.2). With open paths, this can be somewhat confusing. For instance, in Figure 12.3, the inside of the open path can be easily determined. The open path in Figure 12.4,

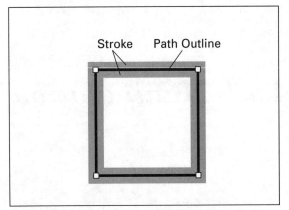

Figure 12.1 *Stroke is applied evenly to both sides of the path outline.*

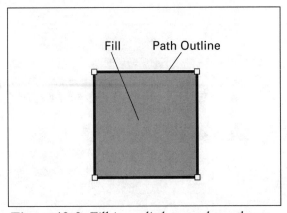

Figure 12.2 *Fill is applied up to the path outline.*

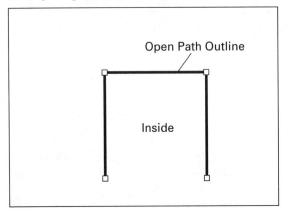

Figure 12.3 *Identifying the inside of an open path.*

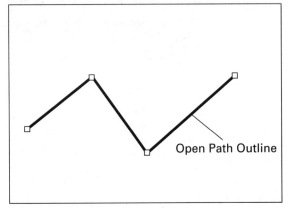

Figure 12.4 *An open path.*

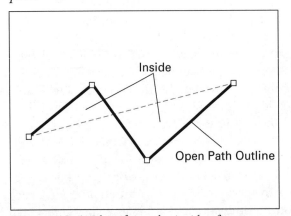

Figure 12.5 *Identifying the inside of an open path by drawing a line between its end points.*

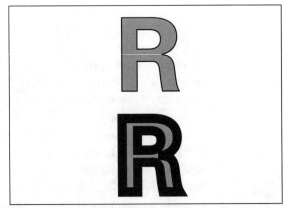

Figure 12.6 *The integrity of a letter is diminished when a thick stroke is applied.*

however, has more obscure inside and outside sections. The best way to determine how this path will be painted is to imagine a line going from one end point to the other (see Figure 12.5). This is precisely how the program determines the fill boundaries on an open path. Keep in mind that even though the program automatically draws a fill boundary, a stroke attribute will not be applied to that imaginary line.

The property of the stroke, which applies half of it on one side of the path and half on the other, creates a certain overlap between the stroke and fill of the path. Since the fill is applied all the way to the edge of a path, and half the stroke width is drawn from that edge and across the fill, the stroke and the fill will occupy the same space. In this case, the stroke is always drawn on top of the fill to show the full stroke width. This can, in some cases, hinder the shape's integrity. Figure 12.6 shows a letter with a thin and thick stroke. The quality of the shape of the letter with the thick stroke begins to diminish. A technique to avoid that problem will be discussed in the "Strokes" section of this chapter.

The Paint Style Palette

The *Paint Style palette* is used to change or display the current paint style attributes of a selected path. To view the Paint Style palette, go to the Object menu and choose Paint Style or press **Command + I**. To hide the Paint Style palette, click the close box in the upper right-hand corner of the Paint Style palette, or press **Command + I** again. The Paint Style palette may also be shown or hidden by choosing the corresponding option under the Window menu; you may move the palette around the screen by dragging its title bar.

The Paint Style palette is comprised of three main panels: the *Color Swatch panel,* the *Stroke Style panel,* and the *Main panel* (see Figure 12.7)—each panel may be viewed separately to save precious screen space. Click on the Pop-Up menu triangle located in the upper right corner of the Paint Style palette, and drag downward to select the desired panel.

The Color Swatch panel includes the *Fill* and *Stroke* squares, the *Color Swatch* squares, and the *Color Information Line* (see Figure 12.8). The fill and stroke squares represent the current paint style attributes of a selected object. To change those attributes, click on the appropriate square; that square will become underlined and the paint style changes will be applied to it and to the selected object. The color information lines display—in words and numbers—the attributes of the selected stroke or fill square. The color swatch squares are used to apply paint style attributes to the stroke and fill squares quickly without having to navigate through the whole Paint Style palette. You may set up color swatches for those colors, gradients, and patterns used most often to save yourself time when applying paint style properties to an object.

To create a new color swatch, specify the desired color, gradient, or pattern in the Main panel, and the selected fill or stroke square will acquire that attribute. Click and drag that fill or stroke square on top of one of the color swatch squares. If the color

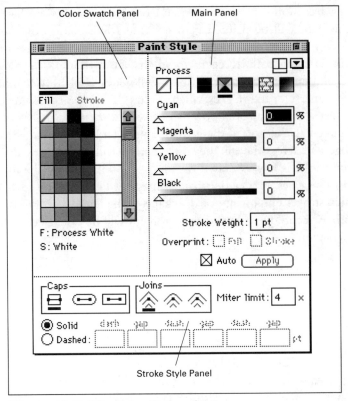

Figure 12.7 *The Paint Style palette.*

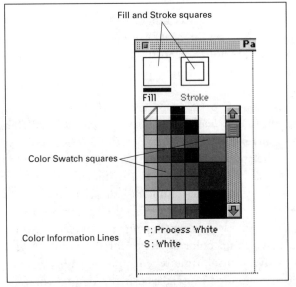

Figure 12.8 *The Color Swatch panel.*

swatch square already has a paint style attribute, it will be replaced by the new one. You can scroll down the list of swatches to find empty color swatch squares.

The Main panel consists of seven *attribute boxes,* the *Stroke Weight text Field,* the *Overprint check boxes,* the *Apply button,* and the *Auto check box.* Selecting the Auto check box will automatically apply the new paint style attributes to a selected object, instead of requiring you to click on the Apply button every time. The seven boxes at the top represent the paint style options, with the currently active option underlined. The first box on the left represents the paint with the None option. Objects filled with None will be transparent, and those stroked with none will likewise not have a stroke.

The next box is a *White Color* box. Choosing this option will paint the fill or the stroke of an object with an opaque white paint. You can automatically change the white color to different percentages of black by moving the triangle on the slider bar (located below the paint style option squares), or by entering a percentage in the text field. Doing this will automatically select the *Black Paint option* square the next time you open the Paint Style palette.

The fourth square will display four slider bars and text fields with each slider bar representing a different process color that you can mix by percentages to achieve desired hues. These percentages may be typed directly into the text fields or achieved by dragging the triangle on the slider bars. When you drag the slider bar triangle back and forth, you will see the gradual color change in the fill or stroke square as you drag. Entering the desired percentage into the text field will move the triangle to the corresponding place on that slider bar. The triangle may also be moved by clicking on the slider bar at the location where you want the triangle to be—the triangle will immediately relocate to that position. To move the triangle in increments of 1 percent, hold down the **Option** key and click on either side of the triangle. To move the triangle in 5 percent increments, hold down the **Shift** and **Option** keys simultaneously as you click on either side of the triangle.

When you are working with the *Process Color* option, the four slider bars can be adjusted, relative to each other, at the same time. Hold down the **Shift** key and drag the triangle of the slider bar that has the highest percentage of color. All the other percentages will then increase or decrease proportionally to create tints of the original mixed color.

The fifth paint style option square represents the *Custom Colors.* Selecting this option will display a list of custom colors available in all the open documents. Creating your own custom colors and acquiring custom color systems, such as Pantone or Truecolor, will be discussed later in this chapter.

The next square represents the *Patterns* option, and selecting this square will display a list of patterns available in all the open documents. Selecting the last square on the right will display a list of gradients available in all the open documents. (Creating patterns and gradients will also be discussed later in this chapter.)

Strokes

The Stroke Weight text field is used to specify the thickness of a stroke in points. The *Overprint* for fill and stroke should be used with caution and thorough understanding of process color separation and offset printing, because the effects of overprint cannot be seen on your screen and are apparent only after the image has been printed by offset printing.

The *Stroke Style panel* consists of options that may be applied to strokes. You can choose from three different Caps or Joins options, set the Miter limit, or specify a solid or a dashed stroke. Figure 12.9 shows just a few options of stroke attribute combinations. Different stroke attributes can create some dazzling effects when applied to duplicates of the same path.

For instance, construct a simple curved path (see Figure 12.10) and paint it with a black 16-point stroke. Copy the path and choose *Paste in Front* from the Edit menu, or

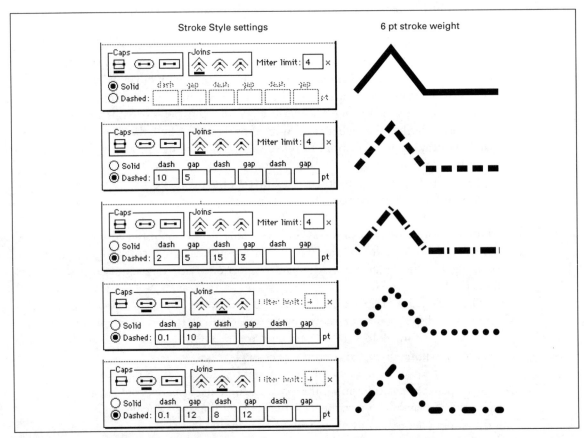

Figure 12.9 *Various stroke settings.*

press **Command + F**. A duplicate of the path will be created and placed in the exact same location on top of the original; paint this path with a white stroke that has a thickness of 14 points. You now have two 1-point black strokes with a 14-point distance in between (see Figure 12.11). Actually, there is a 16-point black stroke with a 14-point white stroke on top. Since all strokes are applied to a path outward from the center, the white rule on top covers 14 points in the middle of the black rule, leaving one point on either side of the black rule (see Figure 12.12). This is ideal for creating perfectly parallel curved lines.

Figure 12.10 *16-pt stroke.*

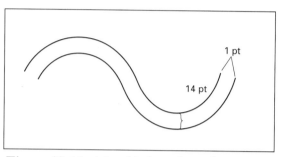

Figure 12.11 *16-pt black stroke with a 14-pt white stroke on top.*

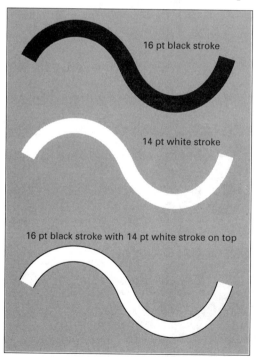

Figure 12.12 *Placing a 14-pt white stroke on top of a 16-pt black stroke of the same shape creates two parallel 1-pt black lines.*

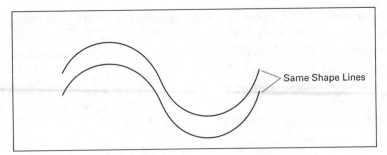

Figure 12.13 *Same shape curved lines placed next to each other are not parallel.*

As I am sure you know, simply duplicating a curved line and placing the two next to each other will not make them parallel. The properties of curves do not allow two curved lines of the same shape to be parallel. Figure 12.13 shows two identical curved lines positioned next to each other; the result is anything but parallel.

Positioning duplicates of paths on top of each other and applying different stroke attributes to them is a very popular technique. Besides being able to create parallel curved lines, many other stroke effects can be achieved. The stroked-letter problem mentioned earlier can also be resolved using this method. Simply paint the original letter with a stroke twice as thick as the one you want, and place a duplicate of the

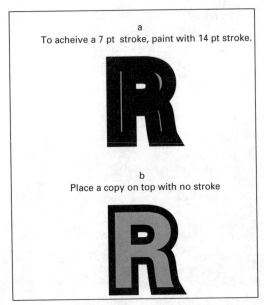

Figure 12.14 *Creating a letter with a thick outline.*

letter on top, painted with no stroke and a solid fill (see Figure 12.14 a, b). Figure 12.15 shows a few of the other effects that can be achieved by placing duplicates of paths on top of each other and applying different stroke attributes.

Custom Colors

When you purchase Adobe Illustrator, files for different color systems are included; these are: FOOOLTONE, PANTONE, TOYO, and TRUMATCH. In order to use custom colors from any (or all) of these systems, that color system file must be opened at the same time as your document. Once you have opened the desired color system file in Illustrator, by selecting the custom color square in the Paint Style palette, you will be able to view a list of all the colors available with that system (see Figure 12.16).

Stroke layering — **Stroke attributes**

	Color	Width	Dash	Gap	Cap	Join
1	Black	10	0	12	Round	Round
2	White	8	0	12	Round	Round
3	Black	4	0	12	Round	Round

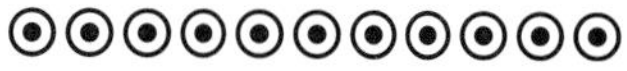

	Color	Width	Dash	Gap	Cap	Join
1	Black	14	0	20	Projected	Miter
2	White	10	0	20	Projected	Miter
3	Black	8	0	20	Projected	Miter
4	White	4	0	20	Projected	Miter

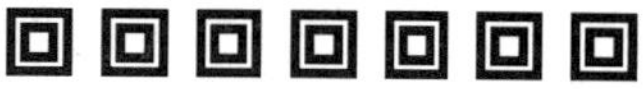

	Color	Width	Dash	Gap	Cap	Join
1	Black	6	0	10	Round	Round
2	Gray	3	10	10	Round	Round

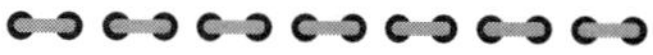

	Color	Width	Dash	Gap	Cap	Join
1	Black	16	0	12	Round	Round
2	White	13	0	12	Round	Round
3	Gray	6	0	12	Round	Round

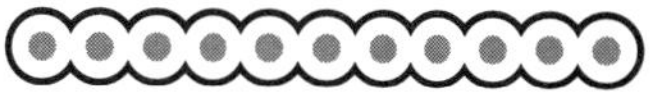

	Color	Width	Dash	Gap	Cap	Join
1	Gray	18	4	6	Butt	Miter
2	Black	11	Solid	Solid	Butt	Miter
3	White	9	Solid	Solid	Butt	Miter
4	Black	7	Solid	Solid	Butt	Miter
5	White	5	Solid	Solid	Butt	Miter
6	Gray	5	4	6	Butt	Miter

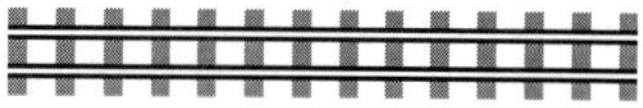

Figure 12.15 *Various designs created by placing strokes with different attributes on top of each other.*

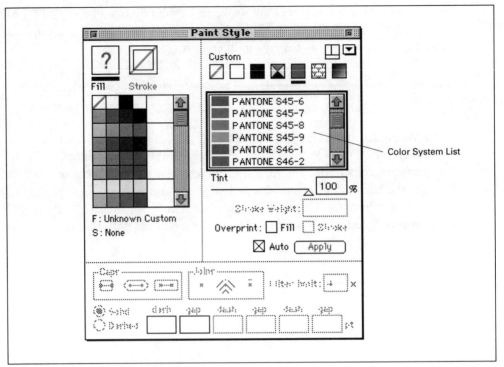

Figure 12.16 *Custom colors list.*

Simply click on the name of the color you wish to use, and the fill or stroke square will acquire that color.

The tint of a custom color may be adjusted by moving the triangle on the slider bar underneath the custom color listing. To create your own custom colors, or to view the process color breakdown of any custom color, choose Custom Color from the Object menu or double-click on the custom color name in the Paint Style palette. The Custom Color dialog box will appear, displaying the list of custom colors, the process color breakdown, and options for creating new or deleting custom colors (see Figure 12.17).

To create a new custom color, press the **New** button. A new custom color will be added to the list consisting of 0 percent of the process colors. You must now specify a name for the new custom color, and adjust the process color percentages to achieve the desired color hues. It is important to give your custom colors very specific names, such as *dark green ball* rather than *dark green,* because colors of the same name will override each other.

For example, let's say that a month ago you created a custom color and named it "dark green." This shade consisted of 100 percent cyan and 100 percent yellow. A week later, while working on another illustration, you created a custom color consisting of 100 percent cyan, 80 percent yellow, and 20 percent magenta and also called it

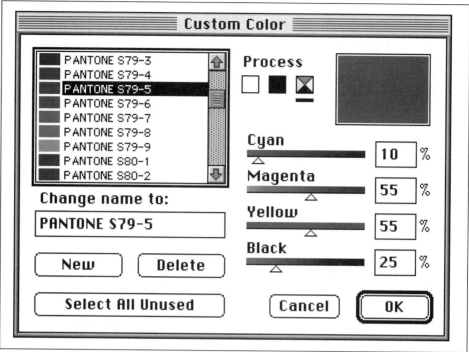

Figure 12.17 *Custom Color dialog box.*

"dark green." Today, you decided to look at both of those illustrations and opened them simultaneously only to find that the "dark green" in one of the illustrations has changed to the green color of the second image. Since the custom color listing displays all the custom colors available in all the open documents at that time, and no two colors of the same name can exist in the listing, one color will assume the attributes of the other.

Creating your own Custom Color palette is a great time-saving—and frustration-reducing—practice, as it assures that objects painted with the same colors in an illustration are consistent. It will also save time by making it unnecessary to enter percentages into the process color text fields each time you need to paint something.

Patterns

Numerous special effects may be achieved with Adobe Illustrator's custom patterns. You can quickly create anything from a tile floor to wallpaper to a great variety of textures and textile designs. To create a new pattern, you will need two things: a *bounding box*—which also serves as the background color for the pattern—and an image to go inside that box. The bounding box is created with the Rectangle tool and should always be located behind the actual pattern image. The pattern image can be created

Figure 12.18 *A star on top of a square.*

with any tools available in Illustrator, provided it does not contain gradient fills or other patterns.

Begin constructing the bounding box by drawing a rectangle. Filling the rectangle with any color will result in that fill being the background of your pattern, so choose a color or None, accordingly. Next, create and place an image inside the rectangle (see Figure 12.18). Select both the bounding box and the image, and choose Pattern from the Object menu. The Pattern dialog box will appear, displaying a list of existing patterns and various buttons for deleting, pasting, selecting, and adding new patterns.

If you click on the New button, the newly created pattern will appear in the dialog box (see Figure 12.19) and you can name the pattern and click OK. Keep in mind

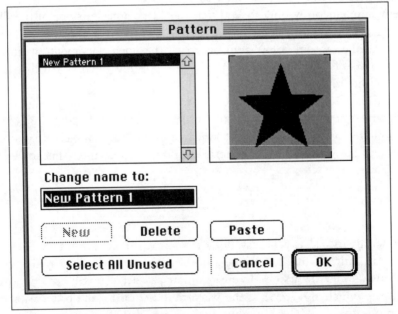

Figure 12.19 *Pattern dialog box.*

that pattern names work similarly to custom colors in the sense that identical ones will override each other. Once the file has been saved with the new custom pattern, that pattern will be available each time you open that file. Once you have added the new pattern to the list, you may delete the bounding box and the pattern image from your document page.

To use a pattern, access the Paint Style palette, select the stroke or fill box, click on the pattern box, and the list of patterns will be displayed. Choose the desired pattern from the list and it will be applied to either the fill or the stroke (see Figure 12.20). Keep in mind that strokes do not display patterns; all patterns applied to strokes will be displayed as gray. When an object has been filled with a pattern, the pattern tile will be repeated as many times as necessary to completely cover that object (see Figure 12.21).

The size of a pattern tile will be the size of the originally created pattern image. Adobe Illustrator provides you with a variety of controls over transforming pattern tiles within pattern-painted objects. For instance, you can move, scale, rotate, shear, and reflect a pattern within an object without affecting the object shape. The dialog boxes for the transform tools include a check box for *Pattern Tiles.*

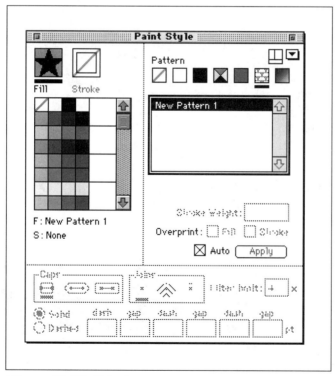

Figure 12.20 *Selecting a pattern.*

Figure 12.21 *Path painted with a pattern.*

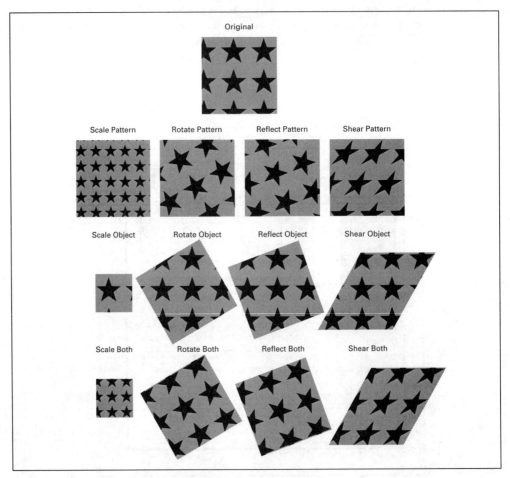

Figure 12.22 *Transforming patterns.*

After selecting the object, accessing the appropriate transform dialog box, and entering the desired specifications, make sure that the Pattern Tiles check box is selected—not the Objects check box—before clicking OK. The transform effects will be applied only to the pattern, leaving the object shape unaffected. Similarly, you may choose to transform the object itself without affecting the pattern, or transform both the object and the pattern together. Figure 12.22 shows the same pattern and object transformed using various options.

If you are transforming objects without the use of dialog boxes, you can still control whether the pattern is affected, as the General Preferences dialog box has a check box for transforming pattern tiles. If this box is checked, all the transformations performed thereafter—without the use of the transform dialog boxes—will affect both the object and the pattern. If the Transform Pattern Tiles box is not checked, only the objects will be affected, leaving the pattern as is. The Object and Pattern Tiles check boxes in the Transform dialog boxes will override the General Preferences setting.

Many different pattern effects may be created in Adobe Illustrator, limited only by your imagination. The pattern image does not necessarily have to fall within the boundaries of the background rectangle, which is useful when you are trying to achieve an effect where the actual tile boundaries are not visible once the pattern is applied to an object. Creating such patterns, however, requires a bit more planning, as, improperly constructed, the pattern image may be cut off in the final result. For instance, if the pattern image in Figure 12.23 is applied to an object, the result will look like the image in Figure 12.24.

To avoid this problem, the part of the pattern that extends past the background boundary must be continued at another location within the background boundary. The best way to do this is by selecting the background rectangle and the part of the pattern image that extends beyond the boundaries, holding down the **Option** key, and

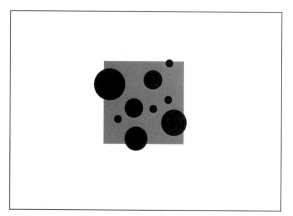

Figure 12.23 *Pattern image falls outside the tile boundaries.*

Figure 12.24 *Parts of the pattern image are cut off.*

moving those elements until the opposite edges of the rectangle align (see Figure 12.25 a, b). Make sure that the Snap to Point option is checked in the General Preferences dialog box to ensure precision alignment.

Repeat this step until you have a duplicate of the rectangle, and the pattern image on all four sides of the original rectangle (see Figure 12.26). Next, select the four duplicate rectangles and the parts of the image that do not fall within the original rectangle boundaries, and delete them (see Figure 12.27). Proceed by adding this tile to the patterns list, as described earlier. Thereafter, when this pattern is applied to an object, the result will be a somewhat irregular pattern with no visible tile boundaries (see Figure 12.28).

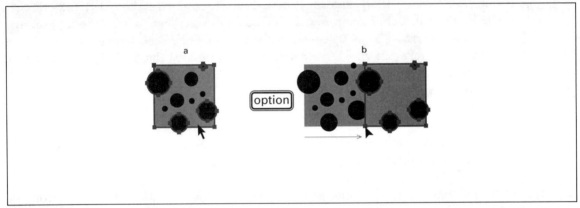

Figure 12.25 *Duplicate the pattern image that falls outside the tile boundaries.*

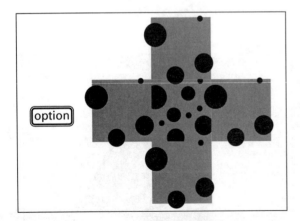

Figure 12.26 *Repeat the pattern image on all sides.*

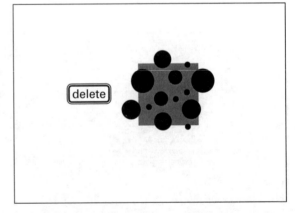

Figure 12.27 *The pattern image that falls outside the tile boundaries must be repeated on the opposite side of the tile.*

Another interesting effect achieved with patterns is *stippling*. If you ever had to shade a rendering using stippling, you realize what a long and tedious process it can be. In Illustrator, you can create a few patterns that can be combined to mimic the stippling effect and reuse them without having to create thousands of individual dots of various densities. Start by creating the background square (0.5 inches × 0.5 inches) and filling and stroking it with none (see Figure 12.29). Next, choose the Freehand tool from the toolbox and start making scribbles within the square—it is okay to go outside of the square boundaries.

Continue scribbling until the inside of the square is somewhat evenly covered (see Figure 12.30). Select all the scribbles you just made and paint them with a 1-point black stroke, rounded caps and joins, and a *Dashed option* of 0.1 (dash), 5 (gap) (see Figure 12.31). Duplicate the whole image, including the square, and select only the

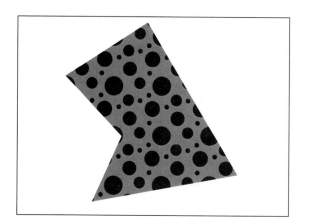

Figure 12.28 *The pattern is no longer cut off.*

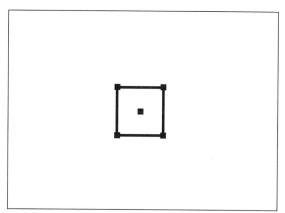

Figure 12.29 *Create a square.*

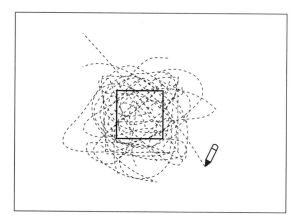

Figure 12.30 *Make scribbles with the Freehand tool.*

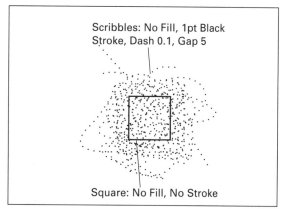

Figure 12.31 *Assign the specified attributes.*

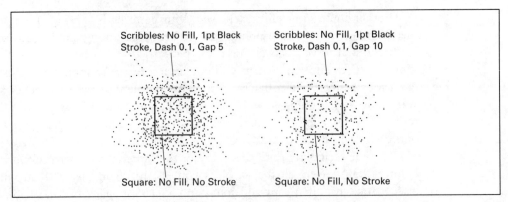

Figure 12.32 *Duplicate and assign the specified attributes.*

scribbles of that copy, painting them with a Dashed option of 0.1 (dash), 10 (gap) (see Figure 12.32).

Duplicate the image again, painting the scribbles with the Dashed option of 0.1 (dash), 15 (gap) (see Figure 12.33). Make one more duplicate and paint the scribbles

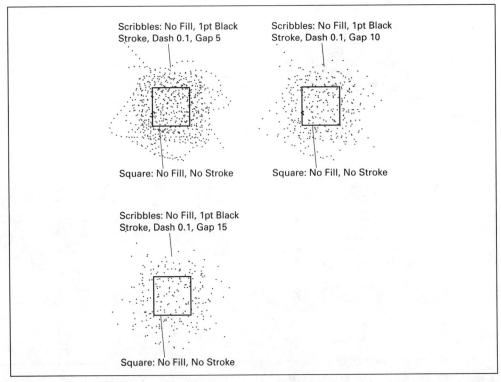

Figure 12.33 *Duplicate and assign the specified attributes.*

with the Dashed option of 0.1 (dash), 20 (gap) (see Figure 12.34). You now have four images, each with a different dot density. Select them one at a time and add them to the patterns list.

You are now ready to create paths that may be painted with those patterns. In this case, we will use simple rectangles, although you may apply the same technique to any shape. Create four rectangles of the same height, but different widths (see Figure 12.35) and position them on top of each other with their left edges aligned (see Figure 12.36).

A second way to do this is to create only one rectangle and scale it horizontally while creating a copy. If you positioned the point of origin along the left edge, the duplicate will already be aligned to the original. After that, simply press **Command + D** twice, and two more rectangles—horizontally scaled in proportion to the first two—will be created with their left edges already aligned. (All these scaling techniques were discussed in earlier chapters. There is, of course, a third way to achieve this result that involves blending paths, which will be discussed later in this chapter.)

As the final step, select the largest rectangle and paint it with the least dense dot pattern. The next smallest rectangle will be painted with the next least dense dot pattern, and so on. Your resulting image should look like a pattern gradually increasing in

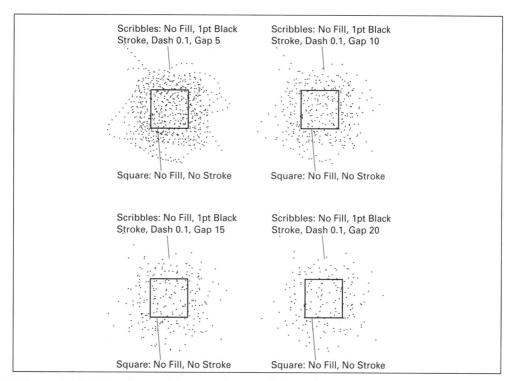

Figure 12.34 *Duplicate and assign the specified attributes.*

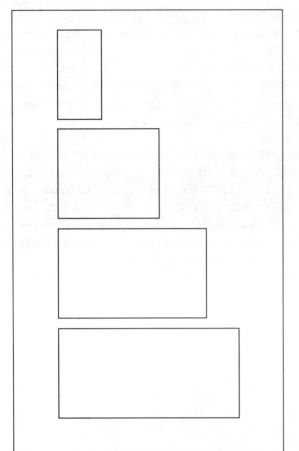

Figure 12.35 Create four rectangles.

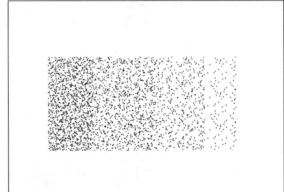

Figure 12.36 Align the four rectangles.

Figure 12.37 Stippling effect.

dot density, which will represent a stippling effect (see Figure 12.37). To achieve an even smoother transition, simply create more dot patterns with less density variations between them.

Gradients

Just as you can fill an object with a flat color, you can also fill objects with gradients that can be created with unlimited combinations of up to 34 different colors per gradient. There are two basic types of gradients: *Radial* and *Linear*. Gradients are named, saved, and retrieved in the same way as custom colors and patterns. To access the Gradient dialog box, go to the Object menu and choose Gradient, or double-click on the name of an existing gradient in the Paint Style palette.

The Gradient dialog box includes: the *gradient slider bar,* the *color options panel,* the *gradients list; New, Duplicate,* and *Delete Gradient* buttons; and the *Linear* and *Radial* buttons (see Figure 12.38). Clicking on the New button will create a basic white-to-black linear gradient and display it in the listing and the gradient slider bar. The gradient slider bar consists of the color guide triangles at the bottom, the gradient midpoint diamond at the top, and the percentage text field. You can toggle between viewing the whole gradient dialog box or just the gradient slider bar by changing the position of the lever under the percentage text field.

The color guide triangles at the bottom of the gradient slider bar are used for placing colors and moving them around within the gradient. Up to 34 different colors can be placed in one gradient. The gradient midpoint diamond, located at the top of the gradient slider bar, pinpoints the halfway point between two blending colors. For instance, if you have a gradient that goes from black to white, the diamond will be at the exact spot where the black is at 50 percent. Once a new gradient has been created, you may change the colors and the positions of the existing color guide triangles, create additional color guide triangles, and change the position of the gradient midpoint diamond.

To add a new color to an existing gradient, simply click anywhere along the bottom of the gradient slider bar, and a black color guide triangle will appear (see

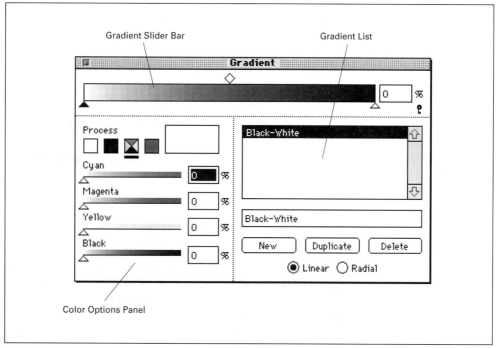

Figure 12.38 *Gradient dialog box.*

Figure 12.39). The color options panel will display the color specifications at that color guide. To change the color at any color guide triangle, click on that triangle and it will turn to solid black, indicating that it is selected. Choose one of the four color options in the color options panel: white, black, process, or custom. The color on the gradient slider bar at the color guide triangle, will change automatically as you assign the color.

You can move any of the existing color guide triangles to anywhere along the gradient slider bar. Holding down the **Option** key as you move a color guide triangle will create a duplicate of that color. The percentage text field, to the right of the gradient slider bar, displays the position of the selected color guide triangle on the gradient slider bar—left being 0 percent, and right being 100 percent. The color guide triangles can also be moved by typing in a desired percentage in the text field.

The gradient midpoint diamonds can also be moved by dragging them left and right along the gradient slider bar, which is useful for adjusting the rate of change in color in your gradient. For example, with a simple white-to-black gradient, the diamond is located at the exact midpoint of the gradient, which is at 50 percent black. If you move the gradient midpoint diamond closer to white, the rate of change will be greater from white to 50 percent black, than from 50 percent black to 100 percent black (see Figure 12.40). This is because the 50 percent change in shading from white to 50 percent black occurs in a much shorter distance than the same 50 percent

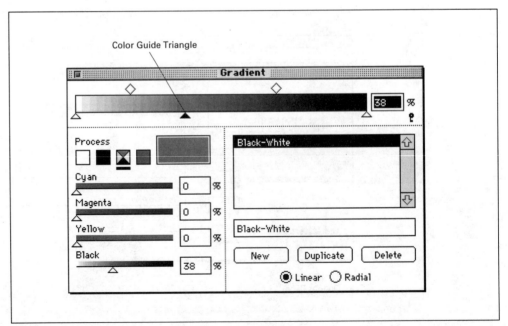

***Figure 12.39** Creating a new color guide triangle.*

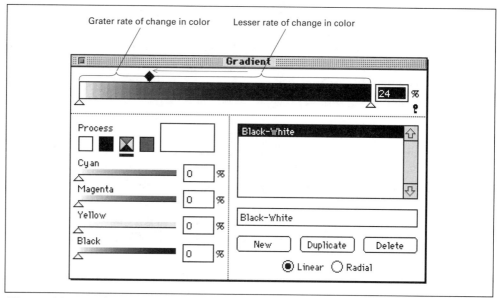

Figure 12.40 *Changing the midpoint of a gradient.*

change in shading from 50 percent black to 100 percent black. This kind of gradient fine-tuning provides tremendous control over how the gradient will look.

The Linear and Radial gradient options also dictate the properties of a gradient: A linear gradient is a straight gradient, blending from side to side; the Radial gradient is circular and blends from a center point out in all directions (see Figure 12.41). After you have created the desired gradient and given it a specific name, it can be applied to an object via the Paint Style palette. Once a gradient is applied to an object, making changes to it in the Gradient dialog box will automatically apply those changes to the

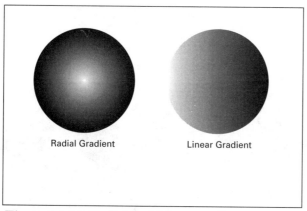

Figure 12.41 *Radial and Linear gradients.*

object, which allows you to see how the gradient will look on your object as you are adjusting it.

The *Gradient Vector tool* controls the direction and the length of a gradient relative to the object. To use this tool, select an object painted with a gradient and choose the Gradient Vector tool from the toolbox (see Figure 12.42). Click the mouse button where you want the gradient to start, and drag to where you want the gradient to end (see Figure 12.43). With a linear gradient, the beginning point is at the left side of the gradient slider bar, and the ending point is at the right. A radial gradient center is at the left of the gradient slider bar, and the outside edge is at the right.

When you use the Gradient Vector tool, the duration and direction of the gradient is determined by the length and angle of the line that appears as you drag the Gradient Vector tool. If you drag past the boundaries of an object, some of that gradient will be cropped off, resulting in only a part of that gradient appearing inside the object (see Figure 12.44). Dragging the Gradient Vector tool for only a section of an

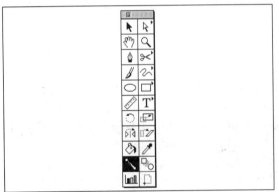

Figure 12.42 *The Gradient Vector tool.*

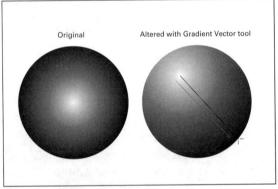

Figure 12.43 *Altering the gradient with the Gradient Vector tool.*

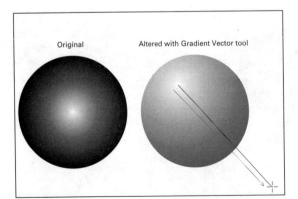

Figure 12.44 *Showing less of the gradient.*

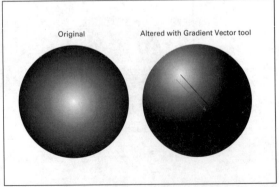

Figure 12.45 *Partially filling a path with a gradient.*

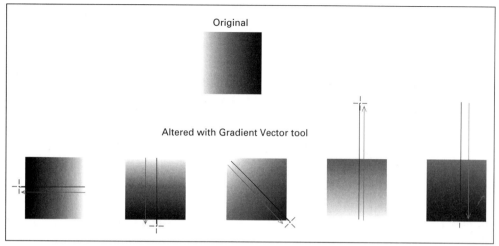

Figure 12.46 *Using the same gradient to achieve different results.*

object will result in a section of that object being gradated, while the rest of the object will be filled with the solid color at the beginning or end of that gradient (see Figure 12.45). This is a great feature, because it allows you to make one gradient look like many different gradients. For instance, you can use one black-to-white gradient for a gradient of any shade of gray. Figure 12.46 shows how one black-to-white gradient is used to shade a rectangle with different gray gradients with the help of the Gradient Vector tool.

The Gradient Vector tool can also be used to apply a shared gradation over a number of objects. For example, create the simple graphic shown in Figure 12.47 and paint all the objects with the same gradient. At this point, every object in this image is filled with the whole gradient. Select the whole image, choose the Gradient Vector tool, and drag it across the image, as shown in Figure 12.48. The individual objects in the image

Figure 12.47 *Every path of the image is filled with the whole gradient.*

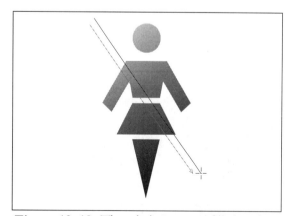

Figure 12.48 *The whole image is filled with the gradient.*

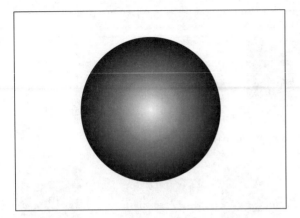

Figure 12.49 *Unaltered radial fill.*

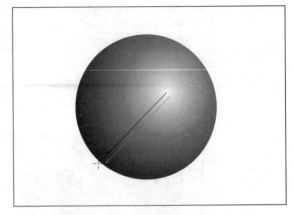

Figure 12.50 *Changing the highlight.*

are now filled with only part of the gradient, while the duration of the gradient stretches across the whole image instead of each object of that image individually.

The amount of special effects and realism that can be achieved just with the use of the gradients and the Gradient Vector tool are virtually limitless. For instance, let us look at a simple circle (see Figure 12.49): After filling it with a basic white-to-black radial blend, some would say it looks like a sphere; others will not. But a simple move with the Gradient Vector tool could make this circle look more like a sphere by simply moving the radial gradient highlight to be slightly off center—this can be done by clicking and dragging the Gradient Vector tool, as shown in Figure 12.50. The image has already changed appearance and performing one more step will make it look like a photorealistic rendering of a sphere.

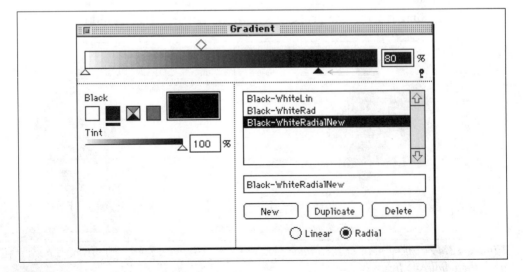

Figure 12.51 *Moving the color guide triangle.*

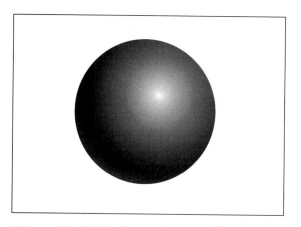

Figure 12.52 *Realistic sphere shading.*

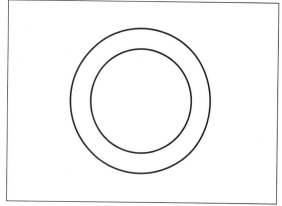

Figure 12.53 *Create two concentric circles.*

Select the gradient from the gradient dialog box and drag the black color guide triangle to 80 percent on the gradient slider bar (see Figure 12.51). Next, insert a new color guide triangle where the black one was and apply a 70 percent black to it. The simple circle shape now has the shading properties of a sphere and looks dimensional and realistic (see Figure 12.52).

The next example demonstrates a technique for creating a dimensional ring. First create two circles of slightly different sizes and place them on top of each other with their centers aligned (see Figure 12.53)—make sure that the smaller circle is on top. Create a radial gradient that goes from black to white to black (see Figure 12.54) and apply it to the large circle, and a white fill to the small circle. Return to the Gradient dialog box and move the left black color guide triangle and the white color guide tri-

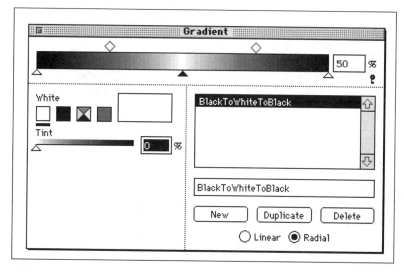

Figure 12.54 *Create a black-to-white-to-black gradient.*

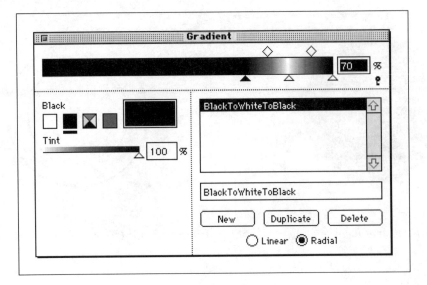

Figure 12.55 *Move the color guide triangles.*

angle to the right (see Figure 12.55). Adjust the position of these two color guide triangles until the full black-to-white-to-black gradient is visible in the space between
the large and small circle (see Figure 12.56). A dimensional ring effect will be
achieved. In this case, however, the hole in the ring is not transparent—compound
paths must be used to create holes in objects and will be discussed later in this chapter.

This same image can be used to create a curved tube. Simply cut the two circles in
the appropriate places, as shown in Figure 12.57, and delete the unwanted portions of
the circles. Send the remaining section of the top circle to the back by selecting it and

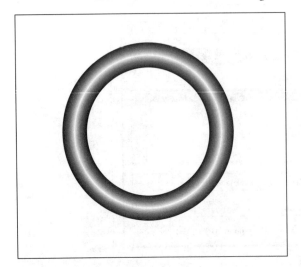

Figure 12.56 *A shaded ring.*

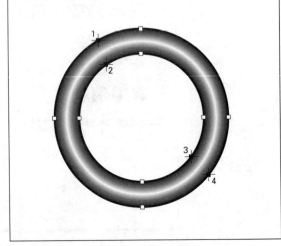

Figure 12.57 *Cut at the specified locations.*

going to Send to Back under the Arrange menu or by pressing **Command + -** (see Figure 12.58). Next, select the corresponding end points of each path and join them (see Figure 12.59). Unfortunately, this technique can be applied to create only tubes that are sections of circles and ovals. To create a dimensional tube of any other shape, a technique involving the *Blend tool* must be used and will be discussed later in the chapter.

Another interesting effect can be achieved by transforming the radial gradient. Create a shape and fill it with a radial gradient, then select the shape and choose the Scale tool from the toolbox. If you establish the point of origin and scale the object

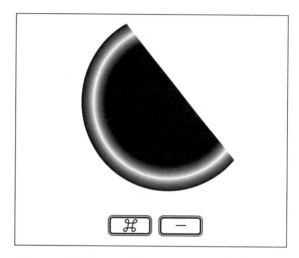

Figure 12.58 *Send the top circle to the back.*

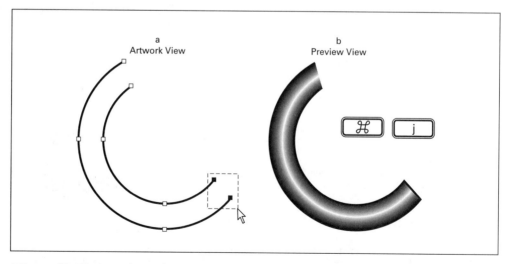

Figure 12.59 *Join the end points.*

vertically, the result will be an oval gradient (see Figure 12.60). The Shear tool can also be used to alter the radial gradient, as shown in Figure 12.61.

The combinations of different shaped paths and the variety of gradient options can result in some amazing-looking illustrations and realistic renderings. The best way to utilize these features is to understand the logic behind how they work, and then experiment with different configurations until the desired result is achieved.

Compound Paths

Compound paths serve two purposes in Illustrator: to create holes in paths and to use several paths as one *mask*. (Masks will be discussed later in this chapter.)

To create a hole in an object, create the object and the hole paths (see Figure 12.62), making sure that the hole path is in front of the object path, and select them both. Choose Compound Path > Make from the Object menu, or press **Command + 8**. The hole path that is on top of the object path will be knocked out and a hole will be created (see Figure 12.63).

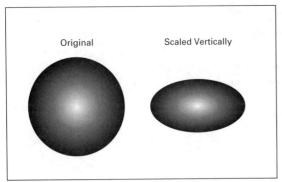

Figure 12.60 *Vertically scaled radial gradient.*

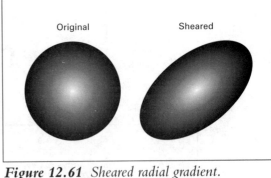

Figure 12.61 *Sheared radial gradient.*

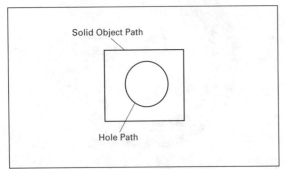

Figure 12.62 *Create a rectangle and a circle.*

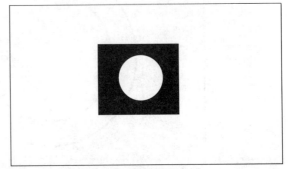

Figure 12.63 *Compound path.*

Placing other objects behind the compound path will make them visible through the hole (see Figure 12.64). More than one hole may be created in any given object; simply create as many hole paths as necessary and place them on top of the object you wish to make holes in. Select all those paths and go to the Object menu and choose Compound Paths > Make, or press **Command + 8**. The backmost path in the selection will be the object in which the holes are punched.

All the objects in a compound path will take on the paint style attributes of the backmost object, regardless of how they were painted previously. Even though an object outlines a hole, the Paint Style palette will show the same attributes for that object as the solid objects in the compound path. Releasing the compound path will result in all the objects belonging to that compound path being solid and painted with the same paint style.

To release a compound path, select the whole compound path by double-clicking on any object within the compound path with the Group Selection tool, and return to the Object menu to choose Compound Path > Release, or press **Command + 9**. When selecting objects to make a compound path, make sure that they are not part of a group or another compound path. Whole compound paths, however, can be selected and made into a larger compound path.

For instance, if you have two compound paths (see Figure 12.65), selecting a part of one and a part of the other will not let you make a compound path (see Figure 12.66), but selecting both compound paths as a whole will make a larger compound path, which will include all the selected shapes (see Figure 12.67). The results of this operation may not be visible and will differ, depending on the layering of the paths; we will return to this issue in the "Masks" section later in this chapter.

You can select parts of or a whole compound path with the Group Selection tool (hollow arrow with a plus). Clicking once on any object within a compound path will select only that object. Clicking for a second time on a selected object within a compound path will select all the objects within that compound path. If you wish to

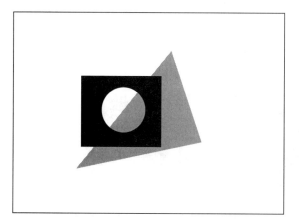

Figure 12.64 *The triangle is visible through the hole in the compound path.*

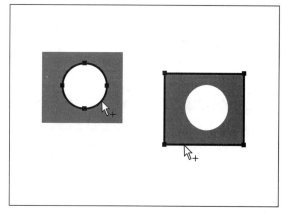

Figure 12.65 *Select portions of two separate compound paths.*

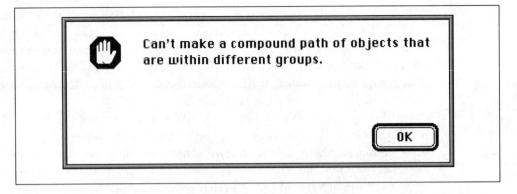

Figure 12.66 *Invalid command dialog box.*

manipulate a section of a compound path, individual anchor points and line segments may still be selected with the Direct Selection tool (see Figure 12.68).

To move a whole object within a compound path, the Group Selection tool must be used first. Click once on the object you wish to move and immediately switch to the Direct Selection tool. Click and drag the object you wish to move (see Figure 12.69). An object can still be moved within the compound path without switching to the Direct Selection tool, provided the object is clicked only once. With the Group Selection tool, click and drag the desired and previously unselected object within a compound path. Only that object will be affected as long as the selection and moving is done in one click and drag.

To move multiple objects within a compound path, click on each object with the Group Selection tool while holding down the **Shift** key (see Figure 12.70). Once the last object has been selected, do not release the mouse button and drag in the desired

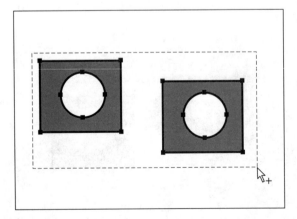

Figure 12.67 *Select whole compound paths.*

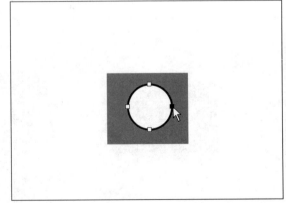

Figure 12.68 *Selecting a single point in a compound path.*

direction. All the selected objects will move simultaneously. If the mouse button was released after the last object was selected, you must go to the toolbox and choose the Direct Selection tool to proceed with the move. Then click and drag any of the selected objects, and the other selected objects will also be affected. The solid objects and holes within a compound path can be transformed and moved without affecting their opaque or transparent properties. If, however, two or more object paths overlap within a compound path, other holes and solid areas are created (see Figure 12.71). The results can be confusing and unpredictable at first, although it is possible to control the outcome by understanding the *Path Direction concept.*

The Path Direction concept is determined when the path is created with the Pen or Freehand tool, and can be changed in the Attributes dialog box found under the Object menu. When a path is created, the direction in which you construct it with the

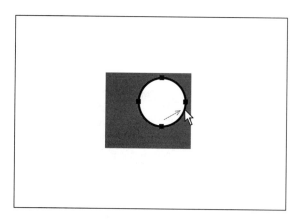

Figure 12.69 *Moving a path within a compound path.*

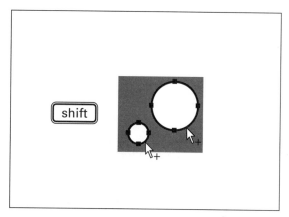

Figure 12.70 *Selecting multiple paths within a compound path.*

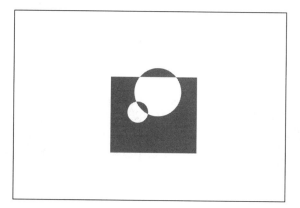

Figure 12.71 *Intersecting shapes within the compound path.*

Pen or Freehand tool is the direction of that path. Objects that are created automatically in Illustrator, such as ovals and rectangles, will automatically have a counterclockwise path direction (see Figure 12.72)

Compound paths work by combining paths with different directions. When you make two objects into a compound path, they are forced to travel in the opposite direction, therefore creating holes. When Illustrator looks at a compound path, it does not see a hole but it does recognize the second path as part of the first one traveling in the opposite direction—therefore assuming that it is another edge of the same path (see Figure 12.73). In a compound path, solid objects traveling in opposite directions will create a hole when intersected (see Figure 12.74). Similarly, objects that already are holes in a compound path will create solid areas when intersected (see Figure 12.75).

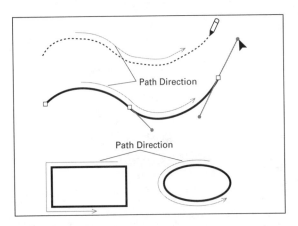

Figure 12.72 *Path direction.*

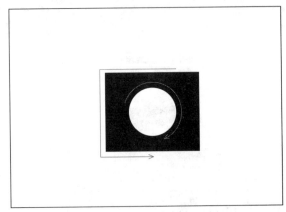

Figure 12.73 *Paths within a compound path travel in opposite directions.*

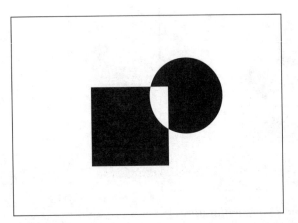

Figure 12.74 *Compound path.*

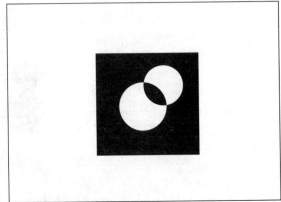

Figure 12.75 *Compound path.*

You can change the path direction to achieve a specific effect by going to the Attributes dialog box under the Object menu. If the *Reverse Path Direction* check box is checked, the path normally has a counterclockwise direction; but if the box is not checked, the direction of the path is clockwise. Be cautious when selecting more than one object, because if the path direction of the selected objects is not all in the same direction, the Reverse Path Direction check box will be gray and clicking on it will make all the selected paths travel in the same direction.

Unfortunately, there is one annoying feature of compound paths: You cannot select other objects through the hole in Preview mode. For instance, if a compound path object with a hole is on top of another object, the object underneath cannot be selected even if it is visible through the hole (see Figure 12.76). Clicking on the hole will select only the path that makes that hole (see Figure 12.77). To select an object underneath a compound path, the whole compound path has to be either locked or hidden (see Figure 12.78 a, b, c). Choosing the Artwork mode from the View menu will also enable you to select any object.

Figure 12.76 *The star is underneath the compound path.*

Figure 12.77 *You cannot select through the hole in the compound path.*

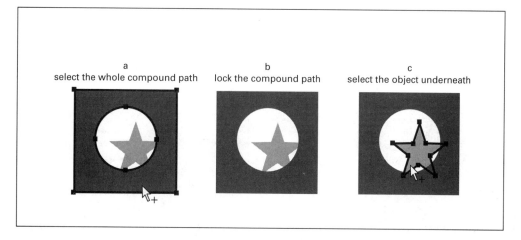

Figure 12.78 *Lock the compound path to select the object underneath.*

There are two ways in which the hole effect can be achieved in Illustrator without using the compound path command: The first requires some cutting and joining. To create a doughnut, construct two circles, as shown in Figure 12.79. Make one cut in each circle with the Scissor tool at the corresponding anchor points, as shown in Figure 12.80; deselect both objects and choose the Direct Selection tool. Hold down the **Shift** key, click on the spots where the cuts were made—one at a time—and move the selected end points a few pixels away, as shown in Figure 12.81. From the Object menu, choose Join, or press **Command + J** (see Figure 12.82).

Next, select the other two end points, or the whole path, and perform the Join command once again (see Figure 12.83). Making sure that the Snap to Point option is checked in the General Preferences dialog box, select the two anchor points that were originally moved out of place, and drag them back on top of their corresponding

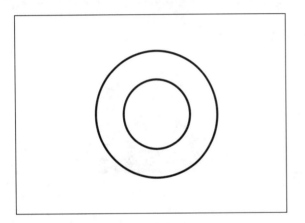

Figure 12.79 Draw two concentric circles.

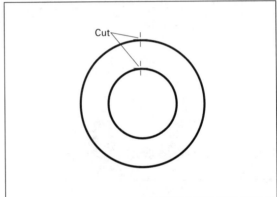

Figure 12.80 Cut as shown.

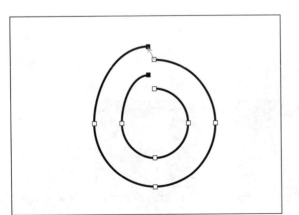

Figure 12.81 Move the two top end points.

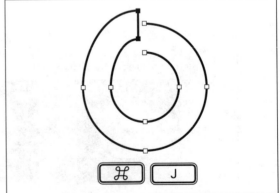

Figure 12.82 Join the two end points.

anchor points (see Figure 12.84). Before the Compound Path option became available in Adobe Illustrator, this technique was the only way to create holes. However, knowing this *old method* will be helpful in your understanding of the program's logic as you develop advanced skills.

By simply following the direction of this path, it will also become clear how the Reverse Path Direction in compound paths is used to create holes. Figure 12.85 shows that even though the doughnut is a single closed path, the inner circle travels in the opposite direction from the outer circle. Unfortunately, in addition to the extra effort necessary to make holes with this technique, there is another drawback: Fill attributes work well on this object, but strokes can be a problem.

The section of the path outline where the two circles are connected will not be visible when the object is filled, but when the object is stroked it will be clearly visible (see Figure 12.86). One way to avoid this is by making a copy of both circles prior to making the cuts. Once the cutting and joining has been made and the resulting path

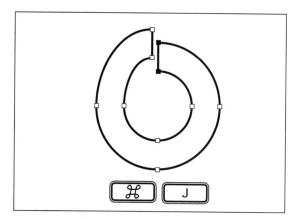

Figure 12.83 *Join the two end points.*

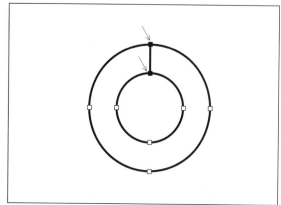

Figure 12.84 *Move the points back.*

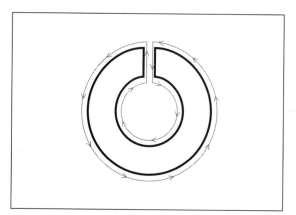

Figure 12.85 *Path direction.*

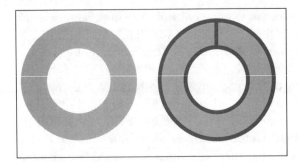

Figure 12.86 *Fill and stroke.*

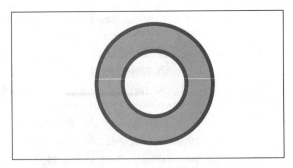

Figure 12.87 *Filled path underneath and two stroked paths on top.*

filled with a desired paint style, paste the two copied circles in front of that shape and paint them with a stroke and fill with None (see Figure 12.87).

Another way to achieve the compound path effect without using the compound path command is by visually mimicking the end result. For this, you must know exactly what will be visible through the holes you will create. For instance, if there is a flat background color behind the object with the holes, simply fill the hole shapes with that color (see Figure 12.88); if the background is filled with a gradient, fill the hole shapes with that gradient. Once the background and the hole shapes are filled with the same gradient, select both the background and the holes, and choose the Gradient Vector tool. If you drag the cursor on the angle and the distance you want the gradient

Figure 12.88 *Faking transparency with solid background.*

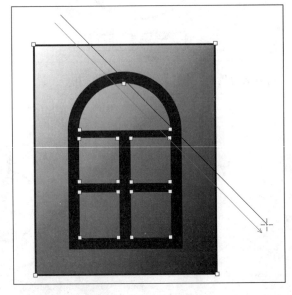

Figure 12.89 *Faking transparency with gradated background.*

to fill the background, the gradient will span across the holes as it does across the background, creating the illusion of transparency (see Figure 12.89).

Of course, in both cases, placing another shape behind the holes will not allow that shape to be visible through the holes. In this situation, a mask must be made from a copy of the hole shapes. This is an advanced technique that will open up a new assortment of special effects.

Mask Paths

The masking feature in Illustrator is used to block out those parts of an image that are not inside the mask—working almost like a cookie cutter. Let's pretend that the dough on the baking sheet is your artwork image, and the cookie cutter is the mask shape. When the cookie cutter is applied to the dough, you are left with a cookie in the shape of the cutter (see Figure 12.90). Similarly, when a mask shape is applied to artwork, the result is a portion of that artwork appearing only within the mask shape (see Figure 12.91).

Figure 12.90 *Cutting dough with a cookie cutter.*

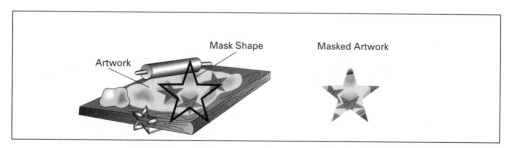

Figure 12.91 *Masking an artwork.*

A mask can be made out of any path or compound path created in Illustrator. To mask an image, create the mask shape and place it on top of the image. Select both the mask shape and all the objects you wish to mask, and from the Object menu choose Mask > Make. Only the portion of the image that is inside the mask shape will be visible in the Preview mode, and the masking path will have no paint style attributes once the mask is applied.

Selecting parts of or a whole mask works similarly to compound paths. Choose the Group Selection tool, click once on any object within the mask, and click on the selected object again. To move some of the objects within a mask, select those objects with the Group Selection tool and then switch to the Direct Selection tool to perform the move. The mask shape may be moved so that you can view different parts of the masked image. First, select the mask shape by clicking on it once with the Group Selection tool, then choose the Direct Selection tool, dragging the mask shape to a new location. A different part of the masked image will now be visible inside the mask shape (see Figure 12.92).

You can place additional objects into the mask in two ways: First, make sure that the new object is behind the mask shape, select the whole mask and the object you wish to add to it, and choose Mask > Make from the Object menu. The second way is by pasting the new object directly in front or in back of other objects already in the mask. Position the new object on top of the mask in the general area where you wish it to be (see Figure 12.93) and choose Cut from the Edit menu, or press **Command + X**. Next, select the object within the mask that the new object should be in front or

Figure 12.92 Moving the mask path around the artwork.

Figure 12.93 Adding another path to the mask.

Figure 12.94 A new path is part of the mask.

in back of and choose Paste in Front (**Command + F**) or Paste in Back (**Command + B**) from the Edit menu. The new object will now be placed within the mask in the specified location (see Figure 12.94).

One or more mask *clusters* can be further masked by another shape. Simply create the mask shape and place it on top of a mask cluster or clusters, then go to the Object menu and choose Mask > Make; a new mask will be created, containing other masked objects (see Figure 12.95).

As mentioned earlier, a mask path cannot have any paint style attributes. If you wish to have a stroked mask outline or filled mask background, duplicates of the mask path must be made. To give the mask shape a stroke, select the mask path and, from the Edit menu, choose Copy or press **Command + C**. Next, choose Paste In Front (**Command + F**) from the Edit menu. Once the duplicate of the mask path has been pasted directly in front of the mask cluster, it will already be selected and you can open the Paint Style palette and specify the desired stroke attributes (see Figure 12.96). Keep in mind that assigning a fill to this path will cover the whole masked image. If you want the mask shape to have a fill as the background of the masked image, another duplicate of the mask shape must be placed behind the mask cluster.

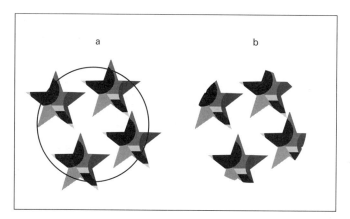

Figure 12.95 *Masking multiple masks.*

Figure 12.96 *Stroking a mask.*

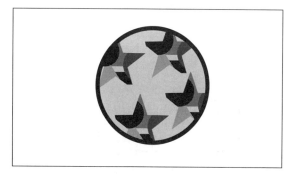

Figure 12.97 *Filling a mask.*

Copy the mask shape, select the whole mask cluster, and go to Paste In Back in the Edit menu, or press **Command + B**. Specify the desired fill attributes in the Paint Style palette (see Figure 12.97).

Masks may be used in combination with compound paths when a mask needs to be made out of several paths simultaneously: for instance, if you want a single image to be masked by a few different shapes. To do this, create and select the objects that you want to be the mask, and choose Compound Path > Make from the Object menu (or press **Command + 8**). Position the objects on top of the artwork to be masked and select both the compound path and the artwork image (see Figure 12.98). Again, choose Mask > Make from the Object menu, and the artwork image will be visible only in the compound path shapes (see Figure 12.99).

As mentioned earlier, masks can also be used to simulate a hole in an object. Construct a black square with a white circle on top, as shown in Figure 12.100; then create a triangle shape and place it behind the square. Be sure that the triangle intersects both the circle and the square and is visible outside the square's edge (see Figure 12.101). Since both the square and the circle are opaque, the portion of the triangle that is behind the square cannot be seen. Make a copy of the triangle, paste it in front of the circle, and the triangle copy will now cover a portion of the square and the circle (see Figure 12.102), while the original triangle is still behind all the other objects.

Next, make a copy of the circle and paste it in front of the topmost triangle. You should now have a triangle, a square, a circle, a second triangle, and a second circle—specifically in that order (see Figure 12.103). Select the top circle and the triangle directly beneath it, and choose Mask > Make from the Object menu. You now have the illusion of the triangle appearing through the circle hole in the square (see Figure 12.104).

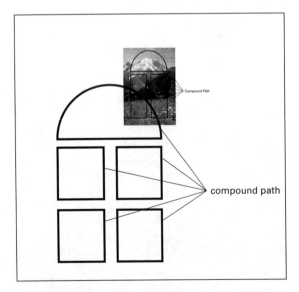

Figure 12.98 *Using a compound path to make a mask.*

Figure 12.99 *Compound mask.*

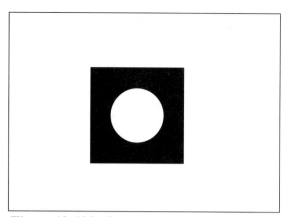

Figure 12.100 *Create a square with a circle on top.*

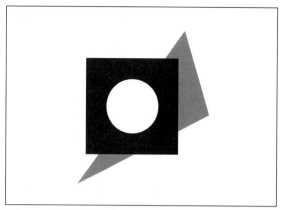

Figure 12.101 *The triangle is not visible behind the square and circle shapes.*

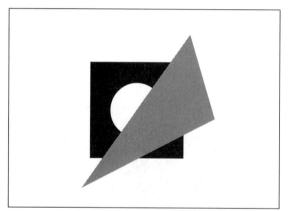

Figure 12.102 *Paste a copy of the triangle on top of the other shapes.*

Figure 12.103 *Paste a copy of the circle on top.*

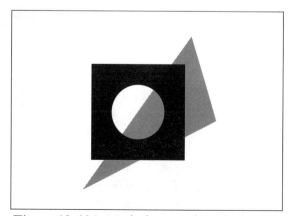

Figure 12.104 *Mask the triangle with the circle to create a transparent effect.*

To summarize, a mask was made out of a copy of the circle. It was then used to mask a copy of the triangle and placed in the exact location on top of the original shapes. Even though the square appears to have a round hole in it, all the objects in this image are very much opaque. The illusion of transparency was created by duplicating the background shape (triangle) and masking it with the circle (hole) so that only the portion of the triangle that is inside the circle (mask) is visible.

This technique can be used to create many different transparency effects, such as intersecting two different colors to create a third color at the intersection, thereby achieving a translucent color property. To see this, create two circles and position them, as shown in Figure 12.105. Paint the bottom circle red and the top one yellow. Next, select the bottom red circle and copy it; select the yellow circle and from the Edit menu choose Paste in Front (**Command + F**). While this circle is still selected, go to the Paint Style palette and paint it orange.

You now have a red circle on the bottom, a yellow in the middle, and an orange circle on top (see Figure 12.106). The bottom red circle cannot be seen because the

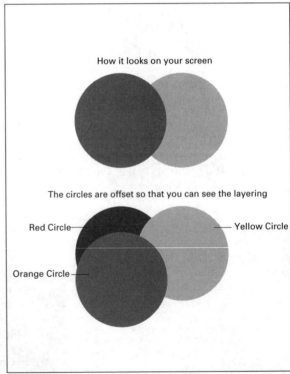

How it looks on your screen

The circles are offset so that you can see the layering

Red Circle

Yellow Circle

Orange Circle

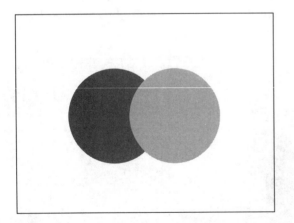

Figure 12.105 *Create red and yellow circles.*

Figure 12.106 *Create an orange circle and place on top.*

top orange circle is completely covering it. Now, select the yellow circle and copy it; select the orange circle and paste the copy of the yellow circle in front of it (see Figure 12.107). The copy of the yellow circle you just pasted in front will be the mask shape, and it will mask the orange circle so that the orange will be visible only in the intersecting area.

Select the top yellow and orange circles and from the Object menu choose Mask > Make. The result, if you followed the steps correctly, is two intersecting circles, red and yellow, which create an orange color at the intersection (see Figure 12.108).

Of course, in Illustrator there is always an easier way to do everything. Similar effects can be achieved by selecting the image in Figure 12.105 and applying a *Pathfinder Soft filter*. A dialog box will appear asking you to specify the percentage of colors you want to mix—you may need to experiment with a few different percentages to find the right translucency. The Pathfinder Soft filter works only with flat colors. So, if you want to make a transparent gradient, the masking technique may need to be used. Also, mastering the transparency effect through the use of a mask is essential in learning to utilize Adobe Illustrator's most powerful features.

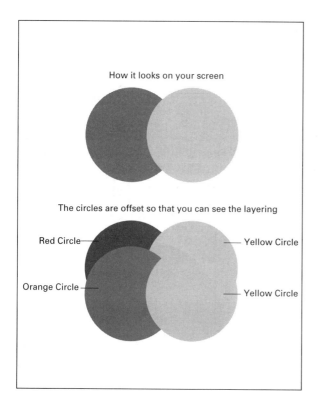

Figure 12.107 *Duplicate the yellow circle and place on top.*

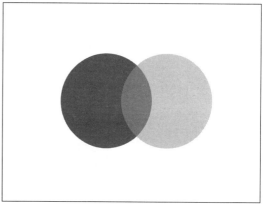

Figure 12.108 *A translucent effect is achieved after the mask is made.*

Blending Paths

Illustrator's Blend tool is used for a variety of effects, such as equally spacing objects in a given area, creating simple object morphing effects, and making gradient color blends otherwise unachievable with Illustrator's gradient feature. The Blend tool has been available since the early versions of Illustrator, when it was the only way to create gradients. With the recently added gradient feature, most people tend to overlook the Blend tool as a gradient creating option. However, avoiding the Blend tool will prevent you from creating about two thirds of the possible gradated color effects (discussed later in this section).

The most basic use of the Blend tool is to evenly space a desired number of objects in a given area. For instance, if you are trying to create a grid that divides an area into ten sections, the Blend tool is the way to go. Start by constructing a perfectly vertical line segment at the end of the area to be divided, and paint it with a 1-point black stroke (see Figure 12.109).

Next, hold down the **Option** and **Shift** keys and drag the line segment to the other end of the area (see Figure 12.110). Select both line segments directly and choose the Blend tool from the toolbox (see Figure 12.111). Click once at one of the end points on the first line segment, and then click on the same end point on the other line segments. The Blend dialog box will appear, consisting of three text fields and the Cancel and OK buttons (see Figure 12.112). The top text field is used to specify the number of steps between the two blending paths. The other two text fields are for percentages of the first and last steps and are rarely used.

Enter the number of divisions you wish to have; for ten equal divisions enter the number 9 and click OK. Nine identical vertical lines will be created, evenly spaced between the two original line segments, creating a total of 11 lines and 10 divisions (see Figure 12.113). For our purposes, we will call the two original line segments the

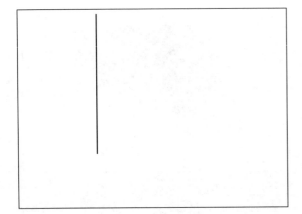

Figure 12.109 *Draw a vertical line.*

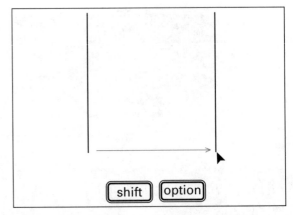

Figure 12.110 *Move and duplicate the vertical line.*

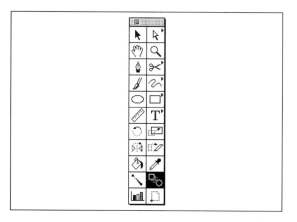

Figure 12.111 *The Blend tool.*

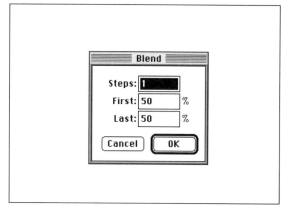

Figure 12.112 *Blend dialog box.*

extremes and the created blend segments the *in-betweens.* The in-betweens are automatically grouped together when they are created, enabling you to easily select and delete them if the desired result is not achieved, and to redo the blend with different specifications.

Another use of the Blend tool is to *morph* shapes from one to the other. There are a few more issues to be considered when using this procedure. When blending between objects of different shapes, the number of anchor points in each object and the anchor points that you select to blend between become very important. As an example, we will blend between a circle and a star—both painted black (see Figure 12.114).

Simply selecting both shapes and performing the Blend function will result in some very strange in-between steps and the end product will not be a nice morphing effect (see Figure 12.115). The problem is that the circle and the star paths have a different number of anchor points: The circle has four and the star ten. Rather than deleting the star's anchor points—which will result in a shape very unlike a star—anchor points

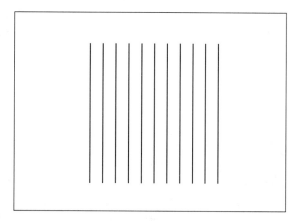

Figure 12.113 *Equally divided area.*

Figure 12.114 Draw a circle and a star.

Figure 12.115 Blending objects with a different number of anchor points.

should be added to the circle path. Even though Adobe Illustrator has an *Add Anchor Points filter,* it is more efficient to manually add anchor points with the *Add Anchor Points tool* located to the right of the Scissor tool. With this tool, you can specify the location and number of anchor points you wish to add. A bit of math will tell us that we need to add six anchor points to the circle.

The locations of those points is important and you should realize the following when adding points to the circle path. The Blend tool works by looking at the anchor points of a path, rather than the line segments. This means that when you choose the two anchor points on the extreme paths to be blended, all the other anchor points will blend relative to the ones you have chosen. If the number of anchor points differs in the two extreme paths, Illustrator adds extra anchor points to the in-between paths to compensate. Controlling where Illustrator places those points is difficult and the results are usually not what you had in mind. Therefore, when you add extra anchor points to an extreme path, remember the location of the corresponding anchor points on the other extreme path.

In our example, we can control which anchor points on the circle will correspond to the anchor points on the star. For instance, to achieve the smoothest possible morph effect between these two shapes, the four existing anchor points on the circle should blend to the four points on the star, as shown in Figure 12.116. Establishing that, we can now determine where the additional anchor points on the circle should be placed (see Figure 12.117).

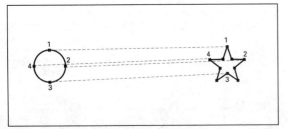

Figure 12.116 Identifying corresponding anchor points in a blend.

Figure 12.117 Add the desired number of anchor points to the circle.

The two shapes are now ready to be blended. Directly select both shapes and choose the Blend tool. Click on the top anchor point of the circle and on the corresponding anchor point on the star. The Blend dialog box will appear, allowing you to enter the number of in-betweens you wish to achieve. Do not enter a very large number, as the shapes will overlap each other, taking away from the full morph effect. I chose five steps in this case (see Figure 12.118). If the images you are blending consist of more than one path, each image should have the same number of paths, and each pair of paths must be blended separately (see Figure 12.119).

Keep in mind that only two closed or open paths may be blended together—you cannot blend between an open and a closed path. When blending between two open paths, you must select the end points of the paths to be blended. Clicking with the Blend tool on an anchor point that is not an end point of an open path will bring up a dialog box telling you to choose the end points.

Besides blending between two different path shapes, the Blend tool can also blend between two different paint style attributes, providing for a whole new variety of special effects. For instance, if our circle and star shapes were both painted with fills of different colors and strokes of different color and weight, the in-betweens would gradually change from one color and stroke thickness to the other (see Figure 12.120). Besides the variety of interesting designs that can be accomplished with this feature, the most popular use for this tool is the unlimited potential of gradient color blend effects.

Figure 12.118 *Blending objects with the same number of anchor points.*

Figure 12.119 *Blending images made up of a number of objects.*

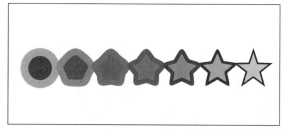

Figure 12.120 *Blending between different paint styles.*

We will start by imitating the linear and radial gradients. Even though this type of color blends can be created in the Gradient dialog box, learning to create them with the Blend tool will help you advance to more complex color blends. Linear color blends can be created in two ways with the Blend tool: by blending between line segments or open paths, and by blending between closed paths. Making a linear color blend between two line segments is similar to dividing an area into equal sections, as discussed previously.

Construct two straight line segments, one where you want the blend to begin and the other where it should end. Paint each segment with a different color stroke of the same weight, and no fill (see Figure 12.121). Select both line segments, choose the Blend tool, click once on an end point of one of the line segments, and click again on a corresponding end point of the other line segment.

A Blend dialog box will appear, showing a number in the Steps text field. This number is the number of steps that Adobe Illustrator recommends. This recommendation is based on the program's calculations of the change in color between the two extremes and its assumption that the file will be printed on a high resolution printer capable of 256 levels of gray. The formula it uses is simple: 256 × largest percentage in color change = number of steps.

For instance, if you were blending from an object painted with 50-percent cyan, 20-percent magenta, and 100-percent yellow, to an object painted with 0-percent cyan, 30-percent magenta, and 60-percent yellow, the largest percentage in color change would be 50-percent (50-percent cyan to 0-percent cyan). The number of steps would then be: 256 × 50 = 126; although the number appearing in the Steps text field would be 124, because the two extreme steps are also counted.

If you wish to calculate the number of steps you need for a different resolution printer, provided you know the dot and the line screen of that printer, use this formu-

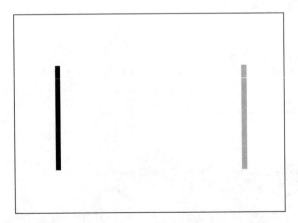

Figure 12.121 *Create two vertical lines, and paint with different color strokes.*

la: (dot screen / line screen) × (dot screen / line screen) = number of grays. Multiply the number of grays result by the largest percentage in color change.

There will be many occasions when you will want to reduce the number of steps regardless of the output resolution. For example, if you are blending between two drastically different colors in a very small area, the program will recommend the same number of steps as if you were blending in a large area. Using more than 100 steps in an area smaller than one inch is a bit excessive. If you are creating a complex illustration, your files may have many blends that consume a lot of memory. Trying to keep the number of steps in a blend to a minimum without causing adverse effects on the quality of the blend is not an exact science, but can be perfected with experience. In the interim, a little common sense will steer you in the right direction.

For instance, if you are creating a drastic color change blend in a large area—a quarter of a letter page or larger—in most cases, you should stick with the number of steps recommended. If, on the other hand, you are using the same drastic color change blend in a small area, a couple of inches or smaller, you may need to input a smaller number in the Steps text field. In most cases, you can input a number that is at least half of the recommended steps.

Once the desired number of steps has been specified, click the OK button to create the in-betweens. Remember that the effects of a color blend can be seen only in the Preview mode, and you may need to deselect the in-betweens—which are automatically selected upon creation—to see the blend clearly (see Figure 12.122). Adobe Illustrator users debate the use of line segments or closed paths for color blends. Even though line segments consume less memory and may be simpler to use than closed paths, other problems are encountered that may negatively affect the quality of the blend. If the stroke weight of the line segments is too thin or the number of steps too small, gaps between the steps may occur (see Figure 12.123). Based on personal experience, I recommend that you use closed paths in all your color blends.

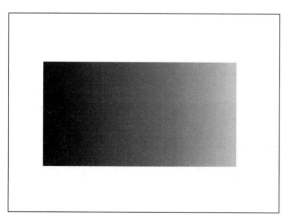

Figure 12.122 *Linear blend.*

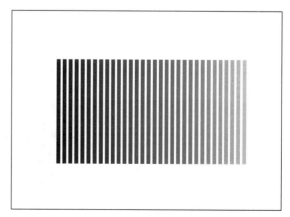

Figure 12.123 *Not enough steps.*

Linear blends can still be created in two different ways with closed paths. First, instead of using two straight lines painted with a different color stroke, create two thin rectangles and paint them with different color fills, but no stroke (see Figure 12.124). Select both rectangles and blend the corresponding anchor points, keeping in mind that if you click on the upper right anchor point of one rectangle, you must also click on the upper right anchor point of the other rectangle. Clicking on anchor points which do not correspond to each other will produce some strange blend shapes (see Figure 12.125).

Even though this blend technique is somewhat more efficient than using line segments, similar problems may occur if the rectangles are made too thin or not enough steps are used in the blend (see Figure 12.126). The best way to create color blends with closed paths—and to ensure that all the in-betweens overlap and do not create gaps between them—is by overlapping the extremes when you begin. This method may be a bit confusing at first, but once understood can be used for even the most complex color blends.

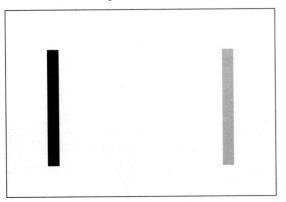

Figure 12.124 *Create two rectangles, and fill*

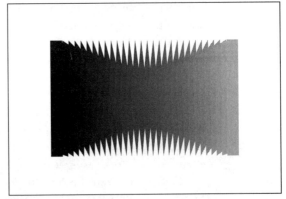

Figure 12.125 *Blending between anchor points that do not correspond.*

Figure 12.126 *Not enough steps.*

Start by creating a rectangle the size of the whole color blend (see Figure 12.127) and then a thin rectangle of the same height, aligning it with one of the side edges of the large rectangle (see Figure 12.128). Be sure that the smaller rectangle is on top of the larger one, or the smaller one will not be visible. Paint each rectangle the desired extreme colors, and blend between the two corresponding anchor points. In a situation such as this, it is easier to click on the corresponding anchor points at the corners that are not aligned with each other (see Figure 12.129). This is because clicking on the anchor points located at the aligned corners will be difficult, as they are on top of each other. Input the desired number of steps and click OK.

Creating color blends with this method assures that there will never be any gaps between the steps. Since the two extremes are on top of each other, all the in-betweens are sandwiched between them and are overlapping each other. Inputting even a very small number of steps will still cover the blend area solidly (see Figure 12.130). Keep in mind that if not enough steps are used in a given size area, some

Figure 12.127 *Create a large rectangle.*

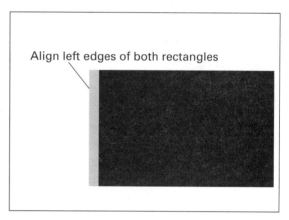

Figure 12.128 *Align the two rectangles.*

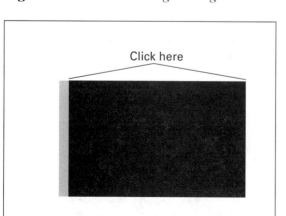

Figure 12.129 *Blend the two rectangles.*

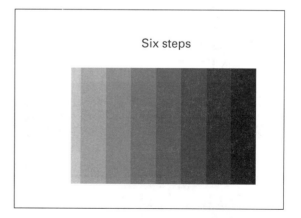

Figure 12.130 *Not enough steps.*

color banding may occur. Banding is evident in a blend when the change from one shade of color to the next is not smooth, but rather abrupt with visible lines between the different shades. This is usually a result of not enough blending steps, or a very subtle color change over a large area.

If you do use the overlapping closed paths method to create blends, there is still a better way to construct the extremes: Start by creating the large rectangle in the same way, but to create the small rectangle on top aligned with one of the large rectangle edges, select the large rectangle and choose the Scale tool. Click to establish the point of origin along the edge of the large rectangle where you want the two rectangles to align (see Figure 12.131). Move to the opposite side of the rectangle, hold down the **Option** and **Shift** keys, and drag horizontally toward the point of origin to scale a duplicate of the rectangle horizontally. A duplicate rectangle will be created on top of the large rectangle and aligned with its edge. Release the mouse button when the second rectangle is of desired thickness (see Figure 12.132).

This is a good technique to become accustomed to using, because when you start creating blends using more complex paths, you will not have to worry about maintaining the same number of anchor points in the extremes. Once you are comfortable creating linear color blends in this way, the transition to creating radial and complex path color blends will be a breeze.

To create a radial color blend, create a circle that will describe the outer edge of the color blend (see Figure 12.133). Select the circle and choose the Scale tool; clicking to establish the point of origin where you want the color blend to end (see Figure 12.134). Hold down the **Option** and **Shift** keys to scale the circle uniformly while making a duplicate (see Figure 12.135). Paint each circle the desired extreme colors and blend by clicking on the corresponding anchor points. Once you input the number of steps, click OK and the radial blend will be created (see Figure 12.136).

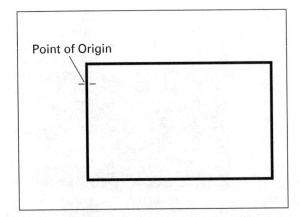

Figure 12.131 *Establish the point of origin.*

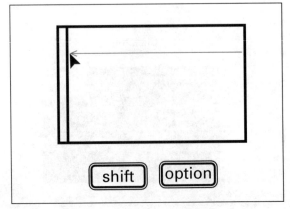

Figure 12.132 *Scale the rectangle horizontally while creating a duplicate.*

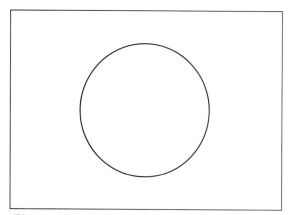

Figure 12.133 *Draw a circle.*

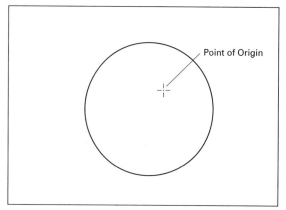

Figure 12.134 *Establish the point of origin.*

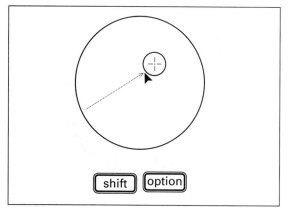

Figure 12.135 *Scale the circle uniformly while creating a duplicate.*

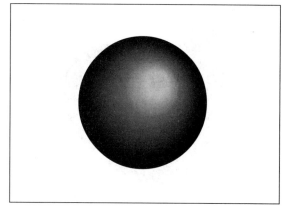

Figure 12.136 *Radial blend.*

To better understand how this blend works, imagine a series of circles stacked atop each other; each circle is a little smaller than the one beneath it and slightly different in color. This arrangement is easy to see when a small number of steps is used. Figure 12.137 shows the same color blend using only four in-between steps, illustrating the basic concept of how overlapping closed path blends work.

With this in mind, let us move to more complex shape blends. In Illustrator, color blends can be created from any path shape, allowing for a variety of color blend effects. For instance, create the abstract shape shown in Figure 12.138. The steps to creating a blend with this shape are similar to those used when creating the basic linear and radial color blends. Simply select the path and scale it to create a smaller duplicate (see Figure 12.139). Paint each shape with a different color, choose the Blend tool, and click on the corresponding anchor points. After clicking OK in the Blend dialog box, the blend will be created (see Figure 12.140).

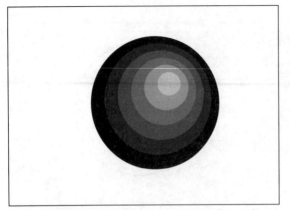

Figure 12.137 *Different size and color circles placed on top of each other.*

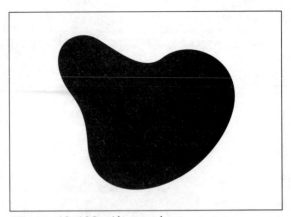

Figure 12.138 *Abstract shape.*

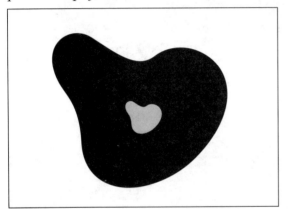

Figure 12.139 *Scaled duplicate.*

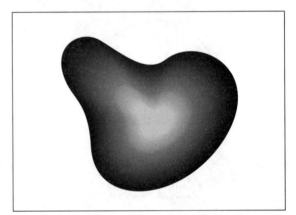

Figure 12.140 *Abstract path blend.*

This type of fluid, irregular color blend is impossible to achieve with Adobe Illustrator's Gradient feature. A blend like this—and ones similar to it—are perfect for creating smooth, uneven surfaces, such as fabrics, clouds, and shading for human features. Figure 12.141 shows an image representing a piece of fabric with subtle folds and creases. Figure 12.142 shows the same image with the extreme shapes before they were blended. The trick to having blends flow smoothly into the background color is to make the large shape, which describes the outside edge of the color blend, the same color as the background. That is why the shapes in Figure 12.142 cannot be seen in the Preview mode.

Taking the fabric rendering one step further, the blends can be created in such a way as to imitate the fabric folds' tendency to be smooth at one place and sharp in another. This effect is achieved by positioning the extreme shapes so that their outlines are closer to each other in one spot and further from each other in another (see Figure 12.143). In those areas where the two extreme shapes are in proximity to each other, the color

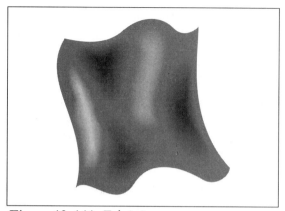

Figure 12.141 *Fabric image.*

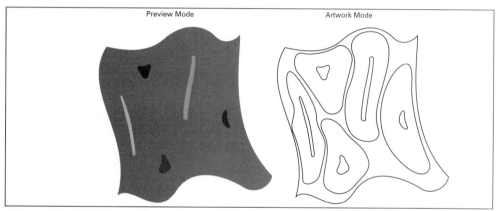

Figure 12.142 *The extreme shapes of the blends in the fabric image.*

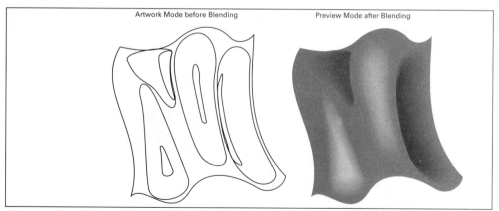

Figure 12.143 *Positioning the extremes with one side aligned.*

blend will be sharp, and vice versa. The realism that can be achieved with these techniques can be quite pleasing.

A few things to keep in mind when creating such complex shaped blends: Sharp corner points, on either of the extreme shapes, can result in a portion of the blend having an edge-like appearance (see Figure 12.144); this characteristic can serve to create a desired effect if used properly. Figure 12.145 shows a closed path color blend created from a star shape. In this case, the edges created by the sharp corners are preferable and give the 3-dimensional star a realistic appearance.

Another glitch that can occur in complex shape blends is the overlap of the in-betweens across the outer edge of the extreme. This will happen when the shape of the two extremes and their relative positions to each other are set in a certain way. There is no rule to help you predict when the overlap will happen; trial, error, and experience are your only guide.

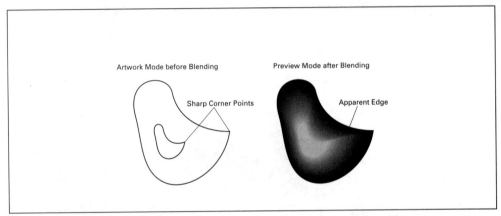

Figure 12.144 *Edges in a blend.*

Figure 12.145 *Desired edges in a blend.*

Figure 12.146 shows two extreme shapes about to be blended. Study these paths closely and note the locations of all the anchor points. Since, in this case, both paths are identical except for their size, the corresponding anchor points between the two paths can be easily identified. Simply draw or imagine straight lines between each pair of corresponding anchor points of the two paths (see Figure 12.147) and you will notice right away that one of the lines crosses over the larger shape and goes outside of it. If the two paths are blended with each other, the in-betweens will also cross the larger shape and go outside of it, creating a sharp overlap (see Figure 12.148).

There may be some occasions when you want this effect, but it can be frustrating if it comes as a surprise. To eliminate this kind of overlap, one of the paths must be reshaped. In most cases, the smaller inside path would need reshaping, because the large path is usually constructed first to a preferred shape. Move the anchor points around and adjust the direction handles, if needed, until the imaginary straight lines between the corresponding anchor points of the two paths all fall inside the larger

Figure 12.146 *Shape and a scaled duplicate.*

Figure 12.147 *Lines between corresponding points cross the larger path outline.*

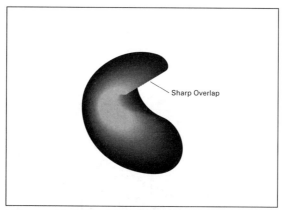

Figure 12.148 *An overlap in a blend.*

shape (see Figure 12.149). The resulting color blend will now be smooth without sharp edges (see Figure 12.150).

Multicolor blends can also be created with the Blend feature in Illustrator. The number of different colors you can have in a blend is not restricted, as with the Gradient feature, although I have never had to use more than 34 different colors in a blend—nor would I want to, since it is very time-consuming. To have more than two extreme colors in a blend, extra paths must be created to provide something to which the colors may be assigned. This, as usual, may be done in more than one way.

First, create the larger shape for the outer edge of the color blend (see Figure 12.151), and then scale this shape down while creating a duplicate. Make the duplicate only a bit smaller than the original shape (see Figure 12.152). Repeat this step using the smaller duplicate shapes until you have the necessary number of shapes (see Figure 12.153). Assign a different fill color to each shape and blend from first to second, second to third, and so on (see Figure 12.154). Instead of scaling each shape separately,

Figure 12.149 *Adjust the shapes so that the lines between the corresponding points do not cross the larger path outline.*

Figure 12.150 *Blend without an overlap.*

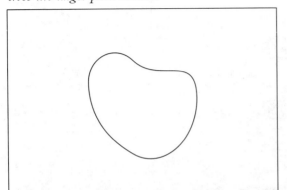

Figure 12.151 *Abstract shape.*

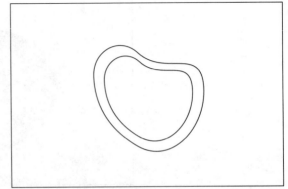

Figure 12.152 *Scaled duplicate.*

you may use the Repeat Transform option after the first shape has been scaled by going to the Arrange menu and choosing Repeat Transform (**Command + D**) once the first shape has been scaled (see Figure 12.155 a-d).

You can also achieve this effect with the Blend tool. This is preferable when you know where the two extreme colors should be and you want the other colors to be equally spaced between them. Create the two extreme shapes with any of the methods described earlier (see Figure 12.156) and select them both, blending them with the number of steps equal to the number of different colors you want in your blend (see Figure 12.157). Select each shape separately and assign colors to them before you proceed to blend each pair of shapes one at a time (see Figure 12.158).

This last technique is especially useful when making multicolor blends between paths of a different shape (see Figure 12.159). Since the scaling method reduces the size of an object without affecting its shape when uniformly scaled, to blend between objects of different shapes, each object must be created separately. Remember that

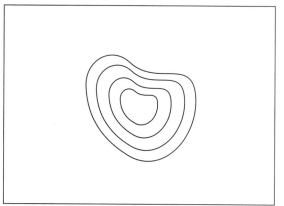

Figure 12.153 *Multiple scaled duplicates.*

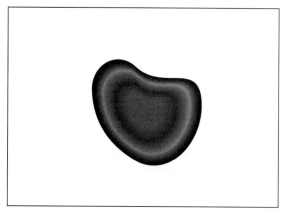

Figure 12.154 *Multicolor blend.*

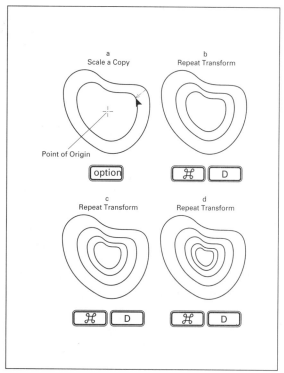

Figure 12.155 *Creating multiple scaled duplicates with Repeat Transform.*

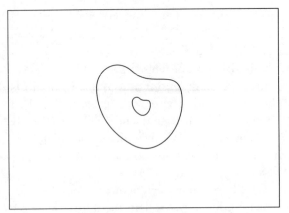

Figure 12.156 *Two extreme shapes.*

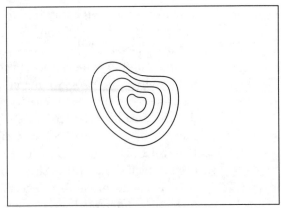

Figure 12.157 *Three-step blend.*

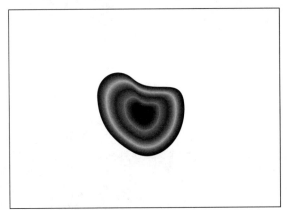

Figure 12.158 *Multicolor blend.*

when the scale method is not used, you must be sure that the number of anchor points on both paths is the same, and that the imaginary straight lines between a pair of corresponding anchor points do not overlap the outline of the larger path (see Figure 12.160). Once that is checked, blend the two shapes with the amount of steps that is the same as the number of different colors you want in the blend (see Figure 12.161), or simply blend the colors of the two existing shapes to create a two-color blend (see Figure 12.162).

Closed-path color blends can be used to create almost any kind of blending effect, except one: To create an image resembling a 3-dimensional wire or tube, open paths painted with strokes are best to use. To create the image shown in Figure 12.163, two open paths identical in shape, painted with different weight and color strokes, and placed directly on top of each other were used.

First, create an open path of a desired shape and paint it with a stroke. The weight of the stroke should be the same as the thickness you want the tube to be, and the color should be the darkest color of the blend (see Figure 12.164). Next, copy the

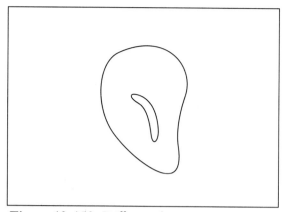

Figure 12.159 *Different shape extremes.*

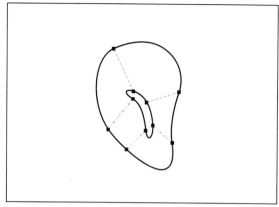

Figure 12.160 *Checking the corresponding points.*

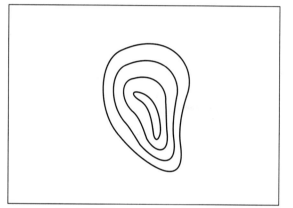

Figure 12.161 *Two-step blend.*

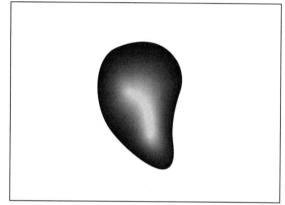

Figure 12.162 *Blending between two different shape extremes.*

path and paste the copy directly in front of the original. Paint the copy with a light color and a much thinner stroke. For this example I used a 100-percent black, 10-point stroke for the bottom path, and a 10-percent black, 1-point stroke for the path on top (see Figure 12.165).

You will now need to blend the two paths, although this may be problematic because all the corresponding anchor points are directly on top of each other and the Blend tool recognizes only the topmost point. To get around this, use the Zoom tool to zoom in—as much as possible—on one of the ends of the paths. The best way to do this is by dragging a small marque around one of the end points with the Zoom tool selected (see Figure 12.166)—that location will be immediately magnified to 1,600 percent (see Figure 12.167).

Now choose the Artwork mode from the View Menu so that the paths and points may be seen better, and choose the Direct Selection tool from the toolbox. Click and drag the end point of the topmost path a very short distance along the outline of the path (see Figure 12.168), just enough so that the end point of the bottom path is

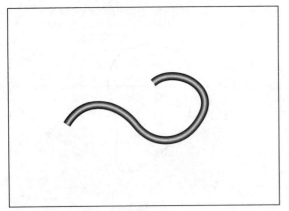

Figure 12.163 Tube blend.

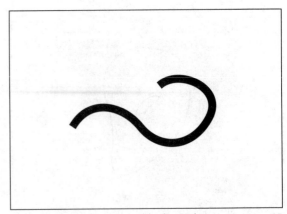

Figure 12.164 10-pt black stroke.

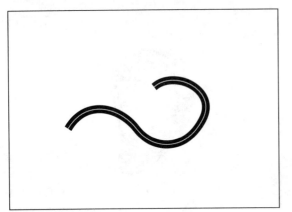

Figure 12.165 10-pt black stroke with a 1-pt gray stroke on top.

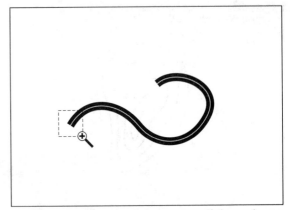

Figure 12.166 Zoom in on one of the ends.

clearly visible. Next, select both paths and click on both end points with the Blend tool. Zoom out and deselect all the in-betweens (**Command + Shift + A**) to clearly see the whole blend (see Figure 12.169).

Another way to access the end point of the bottom path is to move the whole top path a very small amount, about one-half point to 1 point. You can do this by using the Move dialog box discussed in Chapters 3 through 5. This will also produce a highlight that is slightly off center and can add to the realism of the image (see Figure 12.170).

Multicolor blends can also be created with line blends in the same way as with shape blends. Simply blend the two open paths with the number of steps of different colors you wish to have, and use the Blend tool on one pair of paths at a time. When creating multicolor blends with either lines or shapes, it is always best to start from the bottommost path and work your way up. It will be easier to select the anchor points of paths if there are no in-betweens on top, obstructing the view.

Figure 12.167 *Magnified view.*

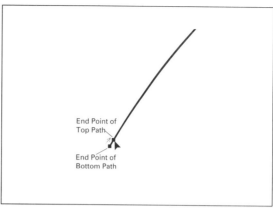

Figure 12.168 *Move the top end point.*

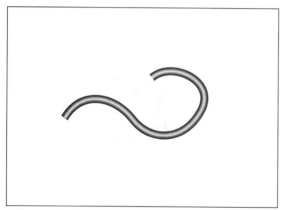

Figure 12.169 *Tube blend.*

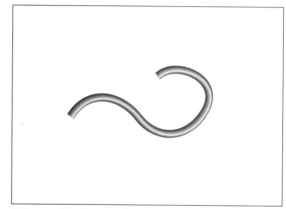

Figure 12.170 *Offset tube blend.*

When creating line blends, keep in mind the Joins and Caps settings in the Paint Style palette; different settings will produce different results, as shown in Figure 12.171. You cannot blend between different Caps and Joins settings, so make sure that all the extreme paths have the same Caps and Joins settings.

Masking Blends

When masks are used in combination with blends, almost any kind of realistic rendering effect can be achieved. To mask a simple linear blend, create the blend as described in the previous section (see Figure 12.172) and construct a path to be used as a mask. For this example, I again used a star shape (see Figure 12.173). Position the mask shape on top of the blend cluster (see Figure 12.174), select the whole configuration and choose Mask > Make from the Object menu. The star's paint style attributes will be disregarded and the linear blend will appear inside the star shape (see Figure 12.175).

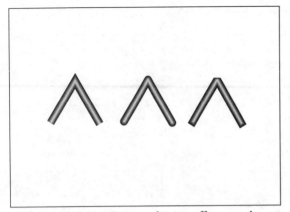

Figure 12.171 *Caps and joins effects on the tube blend.*

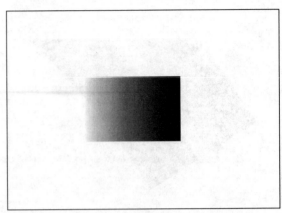

Figure 12.172 *Linear blend.*

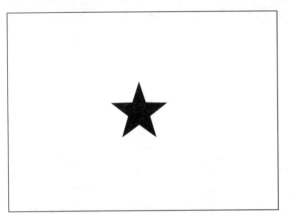

Figure 12.173 *Star shape.*

Figure 12.174 *Star shape on top of a linear blend.*

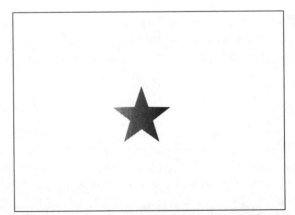

Figure 12.175 *Linear blend masked by the star shape.*

Of course, the same effect may be achieved by simply filling the star with a gradient, but as you already know, not all kinds of color blends can be achieved with the Gradient feature. The next few examples will demonstrate how masks and blends are used together to create realistic rendering effects.

For our first example, we will use shape blends and a mask to render a phonograph record. Start by constructing the triangle shown in Figure 12.176a. Next, create a smaller triangle on top, the same height but thinner so that the top corner and bottom edge align (see Figure 12.176b). Rotate both triangles while making three duplicates using the top corner as the focal point (see Figure 12.176c).

Select two of the smaller triangles and rotate them a few degrees so that they are not centered with the larger triangles underneath them (see Figure 12.176d). Draw a

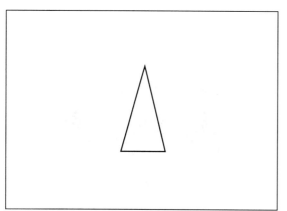

Figure 12.176a *Create a triangle.*

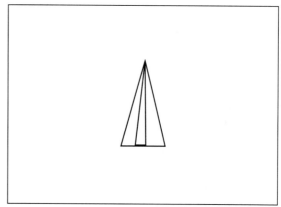

Figure 12.176b *Create a smaller triangle.*

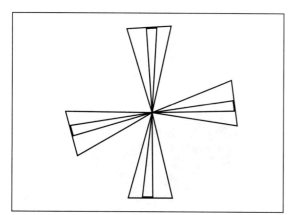

Figure 12.176c *Rotate and duplicate both triangles.*

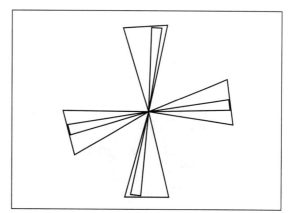

Figure 12.176d *Offset two of the smaller triangles.*

circle with its center point at the location where all the triangles meet, but not larger than the length of the triangles (see Figure 12.176e). Send this circle to the back, painting it and the large triangles 100-percent black. This will be the main color of the record.

Select the two small triangles, which are not centered, with the large triangles underneath them and paint them 20-percent black. Select one of the other two small triangles and paint it 70-percent black and the other 80-percent black (see Figure 12.176f).

Blend each pair of small and large triangles (see Figure 12.176g). Copy the circle and paste it in front of the whole image (see Figure 12.176h), then select the whole image—including the duplicate circle—and choose Mask > Make" from the Object menu (see Figure 12.176i).

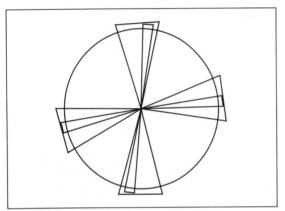

Figure 12.176e *Create a circle.*

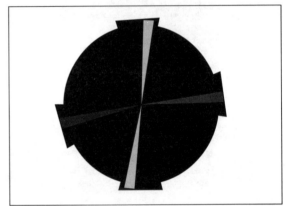

Figure 12.176f *Paint the shapes.*

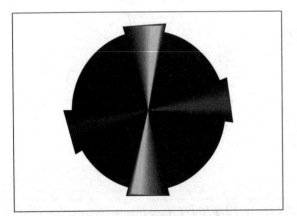

Figure 12.176g *Blend the triangles.*

Figure 12.176h *Paste a copy of the circle on top.*

As the final step, create two smaller circles on top of the whole image and paint the larger one with 60-percent black for the label, and the smaller one white for the hole (see Figure 12.176j). (You can use the same technique with different colors to create a compact-disc rendering.)

The next example will use a more advanced technique of mask and blend combinations to realistically shade a portion of a tree branch. Begin by creating a branch shaped path with the Pen tool (see Figure 12.177). (Because of the color limitations of this book, I will use shades of black, but you should follow along using shades of brown for more realism.) Paint the branch shape with a light shade and then create paths that will be used as the light shade extremes of the blends (see Figure 12.178).

While creating these shapes, a very important concept must be observed. The sections of the extreme paths that fall inside the branch shape outline will be the starting points of the color blends that will be darker as they near the edge of the branch shape. The sections of the extreme paths that fall outside of the branch shape outline will be masked out by the branch shape outline and will not be visible in the final rendering.

To minimize the complexity and memory consumption of the image, maintain the portions of the extreme paths, which are outside the branch shape, as straight line segments. Even if you need to use more straight line segments on each extreme path than if you had used curved line segments, using straight line segments instead of curves will minimize the complexity.

Next, we need to construct the other extreme paths to specify the location of the darkest color shade on the branch. Realistically, the darkest shade of color on the branch will be at the very edge of the branch shape. Create the darker-shade extreme shapes on top of the lighter-shade extreme shapes, as shown in Figure 12.179. Be sure that the number of anchor points of the light and dark extreme shapes is the same, and that the corresponding anchor points line up properly.

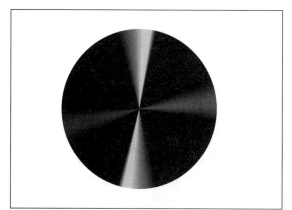

Figure 12.176i *Make a mask.*

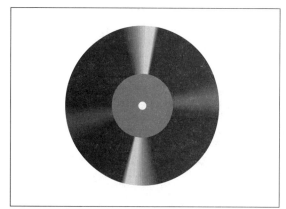

Figure 12.176j *Create two smaller circles to complete the image.*

Paint the smaller extreme shapes on top with a darker shade of color, and blend each pair of extremes. Copy the branch shape and paste it in front of the entire image. Select everything and go to the Object menu to choose Mask > Make. A realistic, 3-dimensional branch will be rendered (see Figure 12.180). This is an ideal technique to use when trying to achieve realism on dimensional, natural objects. such as plants, animals, landscapes, fabrics, and human features.

Another interesting effect produced by the combination of masks and blends is the variation in shading along the edge of an object. For this example, we will use a partially rendered human profile. Use the Pen tool to create the outline of a profile as shown in Figure 12.181. (You can scan the image in Figure 12.181 into your computer to use as a template.)

If you did not have too much trouble drawing this path with the Pen tool, Congratulations! You have done a great job learning the techniques described earlier in the book. If, however, you are still a bit uncomfortable with the Pen tool, you can

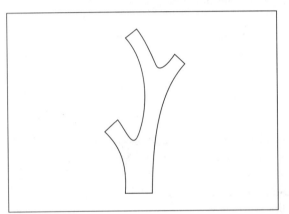

Figure 12.177 *Create a branch shape.*

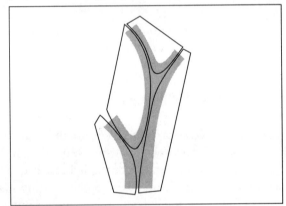

Figure 12.178 *Create the first extreme paths.*

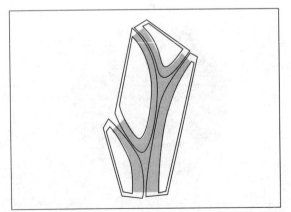

Figure 12.179 *Create scale duplicates of the first extreme paths.*

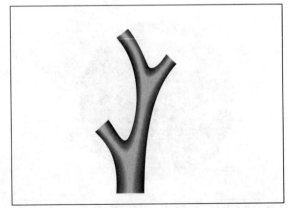

Figure 12.180 *Blend and mask to complete the image.*

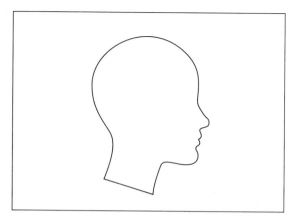

Figure 12.181 *Draw a human profile.*

use the Freehand or Auto trace tools to create this shape. Make sure, though, that the profile shape is a single closed path.

For this example, we will use only one specific technique that will demonstrate one realism effect. (To actually render a full human face, a combination of many different techniques will be required.) When the light hits the contours of a human profile, there is a natural tendency for the shading to be darker at the edges, just as with the branch rendering. In addition, since the profile has many protrusions (e.g., the nose, lips, and chin), the shading along the profile contour has to vary from dark to light. For instance, the top of the nose will be lighter than the space between the nose and upper lip. This is the effect we will try to achieve in this example by positioning different parts of the dark and light extremes of the blend closer to or further away from the profile path outline. The profile path will then be used to mask out those sections of the blend we do not want to show.

As with the branch example, we will need to create a path to be the lighter extreme of the shade blend. This path will be the same color as the profile path and will gradually blend into the darker extreme of the shaded blend as it gets closer to the edge of the profile. When constructing the first extreme path, keep in mind that the further away the outline of this path is from the edge of the profile, the more of the blend will be seen inside the profile shape and the darker the color will be at that place. In the areas where the outline of the lighter extreme is closer to the edge of the profile, less of the blend will show and there will be less room for the blend to get darker.

Therefore, construct the lighter extreme path in such a way that its outline is further away from the profile edge where you want the shading to be darker, and closer to the profile edge where the shading should stay light (see Figure 12.182). Similarly, the darker extreme of the blend will be drawn on the outside of the profile shape and will indicate the areas where the shading will be darker or lighter at the edge of the profile. The areas where the darker extreme will be closer to the edge of the profile will be darker, and lighter where it is further away.

The best way to construct the second extreme shape is to scale a duplicate of the first one and adjust the anchor points and direction handles. This will ensure that both paths have the same number of anchor points (see Figure 12.183). Paint the larger extreme shape a dark shade of color and send it to the back, then paint the smaller extreme shape a light shade of the same color, bringing it to the front. Select the profile path, bring it to the front, and paint it with none. Blend the two extreme shapes, select the whole image and go to the Object menu and choose Mask > Make. Your rendering should begin to resemble the early stages of a realistic dimensional human head (see Figure 12.184). Of course, in order to complete the illustration, eyes, lips, ears, and hair would need to be added. Some or all of the techniques discussed earlier may be used for the facial features and variations in the surface of the face, such as the protruding cheekbones or indented eye sockets.

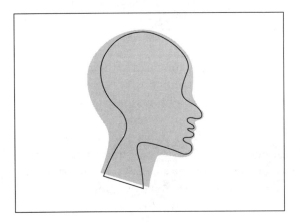

Figure 12.182 *Create the first extreme shape.*

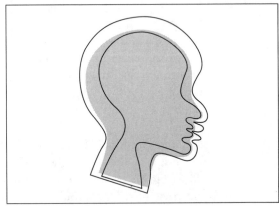

Figure 12.183 *Create the second extreme shape.*

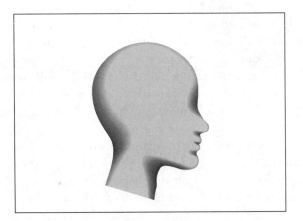

Figure 12.184 *Blend and mask to complete the image.*

As you know, the computer has no imagination or observation skills. To achieve realistic effects in Illustrator, you must decide what the end result should look like and then use different techniques to achieve these results, providing the computer with what, where, how, and when to perform a function.

People observe things differently, as evidenced by the classic optical illusion shown in Figure 12.185; you may see a vase or two profiles. With this in mind, the techniques I use to create certain effects are by no means exclusive and should be looked at as only one of many ways to do something. Ideally, you should combine your own knowledge and imagination to bring your renderings to life.

The next example involves a technique that uses masks to create a transparency effect; as you may recall from the "Mask Paths" section, we used the same method to create two transparent circles (see Figure 12.186). Now, we will try this technique in combination with blends, using the fabric drawing from Figure 12.141 and rendering a translucent shape on top of it so that the fabric shows through and changes color (see Figure 12.187). (Again, due to the color limitations of this book, my rendering will be in shades of black, but you should use color. I suggest simple primary colors: blue for the fabric, yellow for the translucent shape, and green where the fabric shows through the translucent shape—yellow + blue = green.)

Start by creating the fabric image, as described earlier and draw the yellow shape, which will be rendered translucent, on top of it. Be sure that it is a single closed path. At this point, the yellow shape is opaque and will completely cover the fabric where

Figure 12.185 *Optical illusion.*

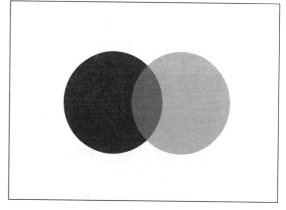

Figure 12.186 *Translucent circles.*

the two overlap (see Figure 12.188). To give the yellow shape a translucent effect, we will create a duplicate of the fabric image and rerender it in green. A copy of the yellow shape will then be used as a mask for the green fabric duplicate so that the green will be visible only inside the yellow shape.

Select the fabric image and yellow shape, and copy them by choosing Copy from the Edit menu or press (**Command + C**). Next, hide both images from the screen by selecting them and going to the Arrange menu to choose Hide, or by pressing **Command + 3**. Use the Paste in Front command from the Edit menu—or press **Command + F**—to paste the copied duplicates in the same spot as the originals. The next step will be a bit more time-consuming, but if the fabric image was built right, it shouldn't be that bad and will be worth it in the end.

Select and delete the in-betweens of all the blends in the fabric image. The in-between steps of a blend are automatically grouped together so that when you use the Group Selection tool to click twice on one of the in-between paths, all of the in-between paths of that blend should be selected. Press the **Delete** button to clear them from your document, making sure that only the in-betweens are deleted and the extremes remain (see Figure 12.189).

After you have deleted all the in-betweens, select all the extremes of the same shade of blue and change them to a green of similar intensity. Repeat this with the other extremes of the same shade of blue, including the background fabric shape itself (see Figure 12.190). Once you have changed all the dark-shade extremes to a dark shade of another color, and all the light-shade extremes to a light shade of another color, reblend the extremes as they were originally. You should now have a fabric image with all the same folds and wrinkles as the original, but in a different color (see Figure 12.191).

The yellow shape should still be on top of the new fabric image. Select both the yellow shape and new fabric image, and choose Mask > Make from the Object menu. The green fabric should now be visible only within the mask shape (see Figure 12.192). Finally, go to Show All in the Arrange menu, or press **Command + 4** and

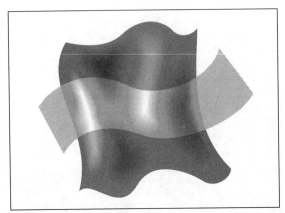

Figure 12.187 *Translucent shape on top of the fabric image.*

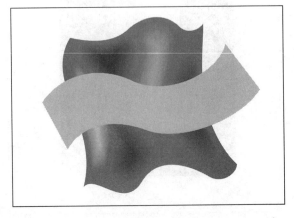

Figure 12.188 *Create a solid shape on top of the fabric image.*

the original fabric and yellow shape should be visible under the new masked fabric image. This will create the illusion of a translucent yellow color on top of blue fabric (see Figure 12.193).

To summarize this technique, there is a blue fabric image on the bottommost layer; on top of that is the solid yellow shape. The topmost layer consists of a green copy of the fabric image masked by a duplicate of the yellow shape. The green fabric is visible only inside the yellow shape so that the blue fabric underneath it can be seen where the yellow shape does not overlap it. Understanding the concept of layering, by which this effect was achieved, is important as you develop expert Adobe Illustrator skills, and will be mentioned again in the next chapter.

Our final example will incorporate both the Mask and Compound Paths with blends to achieve yet another realistic effect. Let us suppose that the fabric rendering

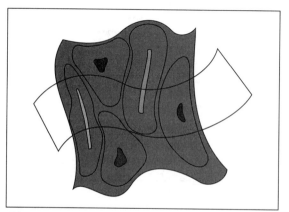

Figure 12.189 *Extremes of the blends in the fabric shape.*

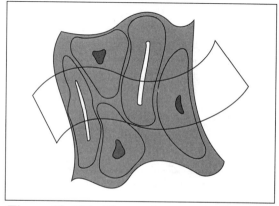

Figure 12.190 *Change the extreme colors.*

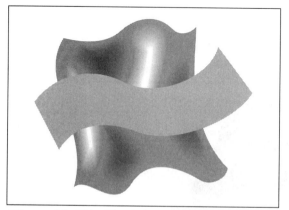

Figure 12.191 *Blend the new extremes*

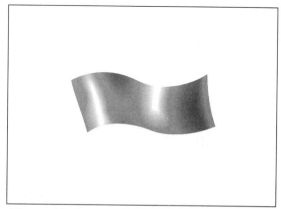

Figure 12.192 *Mask the new fabric image with the top shape.*

has a design on it. The folds and wrinkles in the fabric would also be seen through the design on that fabric. We will start by creating a design for the fabric, made of several closed paths. I will use a number of star shapes, but you can create any other design, as long as it consists of several closed paths that do not overlap each other.

Create the design and place it on top of the fabric image (see Figure 12.194). Select all the paths in the design, not including the fabric rendering, and choose Compound Paths > Make from the Object menu. The paint style of the design shapes is irrelevant at this time. Copy the fabric image and hide the original before pasting the copied fabric image behind the star shapes by selecting the whole star shape compound path and going to Paste in Back in the Edit menu (or press **Command + B**). Delete the in-betweens of all the blends in the fabric image, and duplicate and paint all the extremes and the background fabric shape a different color (see Figure 12.195).

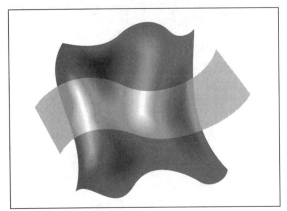

Figure 12.193 The final image.

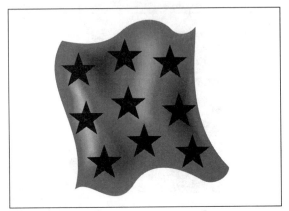

Figure 12.194 Position the star shapes on top of the fabric image.

Figure 12.195 Delete the in-betweens in the duplicate fabric image.

Be sure to keep the color shade relationship between the extremes the same as it was on the original. This color will be the color of your design. After changing the color of the extremes, reblend them (see Figure 12.196). Next, select the new fabric image and the star shapes, and choose Mask > Make from the Object menu. The new colored fabric image should now be visible only inside each star shape (see Figure 12.197).

Go to Show All under the Arrange menu to see the original fabric image. The star design should now look like it is part of the whole fabric image, with all the folds and wrinkles matching between the fabric and its design and only the color change occurring within the star shapes (see Figure 12.198).

The preceding techniques are complex and may not look exactly like my figures after your first attempt. You may want to look through the book to reinforce what you have learned and then try again, carefully following all the steps outlined. As with any

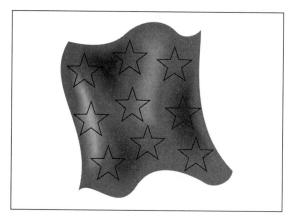

Figure 12.196 *Reblend the extremes in the new fabric image.*

Figure 12.197 *Mask the new fabric image with the compound star shapes.*

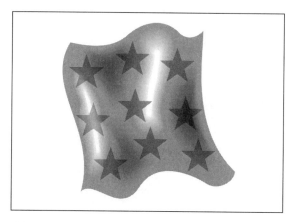

Figure 12.198 *The final image.*

program, it is essential that you understand a number of concepts to successfully create graphic images; these concepts are defined and illustrated throughout the book. Do not feel pressured or frustrated; take the time to read the book carefully and progress to the next topic only when you are comfortable with each technique. This way, you should have no difficulty completing the examples as I have.

The final chapter of this book will bring together many of the concepts discussed previously, so you will want to be sure that you are confident about your skills to fully appreciate the remaining discussion.

13 Combining Paths to Create Images

Welcome to the final chapter of the book. Assuming you have read the previous chapters thoroughly and are comfortable with the techniques described, you should be ready to dive into a serious illustration project. As with any project, preparation is the key to successful and trouble-free completion. Researching your subject, acquiring reference materials, making sketches, and eventually scanning a template are all very important steps. How your illustration will look and what techniques you will use will depend a great deal on the subject matter and your style. If you are creating an abstract illustration, it will not be as important to use a specific effect in a specific situation as it would be in a realistic illustration. An abstract image is just that, and it would be hard to say that a certain blend is in a wrong place or that a path is not shaped correctly. If, however, you are trying to achieve realism in your work, the use and placement of blends, gradients, patterns, strokes, shapes, and paths can contribute to or detract from the image.

It is difficult to generalize about the usage of techniques necessary to achieve a final product, as everyone's methods are unique. You may be the type of person who can sit in front of a blank computer screen and create a beautiful piece of artwork without any reference materials, sketches, or templates. There are, however, still a few guidelines and basic rules that you should be aware of for your artwork to be as efficient as possible. Following these guidelines will ensure that your artwork will print without any unpleasant surprises.

One of the questions most commonly asked about creating illustrations with Illustrator is: Where do I start? Even if you are aware of the different features of the program and are comfortable executing them, knowing where to start can still be a burden if you haven't had much experience. This situation is not limited to computer illustration.

Confronting a blank anything with only an artist's tool can be intimidating in any medium: A painter faces a blank canvas with just a brush; a sculptor, a block of wood or stone with only a chisel and mallet; and a computer graphics artist has to create artwork on a document page with the program's tools. When I sit down in front of a computer screen, I still start with the methods I learned in art school drawing and painting classes. That is: Start with a general layout to fill the page and add detail as you go.

Of course, the work you do before you first go to the toolbox to choose a tool is crucial in determining the difficulty or ease of your work. As mentioned earlier, I cannot stress enough the importance of reference sketches, templates, and choosing a general color palette. There is nothing more annoying than having to decide on and create colors when you are in the middle of working on your illustration. Please make it easier on yourself by creating a custom color palette of any colors you may use in your illustration before you begin.

The next stage begins when you first get an idea to do an illustration, and ends when the illustration is complete; that is, the analysis of the sketch or the reference. What you are basically doing is deciding how a certain image, shape, or effect can be rendered in Illustrator. For me, this process never ends. If you do become a frequent and proficient Illustrator user, you will instinctively start translating everything you see into how it would be constructed in Illustrator. Look at this book and think about the shapes of paths you would have to create to represent it in the program. How will those paths be positioned in relation to each other? Which path will go on top and which on the bottom? Should you use a gradient, or will you need to use a blend for the shading? Will you need to use strokes? Will there be any patterns? These are only a few of the questions you must ask yourself before the illustrating process begins. This chapter will take you through the steps and methods of combining paths to create images.

Overlapping and Layering

Creating illustrations with Adobe Illustrator is easy as long as you always approach it with one basic concept in mind: Working in Illustrator is like working with cut-out pieces of paper.

Imagine that you have a vast assortment of paper painted with any color, gradation, or pattern you can imagine. You are able to cut any 2-dimensional shape from those pieces of paper. Then you can arrange those different shaped pieces of paper on a page to create an image. In Illustrator, the cut-out pieces of paper are the paths you create with the drawing tools. The colors, gradations, and patterns are the attributes available in the Paint Style palette, and by using the Blend tool. All that is left to do is to arrange those paths on the document page.

We note, however, that—like the colored paper—the painted paths in Adobe Illustrator are opaque, and placing one path on top of another will obstruct the bottom one. The effects of transparency or translucency must be simulated by using masks and layering techniques. If you have read all the previous chapters in this book, you know how to make a variety of different shapes and paint attributes with the available tools. Now, we will concentrate on how to arrange those shapes using *Layering* and *Overlapping* to construct a desired image.

When two pieces of paper are placed on a page, they can either not touch at all, abut each other, or overlap (one atop the other). Adobe Illustrator provides you with commands to control the layering of paths on the page. These are Paste in Front (**Command + F**), Paste in Back (**Command + B**), Send to Back (**Command + -**), and Bring to Front (**Command + =**). As you create the paths in Illustrator, they build logically in sequence so that the path that was created last is on top of the paths created previously. Therefore, it makes sense to start your image with the backmost objects and work your way toward the front.

If you wanted to create a square with a circle on top of it, you would naturally construct the square first and then the circle (see Figure 13.1). Now, let's say that part of the circle needs to be inside the square and part outside (see Figure 13.2); you can easily figure out the layering and positioning of the two paths. The whole square should be created first, and the circle positioned on top of it at the desired location. The portion of the square that is overlapped by the circle is not visible, because it is beneath the opaque circle path.

Inexperienced Illustrator users tend to overlook this concept. As a result, when creating intersecting shapes, the paths do not overlap but rather abut each other. This is mainly because of a failure to see intersecting paths as existing on different layers, and a tendency to arrange all objects as if they were on one layer. This means that the intersecting square and circle in Figure 13.2 would not be placed one on top of the other, but rather next to each other.

To achieve the same effect without overlapping the paths, a great deal of extra work would need to be done. The circle can remain the same shape, but the square must be constructed in such a way that the portion that would normally be covered by the circle is actually cut out of the square shape (see Figure 13.3). A circle is then created to abut the cut-out portion of this square to achieve the same result without overlapping the shapes (see Figure 13.4). I do not believe that even an ambitious novice would choose this method over the overlapping technique. Nonetheless, many people who have been using Illustrator for quite a while still abut paths. Besides the obvious time-consuming drawback, abutting paths creates a very distinct visual problem.

Let's return to the cut-paper analogy. If you had to actually cut out the portion of the square where the circle intersects it, how precisely do you think that cut out would match the outline of the circle? I am sure that you would agree that, without the aid of a precise cutting machine, it would be impossible to do. Unless the abutting shapes are cut so that the outlines match perfectly, gaps between those two shapes are likely to result. Fortunately, Adobe Illustrator does have a precise cutting machine: the *Minus Back* or *Minus Front filters*.

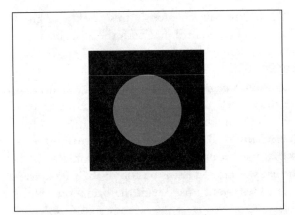

Figure 13.1 *A square with a circle on top.*

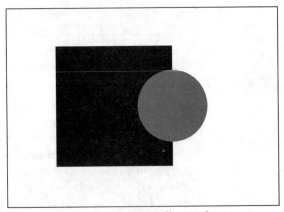

Figure 13.2 *A circle partially overlapping a square.*

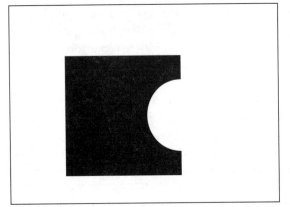

Figure 13.3 *Circle knocked out of the square.*

Figure 13.4 *Abutting the circle and the square.*

The Minus Back filter removes the portion of a shape where another shape underneath it intersects it, while the Minus Front filter cuts out the portion of a shape where another shape on top of it intersects it (see Figure 13.5). To use these filters, you would need to construct overlapping shapes atop each other, and would have then already created the desired image. Although overlapping shapes instead of abutting them is faster and more precise, there will be some cases where abutting paths cannot be avoided.

Figure 13.6 shows three intersecting shapes, each positioned in such a way that it is simultaneously on top of one shape and beneath another. You can see that the circle is on top of the square, but underneath the triangle, which is underneath the square. Since the circle cannot be on a layer on top of the square and underneath the square at the same time, some shapes must be abutted. As a general rule, it is always better to abut shapes that have straight edges instead of curved. This is primarily because it is much easier to align straight lines to each other than curves and because a certain amount of memory is saved.

Memory becomes a factor, because when you abut shapes, you create two outlines where there was only one. Creating two adjoining outlines with straight lines takes up less memory than with curves. Remember that when you are abutting paths, the Minus Back and Minus Front filters will be the best features to use since it is very difficult—even with the precision of the Pen tool—to draw a path that perfectly mimics another path's outlines. When you do use the Minus Back and Minus Front filters, be aware that the path that is being minused from another path will be deleted. There, you should be sure to make a copy of that path before executing the filter command so that you can paste it back into your document later.

When you are constructing an image in Illustrator, it is not always feasible to create the backmost objects first and the frontmost objects last. For instance, if you were drawing a human head (as shown in Figure 13.7), you would first need to analyze the shapes of paths necessary to create, as well as their layering. The most difficult aspect of analyzing an image is deciding where one path will end and the other begin; the cut-paper analogy can be helpful once again.

If you were in fact constructing this image out of cut pieces of paper, how many different shapes would you need? You can quickly and easily see that the image consists of hair, two ears, and the outline of the face. Those are exactly the paths you will need to create. Concluding the layering of these paths will again be pretty easy as you realize that the hair is on top of the face, and the ears are behind the hair. This is all the information necessary to construct this image. Since it would be difficult to create the ears before the face and hair, they should be drawn last, which would leave them on the layer atop the face and hair. Even if you cannot build your image in the proper layering, the other layer-shuffling commands may be used to adjust the layering of paths. The shuffling commands include: Paste in Front, Paste in Back, Bring to Front, and Send to Back.

In this case, simply select both ears and send them to the back (**Command + -**). The face image also brings up another important aspect of layering and overlapping

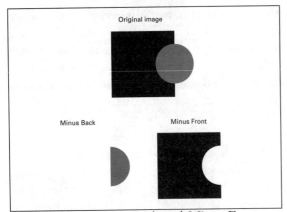

Figure 13.5 *Minus Back and Minus Front filters.*

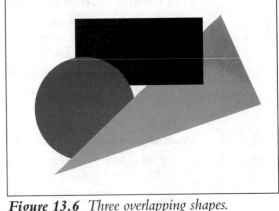

Figure 13.6 *Three overlapping shapes.*

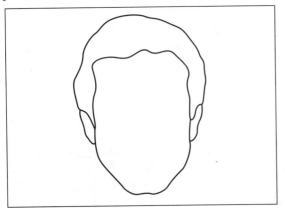

Figure 13.7 *Human face outline.*

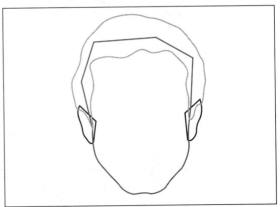

Figure 13.8 *How the shapes are constructed underneath other shapes.*

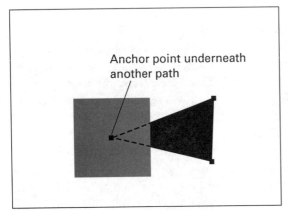

Figure 13.9 *Overlapping shapes.*

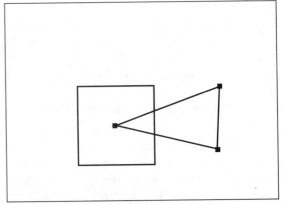

Figure 13.10 *Artwork mode.*

paths: What should the rest of the face outline path look like underneath the hair? The answer is: It does not matter, because that portion of the face path will be covered by the hair path. The aesthetics are of no consequence. However, keep in mind that curved line segments consume more memory than straight line segments, so it is always a good idea to construct the portion of a path covered by another path with straight line segments. Figure 13.8 shows the head image in Artwork mode to allow you to see how I chose to construct each path.

Selecting and Working with Layers

Selecting Obstructed Paths

One of the most beneficial aspects of creating artwork with Illustrator is the ease with which it can be edited. If the shape of the face you just rendered is not quite right, you can quickly and easily adjust the path until it looks correct. Of course, before any adjustments can be made, you must select the desired anchor points and/or direction handles. This can be difficult if the direction handle or anchor point you are trying to adjust is beneath another path (see Figure 13.9). One way to avoid that is to simply switch to the Artwork mode. This mode displays all the paths without their paint style attributes, allowing you to see sections of paths otherwise obstructed by paths on top of them (see Figure 13.10). However, this may not always work: for instance, if the anchor point you are trying to select is located directly underneath another path's out-line (see Figure 13.11).

In this case, a number of other methods may be used to access the desired anchor point: The top path can be locked, hidden, or toggle selected. By selecting the top path and locking it, you make that path unselectable and, therefore, you are able to select any path or point underneath it. The advantage to using this method is the ability to still see the top path while adjusting the one underneath it, which is helpful when the path underneath must be reshaped in relation to the path on top. Hiding the top path will also allow you to select the one underneath it, which is beneficial when the adjustment of the bottom path must be done without any visual interference from the one on top.

An example of when this would be most relevant is when the path you are trying to adjust is underneath a blend. Since blends tend to be composed of many objects placed very closely to each other, being able to see through them—even in the Artwork mode, with the blend being locked—can still be almost impossible (see Figure 13.12). Being able to select the whole blend with only one click becomes very important and is one of the reasons why the in-betweens of a blend are automatically grouped. Sometimes, a line segment or an anchor point can be obstructed by hun-

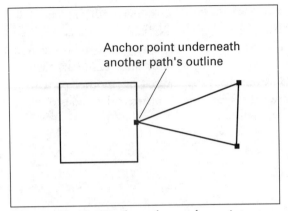

Figure 13.11 *Hard to select anchor point.*

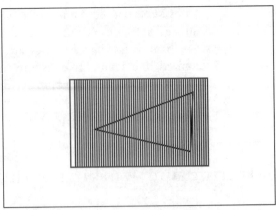

Figure 13.12 *Hard to select path.*

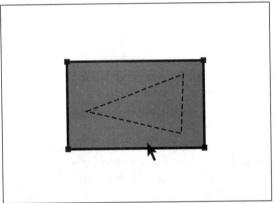

Figure 13.13 *Select the top path.*

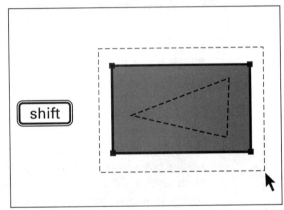

Figure 13.14 *Toggle selection.*

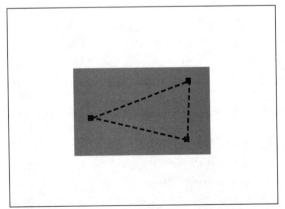

Figure 13.15 *The path underneath is selected.*

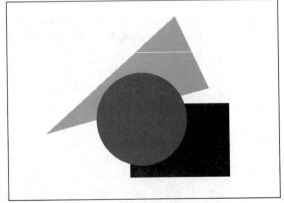

Figure 13.16 *Circle is on top.*

dreds of paths that are not part of any blend, but are simply a part of a very complex illustration. You should follow the example of the creators of Adobe Illustrator and group those sections of your illustration that consist of many different paths. This will enable you to select that whole section with one click to perform any number of editing procedures. Grouping objects is discussed in Chapter 5.

There will be some cases where locking or hiding paths that obstruct the one you need to work on is not desirable: for instance, if you already have some paths that are locked and others that are hidden. Adobe Illustrator's Hide and Lock features allow you to hide and lock paths or a number of paths one at a time, meaning that you can keep adding more and more paths to those already locked or hidden. You cannot, however, Unlock or Show some of the locked or hidden paths, as unlocking or showing will unlock or show all the paths that were locked or hidden, regardless of the order in which they were locked or hidden. This can create a problem when you have already locked or hidden a certain section of your illustration and now are working on another section in which a path is still in the way of another path. You need to be able to adjust the obstructed path of this section without adding any paths from this section of your illustration to the paths of the hidden or locked section.

To select an anchor point, line segment, or path without hiding or locking the one on top of it, a *toggle selection* can be used. Begin by using the solid arrow selection tool to select the top path (see Figure 13.13). Then, with the Direct Selection tool, hold down the **Shift** key and drag a marque across the whole top path, including the obstructed section of the path you wish to select (see Figure 13.14). The top path will be deselected, while the desired section of the path underneath will be selected (see Figure 13.15).

Your choice of selection tools will depend on the kind of selection you need to make. For instance, if you need to select the whole bottom path, use the solid arrow selection tool in both steps. In this example, to select the whole triangle path, the toggle selection is not necessary, because you can simply click with the solid arrow on any part of the path to select the whole path. If, however, you have two paths of exactly the same shape, one on top of the other, there is no way to access any section of the path on the bottom, because it is completely covered by the path on top. In this case, the toggle selection should be used.

Changing the Layering of Paths

As mentioned earlier, an illustration cannot be rendered with all the paths in the correct layers without having to shuffle the layering of some of those paths. Path layering can be changed with a combination of the four layer adjusting features mentioned in the beginning of this chapter: From the Arrange menu, the Bring to Front command (**Command + =**) puts the selected path or paths on top of all the other paths, and the Send to Back (**Command** + **-**) command puts the selected path or paths underneath all the other paths.

Greater control over the exact placement of the selected paths is achieved by using the Paste in Front (**Command** + **F**) or Paste in Back (**Command** + **B**) from the Edit menu. These commands allow you to place a path or paths precisely on top or beneath a specified path. For instance, to place the circle in Figure 13.16 between the square and triangle, select the circle and choose Cut from the Edit menu (or press **Command** + **X**). Next, select the square and choose Paste in Front from the Edit menu (or press **Command** + **B**). The circle will be placed underneath the square, but on top of the triangle (see Figure 13.17).

If no paths are selected, the circle will be pasted in back of all the paths in the document (see Figure 13.18). You can also select the triangle and choose Paste In Front, or press **Command** + **F**, for the circle to be placed on top of the triangle and underneath the square to achieve the same result as shown in Figure 13.17. If no paths are selected, the circle will be pasted on top of all the paths in the document (see Figure 13.19). Multiple paths can be cut and pasted in front or behind other paths using the same procedure.

After being able to create paths, having control over their layering is one of the most important factors of learning Adobe Illustrator. Since Illustrator works very similar to cut paper collage, proper positioning and layering of paths is crucial to the final outcome of your work. You cannot create an image in Illustrator without placing paths in specific layer combinations.

The Layers Palette

Adobe Illustrator provides you with yet another way to control the layering of paths. The *Layers palette* can be a powerful layer editing and control feature if used properly, but realize that improper use can be more detrimental to your work than not using this feature at all. An important thing to remember when using the Layers palette is that it should be used only with complex illustrations and a few unique instances when placed EPS images or extensive patterns and blends are present.

The primary objective of the Layers palette is to separate a complex illustration into sections consisting of multiple paths, and to assign them to their own layer in the document. For instance, if an illustration incorporates a sky with clouds and birds in the background, a forest with trees in midground, and a person in the foreground, these elements can be assigned to specific layers and controlled with the Layers palette. The difference between the usual layering of paths in Illustrator and using the Layers palette is that a layer created with the Layers palette can consist of any number of paths each on their own layer and all a part of a larger layer. These larger layers may be viewed separately and locked, hidden, or rearranged in relation to each other without affecting the layering of the paths within them. The Layers palette also allows you to set different colors for path outlines and anchor points for each layer so that they can be easily distinguished from other layers.

To access the Layers palette, go to the Window menu and choose Show Layers (or press **Command + Control + L**). When the Layers palette appears, it will display the existing layers and their controls (see Figure 13.20). The left column contains circles that indicate the status of the existing layers. The *eye* icon at the top of the left column represents the Show/Hide controls, and the *pencil* icon represents the Lock/Unlock controls. A solid black circle under the eye icon indicates that the layer is being shown and is in Preview mode. Clicking once on that circle will hide that layer and the circle will no longer be displayed. The circle under the pencil icon for the same layer will then be displayed as solid gray, indicating that the layer is hidden, but not locked.

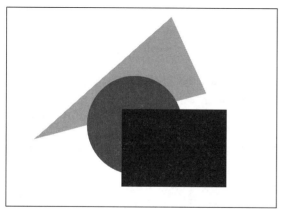

Figure 13.17 *Circle is on the middle layer.*

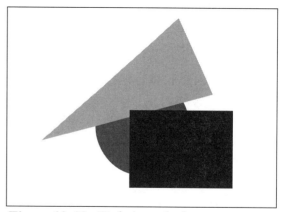

Figure 13.18 *Circle is on the bottom.*

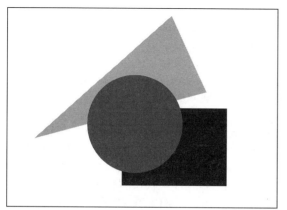

Figure 13.19 *Circle is on top.*

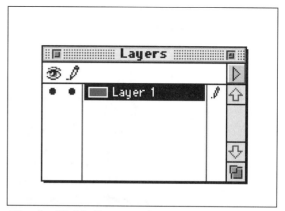

Figure 13.20 *Layers palette.*

Clicking again in the spot where the circle was displayed under the eye icon will show the layer.

The black circle under the eye icon will once again be visible, and the circle under the pencil icon will become solid black. Clicking on the black circle under the pencil icon will lock that layer and cause the circle to no longer be displayed; this does not affect the circle under the eye icon. Clicking again in the empty spot under the pencil icon will unlock that layer and display a solid black circle. A white circle with a black outline under the eye icon indicates that the layer is being shown and that it is in Artwork mode. To change the layer display from Artwork to Preview, and vice versa, hold down the **Option** key and click on the circle under the eye icon next to the desired layer.

The center column of the Layers palette contains the names and colors of all the layers in the document. As a default, there is always one layer called Layer 1 and it is blue. Clicking on the layer name will highlight that layer, indicating that the layer is active. A pencil icon will also be displayed in the right column of the Layers palette next to the active layer. A slash on top of that pencil icon appears, showing the active layer is locked. All the new paths created in the document will belong to the currently active layer.

Multiple layers may be selected by holding down the **Shift** key and clicking on the desired layers, or by dragging across a number of layers. Once a layer is made active, it can be moved around in relation to other layers in the Layers palette, and the options for that layer can be changed. The top layer in the Layers palette is the topmost layer in the document. To change the position of the active layer, click and drag that layer up or down to place it on top or underneath other layers.

Clicking the triangle in the upper right of the Layers palette displays a pop-up menu with the options available for the active layer. This menu also contains the *New Layer options*. Choosing *Delete Layer* from the pop-up menu will delete that layer and all the objects belonging to it. The *Hide Others/Show All, Artwork Others/Preview All*, and the *Lock Others/Unlock All* options produce the same results as clicking the circles under the eye and pencil icons in the Layers palette.

Choosing the *Paste Remembers Layers* will paste a copied object into the same layer it was copied from. Choosing the *New Layer* or *Layer Options* for the active layer will bring up an identical dialog box, which allows you to specify the name of the layer, its color, and Show, Preview, Lock, Print, and *Dim Placed Images* options. The Show, Preview, and Lock options have the same effects as clicking on the circles under the eye and pencil icons in the Layers Palette.

Checking the Print option will print that layer when the document is printed. Realize that if this option is not checked, the objects in that layer will not be printed. The Dim Placed Images option dims the placed EPS image by approximately 50 percent. If you choose New Layer from the pop-up menu, clicking OK will create a new layer with the specified options. If Layer Options for the active layer was chosen, clicking OK will change the attributes of that layer to the specified options.

Remember that it is a good idea to assign different distinct colors to each layer so that objects can be easily identified with the layer to which they belong. There is virtually no limit to the number of layers you can create with the Layers palette, but having too many layers will slow down the processing time of your computer. Personally, I have never had the need to create more than ten layers.

To move objects between layers, select the objects you wish to move and choose Show Layers from the Window menu. A small square will be displayed in the right column of the Layers palette next to a layer's name, representing the selected objects of that layer. Simply click and drag that square until it is next to the layer to which you wish to move the selected objects. A triangle will appear next to the name of the layer where the objects are being moved. Release the mouse button and the square will change to the color of that layer. All the selected objects will now be part of that layer, and their path outline and anchor point colors will change accordingly.

The Layers palette's main application is its ability to control the Hide, Lock, and Preview of the sections of a complex illustration. This allows you to work on the foreground portion of an illustration without any interference from the background image. Also, if a section of your illustration contains patterns or blends that take a long time to preview, you can set that section to Artwork mode while working on another section in Preview mode. The Layers feature is also helpful when using a placed EPS image instead of a template.

Assign the placed EPS image to a background layer, check Dim Placed Images in the Layer Options dialog box, and lock that layer. Create a new layer for the paths you will be constructing while tracing the placed EPS image. The advantages to tracing an EPS image—as opposed to a template—is being able to see more detail and subtle changes in shading, which are not visible in a template. Tracing templates and EPS images is discussed in Chapter 10.

Using the Layers feature also eliminates the layering problems discussed in the previous section. While you are working on a complex illustration, if a portion of it is already hidden or locked, hiding or locking additional objects will not allow you to show or unlock those objects without showing or unlocking all the previously hidden or locked objects. The Layers feature avoids that by allowing you to show, hide, lock, and unlock different sections of an illustration without affecting objects on other layers. This means that you can hide or lock all but the section you are working on. While you are working on that section or layer, you can hide and lock separate objects within that layer using the Hide and Lock commands in the Arrange menu. Those objects can then be shown or unlocked while other sections or layers of your illustration remain locked or hidden.

When you are working on a complex illustration or design, the Hide and Lock commands and the Layer shuffling features will be used frequently and will become routine operations. How you utilize these features will directly affect the quality and speed of your work. Understanding how Adobe Illustrator layers and displays paths, and being able to relate to the cut-paper-collage theory will eliminate a lot of frustration as you work with Illustrator.

Analyzing Image Construction

After you have learned all the features to create and manipulate paths with Adobe Illustrator, the hardest part remains interpreting what you see. Whether it is a reference photo, a drawing, a sketch, or an image from your head, you must still decide how it will translate into Adobe Illustrator artwork. Of course, certain images lend themselves more readily to translation than others. A photograph, for instance, is the hardest reference to interpret. Because subtle changes in color, shade, and detail are the hardest aspects to mimic with the Illustrator's tools, more interpretation is needed. A line drawing or a sharp-edged rendering requires less interpretation, because those properties are easier to mimic in Illustrator. This process becomes easier with experience but is never fully resolved, because each project presents a unique set of interpretation challenges that will differ with each image you choose to render.

Adopting the cut-paper-collage analogy is the first step to being able to translate what you see into what you render with Illustrator. Once you have acquired the reference material or sketch, imagine how you would represent that image with cut pieces of paper. This interpretation begins with a breakdown of the reference image into sections, and then further separating those sections into smaller parts or shapes. It is helpful at this point to draw a pencil sketch clearly outlining those shapes. For instance, Figure 13.21 shows a photograph that might be used as reference; after restudying this image, try breaking it down into smaller sections.

A number of methods can be used to help you better visualize general shapes of this image without concentrating on every single detail. First, try to blur your vision while looking at the photograph. The details seem to get lost and only the main, general shapes are visible. This particular technique is used by most artists almost instinctively, but if you have never tried this, it may take a little while to make your vision blurry instead of sharp. Once your vision becomes blurred, you should be able to almost count the different general shapes in the image. That will be the number of paths you begin with in Illustrator. At this point, you should not concern yourself so much with the shading and the detail of object in the image. The important thing is to establish a general layout of the image so that you have a basis to which the shading and details will be added.

Another technique for visualizing the general shapes in an image is adjusting the contrast of that image. This can be done with any scanning software or a photo manipulation program, such as Adobe Photoshop. This is like blurring your eyes but in a way is more precise. As you apply more contrast to the image, some of the detail will start to disappear, allowing you to see only the main, general shapes. This technique will also create sharper edges around those shapes by eliminating the subtle shading and bringing out the contrast between objects.

Figure 13.22 shows the reference photograph after its contrast and brightness have been altered in Adobe Photoshop. A template made from this image may look much better in Illustrator than the original photograph before it was adjusted. Since a template in Illustrator can be seen only as a black-and-white image, without any shading, a photograph with a lot of contrast will look more like the final template in Illustrator. To read more about templates, see Chapter 10.

Creating a sketch from reference material is another way to analyze the image before you create it in Illustrator. This is the method I use most often and it is perhaps the most beneficial in helping you translate what you see into what you draw. Placing a tracing paper over the reference shot will obstruct some of the details, allowing you to see the basic shapes. Using a pencil to outline those shapes will help you start the thinking process of how the image will be constructed in Illustrator, since while you are tracing, the interpretation has already begun.

At this point, you will be able to make a few basic adjustments to the general shapes and their layout. You can also make some decisions regarding how much detail to keep in the final illustration. As you outline the general shapes with a pencil, keep in mind the techniques and tools Illustrator offers to recreate those shapes, and how they will be arranged in relation to each other. Think about the paths and their characteristics: Will they be made of straight lines, curves, or a combination of the two? Will they be open or closed paths? Will they be painted with fills or strokes? Can a gradient be used or will you need to create blends? The more decisions you make before launching the Illustrator software, the less interpretation will be required while you are working. Drawing on the computer can be difficult enough without having to focus on the interpretation aspects of the creative process. As I've said previously, a majority of analysis and translation will be done while you are working, but you can save time and avoid frustration by preparing.

Figure 13.23 shows a pencil sketch outline of the reference photo; this is the best material to use as a template in Illustrator. The contours of shapes are clearly visible and will be much easier to trace with Illustrator's path-creating tools. The order of layering of those paths can also be determined (to a certain extent) as you analyze the

Figure 13.21 *Photo reference.*

Figure 13.22 *High-contrast photo.*

sketch. For instance, it may be clear from observation that the path outlining the saucer shape will be underneath the path outlining the cup shape.

Another exercise to help you translate the reference image into its Illustrator construction is to imagine what the paths underneath other paths will look like. In other words, how will the shapes overlap each other. You can even take the pencil sketch a step further by continuing to draw the outlines of shapes behind other shapes—as you would with Illustrator paths. (To make it less confusing, you may want to draw those sections a little lighter so that they do not interfere with the visible outlines.)

Figure 13.24 shows a sketch with the shape outlines drawn as they might look in Illustrator's Artwork mode. This will help you visualize the shapes as continuous, cut-out, solid sections instead of just lines that begin and end at specific locations. For instance, the outline of the saucer shape does not end when it reaches the outline of the cup shape, but rather continues behind the cup. Once you have analyzed the image and estimated how the paths will be constructed and arranged in relation to each other, you should consider how to organize and manage the different sections of the image. This particular picture can be easily broken down into its five main elements: the background, the plate with the croissant, the saucer with the cup and spoon, the newspaper, and the calculator with the ribbon. Establishing that breakdown will help you to better manage the whole illustration as you are working. Because at some point while creating this illustration you may need to work on any one element without the interference of the others, you can plan ahead and organize your artwork accordingly.

There are two main features in Illustrator that help you organize the artwork for easy selection and manipulation of different elements: One way is by grouping all the paths that are part of a specific section; for instance, the paths that make up the plate, croissant, and their shadows. The cup, saucer, spoon, and their shadows would be another group, and so on. This grouping will enable you to select a whole section with only one click, and not affect the other elements.

Figure 13.23 *Pencil outline sketch of the photo.*

Figure 13.24 *Pencil outline sketch showing some of the hidden path sections.*

The Layers palette may also be used to organize different sections of your artwork. Each main element or number of elements can be assigned to their own layers, allowing you to hide, lock, and preview them independently. Since the most time-consuming creative process is done while fine-tuning and detailing the artwork after all the basic elements have been constructed, taking some time in the beginning to organize your work can prove beneficial in the long run.

Working in Adobe Illustrator is not much different than working in any other environment with any other tools. There is a constant drive to accomplish a goal in the fastest, most efficient manner to produce the best possible product. During the Industrial Revolution, those goals provided the principal motivation behind the invention of the assembly line. The main concept behind assembly line production was to divide the construction process into separate steps. To achieve an end result of 100 bottles of soda, for instance, 100 bottles were first made, then filled, then capped, and finally labeled. Making, filling, capping, and labeling 100 bottles individually would have been a much more time- and energy-consuming (and costly) process. The same theory can be applied to many other creation and construction processes. To manage your time and energy while working in Illustrator, the same concepts can be utilized.

We have already discussed how to separate some of the production steps in Illustrator; once you begin constructing an image, these concepts should be put to use. For instance, create all the general shapes before detailing them, establish a general color palette instead of creating a new color each time you need one, and paint paths with the available paint style features before doing manual color blending. Of course, working in Illustrator is not like working on an assembly line, as many times the creative process can take you back a step as you move forward. However, once you become proficient in Illustrator, the creative process will be only a part of image creation, while the rest is manual labor. But, saving time and energy during the manual labor part will leave precious moments and vigor for the creative process.

After analyzing the reference material, thinking about the organization of its sections, and setting up a general palette, I begin the actual path construction. Even though I have already created a basic color palette for a particular illustration, I proceed with construction of the main, general sections using only one color. Since Adobe Illustrator assigns the same paint style attributes to the current path as to the one created previously, it would be too time-consuming to change the paint style attributes of each path as you went. Instead, I create all the basic, general paths first and then begin coloring them. Many of the paths may be painted with the same color fill or stroke or gradient, and those paths can be selected together and painted all in one shot. The time saved by this process alone can range from minutes to hours; imagine what you could do with a few extra hours of creative time.

When I construct the general paths in the same paint style, I usually pick a color fill that will be the most common one in that illustration. The only problem with that, however, is that paths that overlap and intersect each other cannot be easily distinguished. In other words, if you place a circle on top of a large rectangle of the same color, the circle will not be visible in the Preview mode. Switching to Artwork mode will allow you to see the circle, but you will not be able to see whether it is on top of or beneath the rectangle. To avoid this, assign a different color stroke to all the paths so that you will be able to see the outline of all the shapes and their layering.

As I create all the paths of the same color fill and stroke, I make sure that the layering is correct and the grouping follows a logical organization. Once all of the basic general paths have been constructed by outlining the line-drawing sketch template, and they are in the correct layering and grouping order, I select all the objects that will not be painted with a stroke and assign a stroke of None. Following the same procedure, I can select all the paths that will be filled with the same color and assign that color to them. Eventually, I will have to select paths one at a time to assign unique paint style attributes. Paths that get a gradient assigned to them often require those gradients to be adjusted with the Gradient Vector tool. Lastly, I decide which areas will need a manual color blend, and begin working on creating those blends and the masks that may need to accompany them.

This is the basic procedure I use for the majority of my illustration work. The finer points of this routine change occasionally based on the specific requirements of the illustration. As you have become aware from the discussions in this book, there are many different techniques to accomplish all tasks in Illustrator, and most of you will undoubtedly discover your own techniques and methods. Even after eight years of using the program, I still do.

Index